John Bradstreet's Raid, 1758

CAMPAIGNS & COMMANDERS

GREGORY J. W. URWIN, SERIES EDITOR

John Bradstreet's Raid, 1758

A Riverine Operation of the
French and Indian War

Ian Macpherson McCulloch

University of Oklahoma Press : Norman

Library of Congress Cataloging-in-Publication Data

Names: McCulloch, Ian Macpherson, 1954– author.
Title: John Bradstreet's Raid, 1758 : a riverine operation of the French and Indian War / Ian Macpherson McCulloch.
Description: Norman : University of Oklahoma Press, [2022] | Series: Campaigns and commanders ; volume 74 | Includes bibliographical references and index. | Summary: "This comprehensive analysis of Bradstreet's 1758 raid during the Seven Years' War draws on provincial participants' records and French documents to offer a balanced account of a critical moment in early American military history, thereby dispelling many of the myths that have grown up around the operation"—Provided by publisher.
Identifiers: LCCN 2022000556 | ISBN 978-0-8061-9061-7 (hardcover)
ISBN 978-0-8061-9393-9 (paper)
Subjects: LCSH: Bradstreet, John, 1711–1774. | Fort Frontenac (Ont. : Fort)—Capture, 1758. | United States—History—French and Indian War, 1754–1763—Campaigns.
Classification: LCC E199.B823 M33 2022 | DDC 940.2/534—dc23/eng/20220304
LC record available at https://lccn.loc.gov/2022000556

John Bradstreet's Raid, 1758: A Riverine Operation of the French and Indian War is Volume 74 in the Campaigns and Commanders Series.

The paper in this book meets the guidelines for permanence and durability of the Committee on Production Guidelines for Book Longevity of the Council on Library Resources, Inc. ∞

Copyright © 2022 by the University of Oklahoma Press, Norman, Publishing Division of the University. Paperback published 2024. Manufactured in the U.S.A.

All rights reserved. No part of this publication may be reproduced, stored in a retrieval system, or transmitted, in any form or by any means, electronic, mechanical, photocopying, recording, or otherwise—except as permitted under Section 107 or 108 of the United States Copyright Act—without the prior written permission of the University of Oklahoma Press. To request permission to reproduce selections from this book, write to Permissions, University of Oklahoma Press, 2800 Venture Drive, Norman OK 73069, or email rights.oupress@ou.edu.

For the provincial soldiers of New Jersey, New York, Massachusetts, and Rhode Island who caused a legendary French fort to fall and a new British fort to rise up in the wilderness

Contents

Preface	ix
Acknowledgments	xix
1. Antecedents	1
2. Assembly	31
3. Approach	67
4. Assault	89
5. Agony	107
6. Aftermath	125
7. Assessment	139

Appendixes

A. Parade State of Fort Frontenac Garrison, 27 August 1758	149
B. List of the King's Employees at Fort Frontenac, 27 August 1758	152
C. Ships Captured or Destroyed by Bradstreet's Forces, 27–31 August 1758	154
D. Order of Battle and Strengths of British and American Forces at Siege of Fort Frontenac, 1758	156
E. Composite Detachment of Col. Joseph Williams's Massachusetts Regiment, 13 August 1758	158
F. Return Taken of the Detachment of the New York Regiment at Camp on Oneida Lake, 18 August 1758	159
G. Col. Bradstreet's Instructions to the Commander of a Scouting Party	160

H. Meteorological Data (Lake Ontario Leg), 22–31 August 1758 — 161
I. Bradstreet's "Orders for Landing," Cataraqui, 25 August 1758 — 167
J. Conditions of Surrender, Fort Frontenac, 27 August 1758 — 169
K. List of Plunder "divided at Bulls fort," 8 September 1758 — 171

Glossary of Eighteenth-Century and Modern Military Terms — 173
List of Abbreviations — 177
Notes — 179
Bibliography — 209
Index — 221

Preface

In 2000, a steamer trunk was found buried away in a musty Schenectady attic in the Mohawk Valley of upstate New York. When opened, it was found to contain a rare, long-lost portrait of John Bradstreet, still in its original gold gilt frame. Experts quickly attributed the work to Thomas McIlworth, a Scottish itinerant painter, who painted most of the prominent people in Albany and New York society during the years 1755 to 1766.

Just a few months after its discovery, the painting was made the centerpiece of an auction of Bradstreet and Aaron Burr memorabilia held in Clifton Park, New York, on 17 August 2000. The collection, touted as being of tremendous historical significance, consisted of letters, documents, deeds, and maps lovingly collected and preserved by one of Bradstreet's granddaughters, Martha Bradstreet (1780–1871). The auction house paid for Bradstreet's sole biographer to fly down from Canada for a reception given the night before the sale and give a talk on "Bradstreet the Man."

Bradstreet's biographer, the late Dr. William Godfrey of Mount Allison University, explained to his audience that when he had finished his 1982 biography on Bradstreet eighteen years earlier, the publishers asked for a portrait to put on the book cover. Godfrey sadly had explained that no portraits of the general were known to exist. But now he professed delight that all could gaze upon the likeness of the Anglo-Acadian adventurer whose name became synonymous with "The Battoe Service" in the French and Indian War, the common appellation given to the worldwide conflict known as The Seven Years' War in the North American theater.

There was no preauction estimate for the Bradstreet painting, as it was one of a kind. Museum curators, art dealers, and private collectors came from Canada and the United States, all desirous of acquiring the portrait. The bidding rose quickly in $1,000 increments to a final sale price of $40,000. Eventually bought by New Haven dealer William Reese, the portrait was professionally cleaned

A gifted (and sunburned) logistician

The only known likeness of Col. John Bradstreet (1714–74), the Anglo-Acadian officer who created "The Battoe Service," spearheaded the fledgling riverine capabilities of Anglo-American forces in North America, and led the 1758 raid on Fort Frontenac. This portrait, by Scottish painter Thomas McIlworth (1720–69), was painted at Albany after his return from the relief of Detroit in 1764. Courtesy of the National Portrait Gallery, Smithsonian Institute.

and quickly resold for an undisclosed sum to the National Portrait Gallery of the Smithsonian, where it now resides today.

In the portrait, we gaze upon an unhappy man in his fiftieth year. Acutely aware that gold lace embroidery, sashes, and gorgets drew unwarranted attention from enemy sharpshooters, Bradstreet is wearing a simple unadorned red frock coat of the kind favored by senior British officers while campaigning in the North American wilderness—James Wolfe, Lord George Augustus Howe, and Sir William Johnson to name just a few. The collarless jacket is worn over a plain red waistcoat and a white shirt. The buttons are brass or gold gilt, and he sports a silk white roller at his neck. His somewhat disheveled brown wig symbolizes that he is back in polite society, but it rides high, almost an afterthought on his lily-white forehead, sheltered until now by his cut-down tricorn hat. This is a soldier, home from campaign.

Bradstreet looks unwell, no doubt tired and exhausted from traveling in open boats across Lakes Ontario and Erie for the past three months. We also sense that he is a reluctant sitter, out of his element, his portrait a favor to the wife of his protégé Philip John Schuyler, who was also painted the same year by the same artist. We sense this from what is not in the portrait. It is strange indeed that the background of the only known portrait of such an accomplished egotist is devoid of his participation in any previous successful campaigns such as the capture of Louisbourg in 1745, or his hit-and-run raid on Fort Frontenac in 1758.

By contrast, most commanders in the French and Indian War had their exploits of derring-do commemorated and immortalized in fine baroque style with a relevant action or edifice captured over their right or left shoulder. For example, when Sir Jeffery Amherst was painted in ceremonial armor in 1765 by Sir Joshua Reynolds to mark the surrender of New France, the background prominently featured the descent of his "American Army" shooting the rapids on its way to capture Montreal in 1760. The same applied to officers of a lesser rank but future station. In later life, the Honorable Hugh Montgomery, who had served as a subaltern in Montgomery's Highlanders (77th Foot) and as captain in the Fraser Highlanders (78th Foot), chose a background of a burning Cherokee village in Carolina to commemorate his French and Indian service.

Sitting for the painting must have been pure agony for Bradstreet, who was never wont to remain still for long. Impatience, with a dash of defiance, oozes from his cold gray-blue eyes, his sunburnt, weathered face a crucial key allowing us to date the painting with some degree of certainty—October 1764. Bradstreet has just returned to Albany from trying to subdue the Amerindian tribes taking part in what came to be known as Pontiac's Rebellion, or Uprising. Instead of receiving a hero's welcome and his nation's thanks for his relief of the besieged Detroit, Bradstreet has been raked over the coals by the commander in chief in America—Gen. Thomas Gage—for making an unauthorized peace with the Shawnee and Delaware. Bitter and unrepentant, Bradstreet is in the process of waging a caustic correspondence with his superior. It is from this point that his career will go into a sharp decline, and he starts drinking heavily. Ten years later, he will be dead from cirrhosis of the liver.

I first encountered the historical John Bradstreet as a young infantry officer thirty years ago. I was attending the Canadian Army Staff College in Kingston, Ontario, and every morning of the six-month course I would peer out my window located on the third floor of "Bradstreet Block." Directly below me, I could see a sunken oval excavation complete with retaining walls preserving the foundations of the St. Claude Bastion of the original Fort Frontenac. Despite my curiosity, it was only toward the end of my stay at the college that I found time from my studies to learn more about Bradstreet the man and his relationship to the exposed French masonry on display below my window.

I found that the gentleman in question was born Jean-Baptiste Bradstreet in 1714 in Annapolis Royal, Nova Scotia, to an Anglo-Irish officer and an Acadian mother. His early military career as an officer in the 40th Regiment

The Underground Fort
The original Fort Frontenac now lies beneath the modern-day Fort Frontenac, which serves as the Canadian Army's staff college in Kingston, Ontario. Two of the original corners of the old French fort have been excavated and are on view: the St. Michel Bastion outside the staff college (*above*); and the St. Louis Bastion, the old powder magazine, found inside its limestone walls (*left*). Author's photos.

of Foot (Hopson's) was uneventful until the outbreak of the War of the Austrian Succession. In 1745, he became one of the principal promoters of the operation that led to the capture of Louisbourg by New England forces. When Gov. William Shirley, his supporter and fellow promoter of the Louisbourg expedition, asked him back from obscurity to act as adjutant general for his upcoming expedition to take Niagara in 1755, Bradstreet jumped at the chance. He quickly established an excellent reputation as a competent logistician on the Albany–Oswego corridor.[1]

I also learned that Bradstreet was instrumental in establishing "The Battoe Service," which gave the British Army a much needed operational capability to maneuver in the wilderness of North America. The bateau was a flat-bottomed, shallow-draft, all-purpose cargo boat. First appearing in the records as early as King William's War, by the eighteenth century bateaux were the most common and most important cargo carrier found on the inland waters of colonial

North America. The name derives from the French word *batteau* (boat) and plural *batteaux*, which was commonly rendered in English at the time as "battoe/battoes."[2]

It was during 1756 that Bradstreet formulated his plan to take Fort Frontenac, also known as Cataraqui, on Lake Ontario by a coup de main. Various commanders and higher-priority operations put his plan on hold several times until 1758. Then in the aftermath of Gen. James Abercromby's failed assault on Fort Ticonderoga, he was finally allowed, after much cajoling on his part, to put his plan into operation. Bradstreet's colonial force of approximately 3,000 men reached Lake Ontario on 21 August, and four days later his army was laying siege to the small French fort and its vital supply depot at the mouth of the Cataraqui River near the egress of Lake Ontario into the mighty St. Lawrence River. The tiny French garrison of Fort Frontenac surrendered after a token resistance on 27 August 1758.

Bradstreet was promoted to colonel in the British army for his well-publicized exploits and continued to serve as a deputy quartermaster general (DQMG) in America for the remainder of the war. During the Pontiac Uprising (1763–64), he was assigned to lead a northern expedition from Fort Niagara to relieve the besieged Detroit. He accomplished this mission, but while doing so, he overstepped the bounds of his authority by offering peace to the various disaffected tribes. He thus not only incurred the displeasure of the commander in chief, Maj. Gen. Thomas Gage, but more seriously, drew the lasting enmity of the superintendent of Indian affairs, Sir William Johnson.

Bradstreet's military record and reputation never recovered from this 1764 campaign, which overshadowed his 1758 accomplishment. All future requests for governorships or preferment were simply ignored by Gage, who remained as the commander in chief of North America for the rest of Bradstreet's life. John Bradstreet died on 25 September 1774 at New York City, spared the spectacle of armed insurrection that the abrasive, ambitious, but astute harbinger had long predicted to be in the offing.

This book, however, is not just about the raid commander, John Bradstreet. It examines the expedition he led and the many unsung people whose talents and energies he harnessed to achieve his personal goals and objective. The latter, the participants—winners and losers—had their lives changed by their direct or indirect involvement with the 1758 raid on Fort Frontenac. Unfortunately for the ambitious Bradstreet, the raid was not in the public eye for long. It was eclipsed by bigger and more important victories the same year: Gen. Jeffery Amherst's at Louisbourg on Cape Breton Island; and Gen. John Forbes's at Fort Duquesne, situated at the Forks of the Ohio. The turn of events must have been maddening for the junior Bradstreet. Still, the daring raid's success and the logistical savvy required to pull it off, safeguarded his reputation after the bloody repulse of his commander, James Abercromby, on the Heights of Carillon at Ticonderoga earlier in the summer.

At the same time, General Abercromby's effort to use the raid's success to repair his own tarnished reputation frustrated Bradstreet. It was not long after his return from the August raid that Bradstreet realized that his cautious and unimaginative superior had only let him go on the raid in the hope that a resounding success would salvage his career. In a blatant attempt to head off Bradstreet and others from reporting directly to authorities at home after the disastrous defeat at Carillon, Abercromby embargoed all outgoing mail. By controlling the flow of information regarding his actions, he would be able to put his spin on affairs. Content to list all the advantages that had accrued by the capture of Fort Frontenac (according to Bradstreet), Abercromby hoped that these perceived accomplishments would be enough to mitigate his uninspired blundering at Ticonderoga. Undaunted, Bradstreet sought to put his own spin on the story of the expedition by publishing his *Impartial Account* the following year.[3]

This 260-year-old spat has not helped to further modern historians' understanding of the event. To recover what happened and grasp its significance, one has to deal with Abercromby's spin-doctoring and Bradstreet's braggadocio. Too often Bradstreet's less than *Impartial Account* has been accepted as gospel by historians. But in doing so, they fail to listen to the distinguished military historian John Keegan, who cautioned historians against "reconstructing events solely or largely on the evidence of those whose reputations may gain or lose by the account they give." Keegan has cautioned that even if "it is only a warrior's self-esteem at stake, he is liable to inflate his achievements—what we may call the Bullfrog Effect."[4] John Bradstreet's thirst for fame and promotion was legendary in his own time. Lord Loudoun observed pointedly to his friend the Duke of Cumberland that the dynamic and hard-charging Bradstreet had to be "rode with a bridel" at all times. He was what modern-day British army officers would have termed "a thruster."[5]

The raid is often relegated to being an interesting adjunct to the failed 1758 Ticonderoga campaign and a prequel to Forbes's successful 1758 Fort Duquesne expedition. As a result, the expedition's actual participants are forgotten and consigned to the dustbin of history, marginalized by Bradstreet's official version, which was written to enhance his own reputation and luster. After much study and research, I have concluded that Bradstreet, just like his superior Abercromby, attempted to use and manipulate the event to further his own career. In part, he did so by burying, for a second time, the men who died on this expedition.

The commander's assertions in his *Impartial Account* that he only had one man killed and a dozen-plus men wounded on his expedition are false and misleading at best. The exact death toll will never be accurately known, but hundreds of provincials who participated in the raid subsequently died on the return leg of the journey from Cataraqui or, weakened in constitution, shortly thereafter at Fort Stanwix from nervous exhaustion, dysentery, typhus, or smallpox. Ironically, Bradstreet is hoist on his own petard when he admits in the first few pages of his *Impartial Account* that two men of his reconnaissance forces were killed and scalped by Indians at the very outset while making their way down to Lake Ontario. With the exception of his beloved battoemen, the remainder of the provincial forces that accompanied him were viewed as disposable, and he quickly moved to disassociate himself from the regiments or any responsibility for them on his return. They simply were no longer his problem.

I am, however, concerned with these men and what their stories, and not just John Bradstreet's, can tell us about the Seven Years' War in North America. I am also interested in critically examining John Bradstreet's command abilities and how he fitted into the campaign planning process for 1758, William Pitt's first year at the helm directing the war in America. Because of this interest, I have written a book that deals broadly with the participants whose lives were changed by their involvement with the 1758 raid. The *hundreds* of provincial soldiers who died, and those who survived, left legacies that differed from and outlasted Bradstreet's self-serving account.

The raid's success was instrumental in the restitution of pride and morale of the provincial regiments in which these men served, and in the colonies that had raised them, especially after the incomprehensible defeat at Ticonderoga. One American-born officer claimed with some justification in a letter that the taking of Fort Frontenac and its destruction "gave more joy to the inhabitants of this place [Albany] than even Louisbourg itself for it more nearly concerned them and they say now there will be no more scalping."[6]

In sum, this will be a critical study of the 1758 expedition that led to the destruction of Fort Frontenac, which had traditionally been a key gathering point for Canadian trade, diplomacy, and mounting military operations in the Great Lakes region since 1673. The tactical raid, which was a part of the larger 1758 Ticonderoga campaign, would unnerve the French high command, demoralize the Canadian population, and impact indigenous politics in the west.

I focus my attention on the actors at every level and range from the heights of command to the realities of the foot soldier. The military records, private journals, and correspondence of the men involved have been mined to provide information about decision-making, attitudes and motivation, conditions and terrain, movements and results. Some of the personal stories lie scattered

Goose's orderly book, 1758

The orderly book of Capt. Goose Van Schaik (1736–89) of the 2nd Battalion, New York Provincial Regiment. This facsimile page, dated 24 May 1758, reveals that while the Yorkers waited at Niskayuna on the Mohawk River just east of Schenectady for the rest of the army to gather for the campaign, Van Schaick's 101-man company was whittled away to just 35 men, a weak platoon. One officer, four NCOs, and 42 men were detached on the "Battoe Service," and another 21 are indicated as wagoners. Courtesy of Fort Ticonderoga Museum Collection.

or buried away in various nineteenth-century town and county histories or genealogical magazines of New England, New York, New Jersey, and Rhode Island. From the words of the common soldier, I hope, a new view of the raid will emerge that places it in context with other events and processes at play in the middle stages of the Seven Years' War in North America.

I interrupt my story occasionally to ask, and answer, questions—especially about inadequate or dubious evidence, or the credibility of witnesses on both sides. My intention is that a subtext of analysis and argument will make the participants' stories more compelling. Therefore, this account will scrutinize and test the claims made by the commander of the attack, John Bradstreet, and take a hard look at his *Impartial Account of Lieut. Col. Bradstreet's Expedition to Fort Frontenac* (London, 1759), on which many previous historians have relied uncritically. It will correct the common narrative of this part of the Seven Years' War as presented by historians from Francis Parkman in the nineteenth century to Fred Anderson at the turn of the twenty-first.

Destruction of the fort, its fleet, and its stores inflicted significant damage on French war-making capabilities. It also intensified tensions within the *Canadien* high command between the civilian governor and the military commander in chief. But it was not the strategic masterstroke that Bradstreet and his later admirers maintain. If anything, it resulted in a deflection of Anglo-American resources from a strategic center of gravity (the Lake Champlain–Montreal corridor). Moreover, the raid inflicted far more casualties on the Anglo-American forces than is generally recognized.

John Bradstreet was certainly a gifted logistician who accomplished much to develop the fledgling riverine capabilities of Anglo-American forces in North America and to provide the mobility needed for operations in a riverine environment. That capacity was tested and proven in the attack on Fort Frontenac. However, the traditional historical emphasis on the commander has created an incomplete picture, one that impedes a complete understanding of the results of the campaign. It also overlooks some key aspects such as the development of command capabilities across a wide set of junior officers—men who would assume critical leadership roles in the next wars, including the Revolutionary War. Among the social impacts of the victory in the colonies were the release of 130 American men, women, and children as well as a sprinkling of British officers from years of captivity in New France and their return home to the bosom of their families.

Before examining the anatomy of this eighteenth-century raid in any detail, I must address a major quagmire that many purported military historians have failed to navigate: namely, the differences between the strategic and tactical levels of war. While modern historians tend to use the terms "strategic" and "tactical" liberally, they often misunderstand exactly what the terms mean. The result is imprecise and unpersuasive analysis and, often, erroneous conclusions. As Donald Stoker observed in 2009 over a decade ago in "The Forum" of the *Journal of Military History*: "We historians too often fail to differentiate between the terms strategy, operations and tactics, sometimes using them interchangeably, and thus incorrectly. We also sometimes neglect to account for the changing definitions and usage of military terms."[7]

Therefore, to orient and anchor the respective strategies espoused by the British and French concerning their colonies in North America in 1758 and, more specifically, to show how and where John Bradstreet's raid is situated within the campaign design of his operational theater commander, it is necessary to briefly articulate the theoretical differences between the strategic, operational, and tactical levels of war. A glossary of the latest modern and eighteenth-century military terms and their definitions can also be found at the back of the book.

While not "terms" in use during the eighteenth century, the three levels of war certainly existed long before being articulated in their modern conceptual construct. These categorizations evolved to help military commanders organize their thoughts and visualize a logical flow of operations with a realistic assignment of tasks and allocation of resources to achieve them. From a purely military perspective, the strategic level is the level where commanders are given a nation's or an alliance's strategic objectives, as well as an allocation of strategic resources, such as fleets or armies, to accomplish those objectives. At this level, commanders are then expected to focus and sagely apply that military force to achieve those assigned strategic objectives.

Below the strategic level is the operational level, where campaigns and other major operations are planned, conducted, and sustained to accomplish overall strategic objectives within individual theaters or areas of operation. Activities at this level link tactics and strategy by establishing operational objectives needed to accomplish the larger strategic objectives. Particularly critical at this level are logistics, which involve the acquisition, movement, and housing of men, equipment, and supplies needed to wage campaigns.

The tactical level of war is the level where battles, sieges, and raids are planned and executed to accomplish the operational objectives assigned by the commander at the next higher level. The operational-level commander, like Gen. James Abercromby in our study (who was carrying out the strategic directives of his political masters at Whitehall), was responsible for determining what capabilities would be needed for achieving victory, then sequencing and synchronizing them in a logical order to achieve his assigned strategic objectives across much broader dimensions of time and space than those concerning his subordinate tactical commanders.

The focus of tactical subordinates must be on maneuvering their forces to achieve their assigned tactical tasks that then lead to the successful attainment of their operational commander's objectives. Horizons for planning, preparation, and execution thus differ greatly at each of the three levels of war, and the correct tactical and operational applications of force through space and time are the key to success. Simply stated, the tactical-level commander is concerned with the art of battle; the operational commander, the art of campaigning; and the strategic commander, the art of waging war.

Acknowledgments

It is impossible to list every individual and institution that assisted me along the way, but I would like to highlight a chosen few who have responded beyond the call of duty in making my labor of love much easier.

Foremost, I would like to thank my talented team of readers, who made this book better. They are, in no particular order, a mentor and kindred soul, Dr. Kevin Sweeney of Amherst University; my editorial partner-in-crime for my last two books, Earl John Chapman; my longtime friend, Dr. D. Peter McLeod of the Canadian War Museum; another mentor and fellow Canadian from across the pond, Dr. John Houlding; and finally my brother, Paul Dixon McCulloch.

Second, a big thank-you to North American marine artist Peter Rindlisbacher, whose artwork graces the cover. Also a sincere thanks to the many friends and colleagues who gladly granted permission for the images, maps, and artwork to be used in this book. They are, in no particular order, Timothy J. Todish, Nicholas Westbrook, Eugène Lelièpvre, Gary Zaboly, Matt Keagle, Robert Griffing, Robin Brass, Jerry Seymour, René Chartrand, Mike Bechtold, Brian Leigh Dunnigan, and Steve Brumwell.

For invaluable help with the indigenous portion of the story, and for assistance in understanding the meaning of certain words in the Haudenosaunee language, many thanks to Darren Bonaparte, a Mohawk writer, artist, and cultural historian from the Akwesasne First Nations; the *Tsi Tyónnheht Onkwawén:na*, or Language Circle, at Tyendinaga, Ontario; and Dr. Jay Cassel, historian and a senior provincial negotiator for Haudenosaunee and Anishinaabe land claims within the province of Ontario.

Finally, an old chestnut bears repetition: Despite the impressive array of talented and knowledgeable folks listed above, any errors or omissions in the book are entirely my responsibility.

"A New Englandman"
After the stunning defeat of the British-American army at Ticonderoga in July 1758, a British newspaper blamed the alleged incompetence, ill-discipline, and cowardice of the provincial troops. A furious Benjamin Franklin, writing as "A New Englandman," refuted the accusations, contrasting Bradstreet's victorious raid with the recent "Regular" defeats of Braddock, Webb, Loudoun, and Abercromby. Courtesy of the National Portrait Gallery, Smithsonian Institution.

CHAPTER 1

Antecedents

When the blast of war blows in our eyes
Then imitate the action of the tiger:
Stiffen the sinews, summon up the blood

—Shakespeare, Henry V

After the stunning defeat of the British-American army at Ticonderoga in July 1758, an anonymous "Gentleman in General Abercrombie's army" tried, in a prominent London newspaper, to lay all the blame on the alleged incompetence, ill discipline, and cowardice of the provincial troops. A furious Benjamin Franklin took up his pen and hotly disputed such unfounded imputations, citing John Bradstreet's raid as just one example of many "Provincial" victories during the present war.[1]

In his 9 May 1759 rebuttal, Franklin warned the editors of the *London Chronicle* that such unfounded allegations when "read in America, will have no good effect, and rather increase that inconvenient disgust that is too apt to arise between the troops of different corps, or countries, who are obliged to serve together." He then compared the dismal war record of the British regulars in the North American theater since 1755 to that of the American provincials, up to and including Bradstreet's raid, which occurred after the offending letter was written. Franklin did not hold back:

> Surely, the return of your first General [Lord Loudoun], with a well-appointed and sufficient force from his [1757] expedition against Louisbourg, is not the most shining proof of his talents for war. And no one will say his plan was marred by us, for we were not with him. Was his successor [James Abercromby],

1

who conducted the blundering attack and inglorious retreat from Ticonderoga, a New England man . . . ? Then as to the comparison between Regulars and Provincials, will not the latter remark;

That it was 2000 New England Provincials, with but about 150 Regulars, that took the strong fort of Beausejour in the beginning of the war, though, in the accounts transmitted to the English Gazette, the honour was claimed by the regulars, and little or no notice taken of the others.

That it was the Provincials who beat General Dieskau, with his Regulars, Canadians, and "yelling" Indians [at Lake George in 1755], and sent him prisoner to England.

That it was a Provincial-born Officer [John Bradstreet], with American battoemen, that beat the French and Indians on Oswego river [in 1756].

That it was the same Officer, with Provincials, who made that long and admirable march into the enemies country, took and destroyed Fort Frontenac, with the whole French fleet on the lakes, and struck terror into the heart of Canada [in August 1758].[2]

Proudly signing off as "A New Englandman," Franklin was more charitable in his concluding remarks, noting that many of his friends were officers who hailed from "a certain northern latitude" and were "men of sentiments concerning the colonies, more generous and more just than those express'd by the letter writer." These British officers, he summed up, were unbiased men "who can see faults even in their own corps, and who can allow the Provincials their share of merit; . . . feel pleasure as Britons, in observing that the children of Britain retain their native intrepidity to the third and fourth generation in the regions of America; together with that ardent love of liberty and zeal in its defence, which in every age has distinguish'd their progenitors among the rest of mankind."

Just a few years later, a more sympathetic London magazine, the *Annual Register*, would categorically tell its readers that the British army's problems of campaigning in the New World were not the fault of its provincial cousins marching alongside them but of the unforgiving wilderness and its climate, which required the utmost "exertions of courage and address." This editor also did not hold back:

In an American campaign, everything is terrible; the face of the country, the climate, the enemy. There is no refreshment for the healthy, nor relief for the sick. A vast inhospitable desert, unsafe and treacherous, surrounds them, where victories are not decisive, but defeats are ruinous; and simple death is the least misfortune, which can happen to them. This forms a service truly critical, in which all the firmness of the body and mind is put to the severest trial; and all the exertions of courage and address are called out.[3]

It took several years for Britons at home unacquainted with the physical geography of North America to understand the vast distances and immense hardships faced by all armies campaigning there during the Seven Years' War. First, "the face of the country" with its attendant climate had to be conquered before one could actually close with and confront an opponent. To most British veterans of soldiering in Europe, campaigning was camping in the open countryside, with its established road networks, or in tidy towns with a tavern or two for a pint of ale or in snug billets provided by a village every few miles along the way. To such men, the North American wilderness came as a rude shock.

By contrast, seasonal campaigning for provincial soldiers, besides being a welcome source of income, was a grand adventure to the elusive frontier, a rite of passage. Others understood themselves to be actors in a prophetic vision in which America was the Promised Land and they were God's chosen people. Many of the young men who joined were heeding their colony's call to arms in the finest militia tradition of their forefathers, New England having borne the brunt of warfare against New France in the late seventeenth and early eighteenth centuries. New Jersey's provincial regiment was the most recent incarnation of the "Jersey Blues," a well-trained, well-uniformed militia first raised in the 1740s during the War of the Austrian Succession.[4]

War in the North American interior for eighteenth-century armies was essentially a daunting problem of maneuver, communications, and resupply. Away from the Atlantic seaboard or the St. Lawrence River, the principal task of effective generalship was marshaling the capabilities needed to move a force of moderate size into contact with the enemy. Any aspiring commander needed a small highly trained army of experts or enablers. And, for those seriously contemplating any waterborne approach, boat builders, battoemen, and sailors were needed to build and sustain the capability to convey large armies along the inland waterways and through the primeval forest. Long lines of communication also necessitated the building of well-garrisoned, defensible forts, depots, and dockyards along the way, usually located at strategic chokepoints where lakes and rivers joined or narrowed. Most were wooden stockades designed to resist Indians or militias but were incapable of resisting artillery. This meant, in order to take a fort, one's opponent was forced to move heavy guns, ammunition, rations, and siege equipment through the wilderness along the waterways. In sum, a mastery of logistics was required in order to master riverine warfare.[5]

This type of warfare in North American history is not well documented and usually starts with discussions of naval warfare on the Great Lakes during the War of 1812 and on through to the subjection of the Seminoles in the Everglades and the operations on the Mississippi during the Civil War

(1861–65). But more than a decade before the American Revolution, riverine warfare was first conducted on a major scale during the Seven Years' War in North America (1755–60). In 1760, three waterborne British-American armies converged on Montreal, the last stronghold of New France. They arrived at Montreal within forty-eight hours of each other, a feat unequaled in North American military history.[6]

The armies involved were not always so proficient in "brown water" operations. It was a capability that simply did not exist in the British navy or the colonial merchant marine at the outset of the war. Thus a basic riverine doctrine was born of operational necessity, then tweaked and tuned through trial and error until the British-American army and navy had it right. John Bradstreet was at the forefront in the development of that operational capability and, as will be seen later, a deft practitioner of riverine warfare.

"The face of the country"

The principal settlements of New France were anchored on each end by the logistical nerve centers of Quebec and Montreal—the former fortified town the western terminus of critical sea lines of communication with France, the latter a poorly fortified fur depot and a collection point for the limited agricultural resources of the colony. Overland access to the core of New France by British-American forces was only possible by utilizing lakes, portages, and rivers as highways, and thus invading armies were restricted to two interior avenues of approach from the south and southwest. The first line of approach ran northward from New York City on the Atlantic to Albany on the Hudson River. It had been used by Amerindian nations as a natural north–south highway for centuries. With a short portage over the watershed into the Lake George and, subsequently, Lake Champlain watersheds, flotillas of boats could then convey armies northward via the lakes and then down the Richelieu River to the St. Lawrence River valley and Montreal.

A variant of this approach branched off the Hudson River just above Albany and led westward up the Mohawk River to a place known as the "Great Carrying Place." At this point, cargo and boats would be carried over a small plateau for one to four miles to Wood Creek on the other side, which ran down into Lake Oneida, the source of the Oswego River draining down into the larger Lake Ontario. This western branch of the first approach then intersected the French line of communications with Fort Detroit via Fort Niagara, located below the giant falls draining Lake Erie into Lake Ontario. Theoretically, the British could also intersect this French line of communications by coming up to Lake Erie through the Ohio country as well. To prevent such a move, the French had built a string of small palisaded forts in the opposite direction to link with the recently built Fort Duquesne (1755) at the Forks of the Ohio (the juncture of the Monongahela and Alleghany Rivers), which in turn, via the Ohio, linked to the Illinois country on the Mississippi.

Canada then was like an immense fortress, with smaller forts dotting the various lines of communication that radiated outward from its central hub like spokes from a wheel. These palisaded forts were, for the most part, fortified trading posts, but, more importantly, pinpoints on the map supporting sovereignty claims. And while most were in easy and direct communication with the center, none were ever designed to mount large military operations or serve as forward logistical bases for offensive operations. Instead, they acted as early-warning posts on the approaches to the center. It was only in the second year of the French and Indian War that the French built their first substantial fortification actually designed to block, delay, or mount a major conventional operation with Fort Carillon (Ticonderoga, NY) on the Albany–Lake Champlain–Montreal axis. A lesser stone fort named Fort St. Frédéric (Crown Point, NY) had been built farther north before the War of the Austrian Succession, but its primary purpose was to serve as a mounting base for raids—large and small—into the Hudson and Connecticut Valleys.

Gen. Louis-Joseph de Montcalm, the commander who replaced Baron Dieskau after the Battle of Lake George in 1755, was committed to keeping the British off-balance with limited offensive-defensive operations. His two most successful military campaigns of the entire war—the capture and subsequent destruction of the British forts at Oswego on Lake Ontario in 1756 and Fort William Henry in 1757 on the southern end of Lake George—were aimed at securing both overland approaches to the core of New France. They were classic preemptive strikes. Both forts, designed by the British to serve as forward operating bases, were razed after their capture instead of being occupied. Not wishing to hold the ground or extend their lines of communication any farther southward, the French withdrew to the status quo defensive line of their established outposts.

Two other key factors besides terrain that bound the French in North America to a defensive theater strategy were the North American winter and their smaller colonial population vis-à-vis the thirteen British colonies that lay to their south. The climate in environs south of Canada saw snow and ice disappear earlier from roads and waterways, allowing British-American forces to mobilize and muster much earlier than their ice-bound adversaries to the north. French forts located on the most southerly lines of communication from Quebec and Montreal, such as Forts St. Frédéric (Crown Point) and Carillon (Ticonderoga) on the southern end of Lake Champlain, were virtually isolated and vulnerable to attack weeks before spring resupply or reinforcements from the north could physically reach them. This advantageous reality for the British was not exploited before 1759; British planners and their commanders could never get organized or concentrate their forces in a timely manner prior to launching on campaign.

The logistical impact of weather was also significant. The St. Lawrence River froze during winter, which meant that resupply and reinforcement from France, if forthcoming, was dependent on the vagaries of spring and the ice breakup in order to get through. By contrast, all American ports were ice-free year-round. Additionally, the growing season for essential foodstuffs in New France was limited compared to its American neighbors to the south who, in some cases, could harvest two crops. While the French needed significant grain and livestock imports from Acadia and France just to survive, the Americans typically produced robust surpluses with enough left over to ship to Britain's West Indian colonies.[7]

The French population in North America was small compared to the potential manpower that lay to the south of the St. Lawrence, but it had grown concurrently with the sixfold increase to the American population between 1689 and 1755; that is, the French were still numerically outnumbered six to one nearly sixty-five years later, even with the addition of French regular troops to the equation. At the outbreak of the Seven Years' War in 1756, the general historical consensus is that New France's ability to project combat power was actually weaker than it had been in previous wars due to a number of significant but subtle shifts and variables within its demography.[8]

The *compagnies franches de la marine*, literally the marines, were soldiers raised by the navy for service on board and garrisoning the forts of New France—effectively, regular troops stationed in the colony. Although the rank and file were recruited in France, its officer corps was increasingly drawn from the colonial aristocracy, while still retaining a significant number of Frenchmen. On paper, the *compagnies franches* numbered thirty companies and a total of 2,760 men with a nominal strength of 2,760 men and were scattered over a very large area in a huge arc from Quebec southward to the edges of the Great Lakes. Their task was to provide small garrisons in the remotest parts of the *pays d'en haut* (upper country) along the farthest lines of communications and outposts. The ability to concentrate their combat power during the war would remain problematic.[9]

The Canadien militia could also be mobilized and, in previous wars, had been called out to repel invading forces, to supply manpower for raids, or to build military roads. Members of the Canadien militia, especially an experienced core of fighters drawn from men used to voyaging through the interior, could prove very effective in hit-and-run raids and other forms of combat now

Colonial marine, ca. 1758

The *compagnies franches de la marine* were soldiers raised by the French navy for service on board ships and for garrisoning the forts of New France. Artist Eugène Lelièpvre, Courtesy of René Chartrand.

associated with guerrilla warfare, but such men were not trained in regular formations and had no experience in conventional regular warfare of the day. The principal limitation to any lengthy deployment was that many of them had to be released for work on the land in the spring and in late summer for the harvest. Others were tapped to serve in the canoe brigades supplying the western posts. A muster roll in 1750 lists 165 companies varying in number from 31 to 176, comprising 724 officers, 498 sergeants, and 11,687 men—in all, 12,909.[10]

By the mid-eighteenth century, the warriors traditionally provided by France's indigenous allies made up a more uncertain source of manpower for use in French military operations. There were two broad groups of allied warriors—drawn from very different cultures: the Anishinaabe of the north (pays d'en haut)—including the Algonquin, Nipissing, Mississauga, Ottawa, Ojibwe, and Potawatomi; and the Haudenosaunee, particularly the staunch Catholic converts who lived in missions near Montreal—the "domesticated Indians." Farther east there were the Abenaki, some of whom had settled at missions near Trois-Rivières (Three Rivers).[11]

There were important differences in the culture and politics of the Anishinaabe and Haudenosaunee, but broadly speaking warriors might engage in private wars, motivated by family or clan objectives, or larger public wars involving the whole community. Warriors conducted themselves according to their own lights, though they had to be mindful of village opprobrium if their conduct was unbecoming, and they typically heeded an experienced and successful warrior who had risen to his position by merit. A war chief's authority was not equivalent to that of a European officer, however, and control was limited by a principle of self-direction, which led to frequent deliberations among members of a group about what was the best course of action and who would join in an attack.[12]

Warriors fought for several reasons: to protect land and resources, to get vengeance (to right a wrong or a killing), to capture and adopt individuals to replace dead members of the community and to gain material plunder, which included the very lucrative ransoming of British captives. The first pioneers remember well the small raiding parties that were the bane of frontier life, but warriors also assembled in larger formations either for siege or battle. Wars in the seventeenth and eighteenth century saw indigenous warriors destroy entire nations (the Huron, Erie, Petun, Neutral, Natchez, and Fox—to name a few).[13]

Destroy did not necessarily amount to killing everyone—the victors might absorb the survivors, especially women and the young. The general preference was to make a strike with minimal casualties to their own side. By the eighteenth century, allied warriors were increasingly inclined to accept smaller gains when attacking the American colonies, returning when they struck a blow, however limited. War parties were not impressed by a plan that appeared to run enormous risks—either wholesale defeat or many casualties to their own side. Either could have disastrous consequences for their community or their particular nation, as they had seen in the wars of annihilation.[14]

Thus, from the outset of the Seven Years' War in North America, French operational challenges were legion and required a pragmatic strategy based on the constraints dictated by their smaller population, long lines of communication, harsh and lengthy winters, restricted ports, and finally, allied warriors whose numbers and resolve were unpredictable. French theater strategy in North America was principally defensive in nature, essentially one of delay along the two main interior lines of approach—the St. Lawrence and the Lake Champlain–Montreal corridors. The contentious part of the French planning process was the answer to the question, How do we do it?

Cooperation by all stakeholders is a key element to any successful campaign planning. During the spring and summer of 1758, such did not occur at the operational level in New France between Montcalm, the senior regular force commander, and the senior civilian commander and head of government, His Excellency Pierre de Rigaud de Vaudreuil de Cavagnial. The Canadian-born governor, ardently devoted to the land of his birth and nicknamed

"Generalissimo" behind his back by Montcalm's metropolitan officers, was determined to do it his way: hold the maximum amount of territory and have the enemy contest everything. But that approach came at tremendous cost: it meant forces scattered over an immense area and unable to concentrate rapidly; large numbers of men and amounts of matériel committed to transportation along some of the longest lines of communication in history instead of to crumbling defenses or to actual fighting. It also placed enormous financial strains on a colony already in freefall with a small agricultural base that could not be adequately supplemented by food from France.[15]

This defend-all approach to a complex problem was in direct conflict with Montcalm's desire to concentrate forces and husband scarce resources to protect the true center of gravity: the Quebec–Montreal corridor. In a somewhat pompous memorandum that he drew up after the loss of Frontenac, the regular force commander likened New France to a large tree: "Nothing less is at stake than the utter and impending loss of the Colony or its salvation, that is to say, the postponement of its fall . . . 'tis the trunk of the tree that's attacked; whatever concerns the branches is of the greatest indifference."[16]

The bottom line was that the defenders of New France were required to stymy British-American efforts to conquer Canada until the war had already been decided on European battlefields and the diplomats had won the peace.

Amateurs talk tactics; professionals talk logistics

By contrast, British planners' attempts to develop a theater strategy that would actually identify and take advantage of French vulnerabilities were, in a word, inept. Given British-American resources, climate, and geographical location, the war in North America could have been won much sooner if the responsible planners had only understood the operating environment and, with that understanding, determined the critical capabilities they needed to muster or develop in order to exploit the weaknesses inherent in the French strategy. It would also take a commander in chief who had some diplomatic skills to deal with individual, and sometimes uncooperative, colonies.

If the core area of New France, bounded by Quebec at one end and Montreal at the other, was to be taken, then all of the three main approaches leading to it had to be utilized simultaneously—the two interior approaches already discussed, as well as the direct maritime approach via the Atlantic Ocean and the Gulf of St. Lawrence. These actions were necessary in order to prevent the French from concentrating their meager forces on any one approach. Early seizure of Quebec was essential to the whole as it offered the vital lifeline back to the mother country, New France's primary source of troops, food supplies, and matériel.

One significant limitation to British operational maneuver was the near impossibility of using surprise as an element of strategy in wilderness campaigning. Knowledge of every pending expedition reached the French, either through colonials who traded illegally with their enemies or through London offices. Added to this situation was the fact that the two main interior land approaches to New France traversed lands inhabited and, to a large degree, controlled by the Haudenosaunee—"The People of the Longhouse." News of any major British movements or pending attacks always reached the ears of the French long before they occurred because of the frequent communication between the Amerindian settlements and their longstanding tribal custom of shielding relatives and brethren from any of the white man's actions.[17]

The 1755 British campaign commenced without any formal declaration of hostilities between Britain and France, and the expeditions that were actually mounted can be viewed as "shaping operations" in preparation for the inevitable war that was looming across the sea in Europe. The principal criterion for targeting the French forts was the perception they were illegally encroaching on British sovereign territory and were, therefore, legitimate objectives.

The British picked four targets and launched. A mixed force of regulars and provincials moved against the newly built Fort Duquesne at the Forks of the Ohio that linked the Great Lakes forts via the Ohio to the Mississippi and the Illinois country. From Albany, a force of regulars and provincials targeted Fort Niagara, on Lake Ontario below the Falls, which was considered to have been illegally built on Seneca lands. Another force, consisting entirely of provincials, gathered in Albany to attack Fort St. Frédéric at Crown Point on Lake Champlain, considered a no-man's-land but used by the French for decades as a jumping-off point for numerous raids into New England.

Finally, a force consisting largely of Massachusetts provincials besieged Fort Beauséjour on the Chignecto Isthmus adjacent to the British colony of Nova Scotia. Only the latter operation was successful: the other three would fail due to varying degrees of mismanagement or bad luck. And while the capture of Fort Beauséjour in 1755 served to secure the Nova Scotia frontier and cow an Acadian population from any further major participation in the war, its importance was minimal in the full-scale fighting that ensued from 1756 through to 1758.

The jumping-off point for the Niagara campaign was to be the aging British trading fort at Oswego on Lake Ontario, which sat astride French lines of communication between Forts Frontenac and Niagara. The post at Oswego was seen by the French as a huge threat to their hegemony in the interior of North America, especially their monopoly on the lucrative fur trade and the important Indian alliances it brought. French fears that it could be used as a secure base for mounting military operations against either Fort Frontenac or Niagara, or as a base for building British warships to gain naval superiority on the lake, were, however, ill-founded. Little attention had been paid to Oswego's defenses, and it had no ship-building or dockyard capability to outfit a lake fleet to compete with the French for control of Lake Ontario. By contrast, Fort Frontenac had both.

Not surprisingly, the Niagara campaign never got off the ground due to the immense logistical problems of just moving men and matériel along the Mohawk–Oswego River corridor to Lake Ontario that had no road system. Added to this mobility problem were the significant inadequacies and weaknesses of the Oswego post itself to serve as a forward operating base without a lake fleet in situ that could project a large force of men and siege guns over the lake, or counter a comparable force striking from Frontenac. It was a failure essentially because the British failed to establish a secure logistical presence at Oswego as well as any operational capability to project power across the lake.

The second expedition, launched from upstate New York against Crown Point, comprised a force of provincials and Indians led by Maj. Gen. William Johnson, the superintendent of Indian affairs for the Northern Department, and ended in stalemate at the southern end of Lake George. French regulars, militia, and Native allies led by Baron Jean-Armand Dieskau preemptively attacked the British. After being surprised, the latter repelled the former, but no further operations were conducted northward that year by British forces. Johnson received a baronetcy for essentially maintaining the status quo in this sector, after being forced onto the defensive by his operationally aggressive opponent.

The third operation was an unmitigated disaster. A large combined force of British regulars and American provincials numbering some 1,200 men and commanded by the newly appointed commander in chief in North America, Maj. Gen. Edward Braddock, were assaulted marching alongside the Monongahela River by a smaller force of indigenous warriors and Canadien militia. Almost surrounded a few miles short of their objective, Fort Duquesne, they were routed with heavy casualties. The scapegoating of Braddock by American and British alike that raged in the aftermath lasted for years but was always looked on askance by George Washington, a firsthand witness of the affair, who no doubt packed it away as a valuable life lesson for his future career.

Blaming "the dastardly behaviour of the Regular Troops," the future commander in chief of the Continental Army would observe: "How little does the World consider the Circumstances and how apt are mankind to level their Vindictive Censures against the unfortunate Chief, who perhaps merited the least of the blame."[18] Some years later, Benjamin Franklin's reflections on Braddock's first and last performance on the North American stage were a more objective and nuanced assessment of the factors at play. He believed that Braddock was "a brave man and might probably have made a figure as a good officer in some European war. But he had too much self-confidence, too high an opinion of the validity of regular troops, and too mean a one of both Americans and Indians."[19]

The simplistic campaign plans that charted the operational course constituting the opening shots of the Seven Years' War in North America were strategically and operationally inept. Whereas successful attacks on the three interior forts—Duquesne, Niagara, and Crown Point—in 1755 would have secured and strengthened British claims to adjacent territories and provided forward operating bases, the details of their execution were amateurish, to say the least. The old military aphorism that amateurs talk tactics while professionals talk logistics would now manifest itself in full measure.

"The Country may be undone"

The sole capture of Fort Beauséjour in 1755 not only secured the Nova Scotia frontier and cowed the Acadian population from further participating in the war; it also denied invaluable food surpluses to the fortress town of Louisbourg on Île-Royale. But its operational and strategic worth was negligible in the full-scale war that ensued from 1756 through to 1758. With Braddock killed on the 1755 Duquesne campaign, Gov. William Shirley took over the reins of planning for the ensuing year's theater strategy. He limited his campaigns to two operational approaches.

One was a strike northward by a large force of provincials under Maj. Gen. John Winslow on the Lake Champlain approach to attempt the capture of Crown Point once again. A second, simultaneous operation, to be led by himself, would launch from Oswego across Lake Ontario to take Fort Frontenac. A possible sequel to this operation was an expedition to capture the remaining posts and forts on Lake Ontario, including Fort Niagara, Fort Rouillé (Toronto), and Fort La Présentation (Ogdensburg, NY).

It was into this operating environment that John Bradstreet was first thrust in 1755. The planning for Shirley's operation was given to him as a secondary duty. His primary duty was forwarding supplies to Oswego in 1756 and building up the riverine capability of the army in a massive bateaux-building program. This latter task would be the genesis of planning for Bradstreet's subsequent raid three years later. Both major operations for 1756, however, were inadequately resourced, led by amateur commanders, and ultimately, became bogged down in logistical details and political infighting.

On Lake Ontario, the French, led by the newly arrived Gen. Louis-Joseph de Montcalm, struck first, mounting a decisive preemptive offensive operation from Fort Frontenac against Oswego in early August 1756. Oswego's three poorly sited and incomplete forts were easily captured and destroyed. More significantly, the entire fleet of British warships that had just been completed were taken and assimilated into the existing French lake squadron. The British not only lost their sole forward operating base on Lake Ontario and thus their capability to project power over the lake but were also forced back on the defensive along this entire portion of the New York frontier. With one stroke, Montcalm had denied this interior approach to the British for the foreseeable future and given the French undisputed naval mastery of the lake.[20]

This loss translated into complete freedom of action for Montcalm and his superior, the Marquis de Vaudreuil (who had arrived the year before). They were now able to concentrate all their resources on defending the only other credible line of interior approach to New France, the Lake George–Champlain corridor.

Lord Loudoun, Shirley's replacement, arrived immediately after the Oswego debacle. His first command decisions were to order the cancelation of the Crown Point operation and to focus all efforts on completing the defensive fort at the southern end of Lake George. This fort, subsequently named William Henry, he reasoned, could be used as a forward operating base the following year, and he set about to improve infrastructure, roads, and services that would enhance his capability to project forces in the next campaign. The rest of the year, and most of the next, saw Lord Loudoun more preoccupied with administration rather than any serious strategic planning, and thus, for 1757, Fort Frontenac was the least of his worries.[21]

For the 1757 theater strategy, Lord Loudoun decided to personally lead a combined operation against Louisbourg, with a sequel plan to take Quebec, the French colony's vital link with its mother country. It was an ambitious and complex plan, and one that ignored the need to exploit the one interior land approach still left open to the British after the debacle at Oswego the year before. He did not even have to invade but, at least, should have made some motions along the Lake Champlain corridor to fix some forces of New France in place and prevent the reinforcement of Louisbourg.

Instead, Loudoun left a small force with an ineffective and timid commander, Maj. Gen. Daniel Webb, to guard his center at Fort Edward, and, in doing so, he handed the initiative to his adversary. Montcalm quickly exploited the situation, striking southward while Loudoun's forces slowly concentrated at Halifax, Nova Scotia, for their projected attempt on Louisbourg. The newly built Fort William Henry at the southern end of Lake George was quickly besieged by superior French forces, captured, then razed to the ground. Montcalm then withdrew with large amounts of captured British artillery and valuable stores, as he had done at Oswego the year before, and strengthened the southernmost French fort, Carillon, at Ticonderoga on Lake Champlain.

On the British home front, William Pitt the Elder appeared on the political scene early in 1757. His arrival was too late to change that year's current operations, but he made it unequivocally clear that he would be more closely involved with the conduct of the war from Britain from that time forward. Loudoun was not impressed. He bluntly informed Pitt that military objectives for the upcoming 1758 campaign should *not* be selected in London by ministers, nor should a commanding general "on the ground" be told *how* those objectives were to be achieved. Loudoun stated for the record that if this was how the new Pitt-Newcastle ministry intended to prosecute the war in North America, then he, as commander in chief, would be left with virtually no latitude in his ability to plan and conduct campaigns, nor any ability to practice what, in modern-day parlance, is called the operational art. Lord Loudoun's fairly caustic response to Pitt in August 1757 was succinct:

> I think it is my Duty to observe to your Lordship, that without a Latitude left in Orders at this distance, to make such Alterations in the Execution of them, as the change of the Situation of the things make necessary, The Country may be undone by a punctual Obedience to the most prudent Orders at the time they were given, or the Person that has the honour to command, must depart from them with a Halter about his Neck.[22]

This observation and others brought an end to Loudoun's command of British forces in North America. Undaunted, Pitt would persevere, leading American historian Stanley Pargellis to observe rightly that the minister's "avowal that he was the only person who could save England was justified in the end by victory." At the same time, it masked "the incongruity of a civilian minister dictating details of a military campaign three thousand miles distant of a country of which he knew nothing first hand. In the American Revolution this same plan, re-adopted, was to end in the disaster it deserved."[23]

Lord Loudoun, by contrast, had learned from his 1757 campaign and had crafted a new and more realistic theater strategy for 1758. The course of action that he sent to London for approval proposed mounting four simultaneous operations along all available approaches: a major expedition against Louisbourg using a few regular troops from Britain but a large contingent of provincials from New England to provide the shovel power for a siege; a strike with a small combined forced of regulars and provincials to capture Fort Duquesne on the Forks of the Ohio in western Pennsylvania in order to secure the western frontier; a major thrust up from Albany and Fort Edward to take Forts Carillon and St. Frédéric with only regular troops, including artillery and engineers; and finally, a diversionary strike across Lake Ontario by a small provincial force of some eight hundred battoemen, as well as the Jersey Blues and New Yorker provincials early in the spring to destroy Fort Frontenac. This latter operation would distract French forces trying to defend Montreal against the major British advance along the Lake George–Lake Champlain corridor. Loudoun promised the command of this last expedition to John Bradstreet.[24]

All these operations, Loudoun argued, would be executed early in the year when the weather favored British-American forces and while their adversaries, the French, were constrained in their ability to react. More importantly, he noted, his strategy would force the French to disperse their combat power, making it impossible to concentrate their forces on any one axis. His letter would cross paths with another letter coming the other way relieving him of command and giving very specific instructions to his successor, Maj. Gen. James Abercromby, on how the various campaigns would be conducted and with what troops. Pitt's theater strategic plan would be very similar to Loudoun's, but with some major changes that had serious ramifications in terms of timings, distances to be covered, and forces available for some of the commanders involved.[25]

The sea approach to Quebec (see map 1) proposed by Loudoun (and Shirley before him) would be used and the siege of Louisbourg executed by a force primarily composed of regulars from Britain commanded by Maj. Gen. Jeffery Amherst and supported by a strong Royal Navy fleet and merchant marine. The seizure of this fortress town before moving on to Quebec was predicated on the idea that it could not be left in the rear of any move on the capital of New France as it would leave any attacker's rear lines of communication vulnerable. What Pitt and his planners failed to appreciate, however, was that without an actual French fleet anchored in its harbor, Louisbourg was just a pile of stone and fishing quays. With French ports blockaded in Europe, and a small British fleet stationed to watch over Louisbourg itself, there were no valid reasons why a strong army and fleet could not bypass the fort and proceed directly up the St. Lawrence against Quebec. As the late W. J. Eccles put it: "A year was wasted in the siege and capture of Louisbourg. Without a navy based there, the fortress was useless, able to do nothing for the French, serving merely as a prison for its garrison."[26]

The second expedition tasked with capturing Fort Duquesne was led by Brig. Gen. John Forbes (see map 1). It was more symbolic and a point of honor in the scheme of things rather than a real attempt to seize a valid military objective whose capture would help British forces achieve the theater strategic end state. Canadian historian George Stanley has noted that to take "Fort Duquesne would not compel the French to abandon the Ohio; at best it would only erase

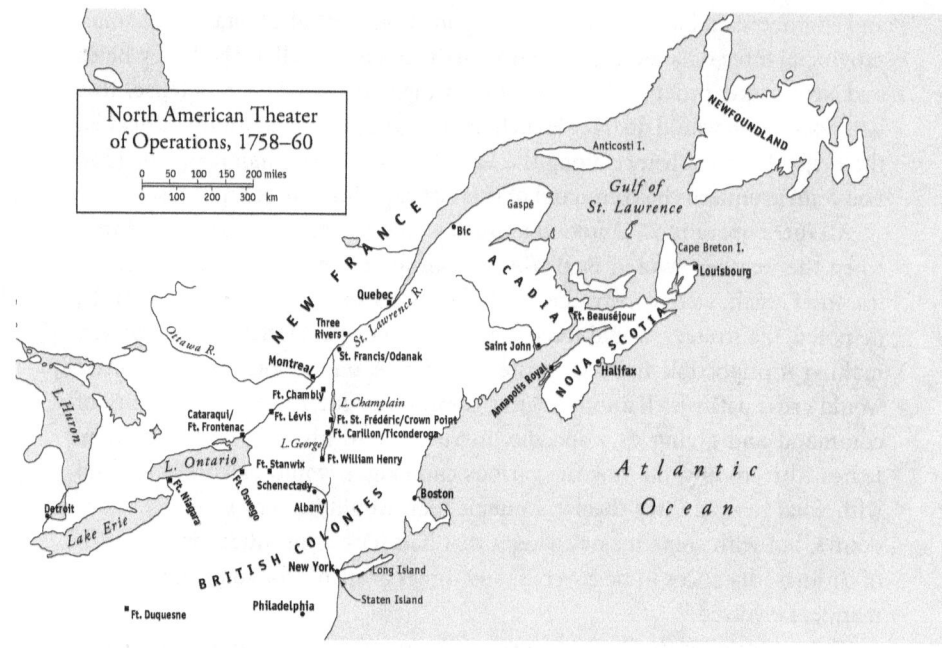

Map 1. Courtesy of Robin Brass Studios.

the memory of Braddock," and that colonial demands for protection, "rather than sound reasons of military strategy, determined that an army should be sent to the Ohio." More charitably, Forbes's expedition could be characterized as a shielding operation designed to try to secure the western frontiers of Pennsylvania and Virginia on which France's Indian allies were raising terror and havoc with colonists. But here again, we see the ignorance and conceit of planners in Whitehall at play and their failure to grasp that seizing static European-style forts in the wilderness was not necessarily the best means of stopping an elusive and unconventional adversary.

Of the two main interior approaches to New France proposed for use by Loudoun in 1758, the diversionary strike across Lake Ontario to reduce Fort Frontenac was canceled by Pitt. To add insult to injury, Pitt's orders reassigned Bradstreet southward to the Forbes expedition in the forests of western Pennsylvania where his talents as a riverine expert and leader of the "Battoe Men" would have been wasted. The blow inflicted by the transfer was softened for Bradstreet with a long-awaited promotion to lieutenant colonel in the British army.

Fortunately for Bradstreet, Abercromby considered the Nova Scotia–born colonel's services invaluable. He retained him as his own deputy quartermaster general (DQMG) for the 1758 campaign, assigning another officer to General

Forbes's southern expedition in his stead. Bradstreet crowed to his influential agent Charles Gould in London: "I find myself set down to serve this Campaign to the Southward but neither General Abercromby or anyone else who are to serve this way are for letting me go fearing the great preparations necessary to be made to transport a large Number of Troops from hence to Canada cannot be executed in time by any other person."[27]

Major General Abercromby was instructed by Pitt to move solely on the Lake Champlain approach; to take Ticonderoga and Crown Point in succession. He was then to continue on to Montreal if possible, all without the benefit of Bradstreet's diversionary raid. The overwhelming force given Abercromby to accomplish this task was Pitt's brainchild. The army Pitt called for—20,000 provincials drawn from the nearest colonies added to Abercromby's regular army component numbering some 5,000—would make a grand army of around 25,000 men. That it would take significant amounts of time to assemble, clothe, feed, arm, and move such a large levy from scratch seems to have been completely overlooked by Pitt and his strategic planners (viz. the logistical requirement). The projections for the numbers of colonial provincials that could be raised were also unrealistic, and, in the end, only about 10,000 arrived in camp. Abercromby's expedition on the Lake Champlain approach would end in a bloody repulse on the Heights of Carillon above Fort Ticonderoga. His 15,000-man army precipitously retreated from Ticonderoga to regroup, and the troops remained for the rest of the campaigning season at their starting point at the southern end of Lake George.[28]

The sequel of pushing on to Quebec City, contingent on Amherst's capture of Louisbourg, had to be curtailed, however, as a portion of those forces were requested by the hapless Abercromby to reinforce his depleted regulars on the central approach. The expedition through western Pennsylvania would see Forbes's 5,000-man army make a laborious march of several months constructing forts and a road as they went before finally arriving at the Forks of the Ohio to take possession of their nonstrategic prize: a smoking, abandoned ruin once known as Fort Duquesne.

Once again, the 1758 campaign in North America would demonstrate the logic that British theater strategic success truly depended on seriously massing and applying effective combat strength *simultaneously* along all the approaches (whether land or sea) leading to the vital nerve center of New France—the Montreal–Quebec corridor. Though Lord Loudoun's draft 1758 campaign plan had proposed such a strategy, its subsequent modification by Pitt removed the offensive strike against Fort Frontenac (designed to split French forces) from the operational design. Taken in tandem with Pitt's adjusting of the forces on the Lake Champlain approach to include a massive, untrained, and unequipped provincial army, it can be clearly seen that Bradstreet's commander was forced to take longer in his preparations to mount his operation and proceed against the assigned objectives. The British being unable to move swiftly in order to exploit their favorable advantages of warmer weather and, thus, earlier mobility, Abercromby's adversary was given critical time and space to mass his own forces on the sole interior line of approach utilized by the attackers. The British operational objectives of capturing Ticonderoga and Crown Point were thus not achieved, which had ramifications for the planned follow-on Quebec expedition from Louisbourg. The end state of the 1758 campaign would be operational failure yet again.

"A miserable shack"

Fort Frontenac, also known as Cataraqui, was the oldest French fort and settlement on the Great Lakes. The stone fort that Bradstreet would attack in 1758, however, was not the first one erected on this site. The original Fort Frontenac was built in the summer and fall of 1673 on the western side of the mouth of the Cataraqui River and at the egress of Lake Ontario into the St. Lawrence River, then partially destroyed and abandoned in 1689 during the Iroquois Wars (1638–98). Upon the return of the fort's namesake, the Comte de Frontenac, in 1695 for his second term as governor, he ordered it reestablished. Despite serious misgivings by many about the suitability of the site, especially its location, which did not actually control or dominate the main outlet of the lake, the French rebuilt the new fort exactly where the first one had stood.[29]

Maures de Malartic of the Bearn regiment, when seeing it for the first time, was not impressed and observed to the Count d'Argenson in 1755:

> Fort Frontenac which is esteemed the strongest in the country . . . consists only of four small stone bastions, the faces of which are no more than six toises, the flanks two and the curtains twelve. The walls are not two feet thick and have neither revetments nor terraces. The terreplein of the rampart is built of plank and masonry; when one of the guns on it is discharged the whole fort shakes. Generally speaking, its situation is very bad, as also is its construction, and it is of no use except for stores.[30]

Viewing the defenses the following year, the Chevalier de la Pause, one of General Montcalm's principal staff officers, was even more succinct. He noted in 1756 that the fort was located "on the west point of the Cataracouy Bay, a short cannon shot from the mouth, built in this place contrary to all the rules of fortification for it is dominated by two positions a musket shot away." He then recommended that if it was considered important enough, an extensive system of earthworks and redoubts would be required to put the fort in a proper

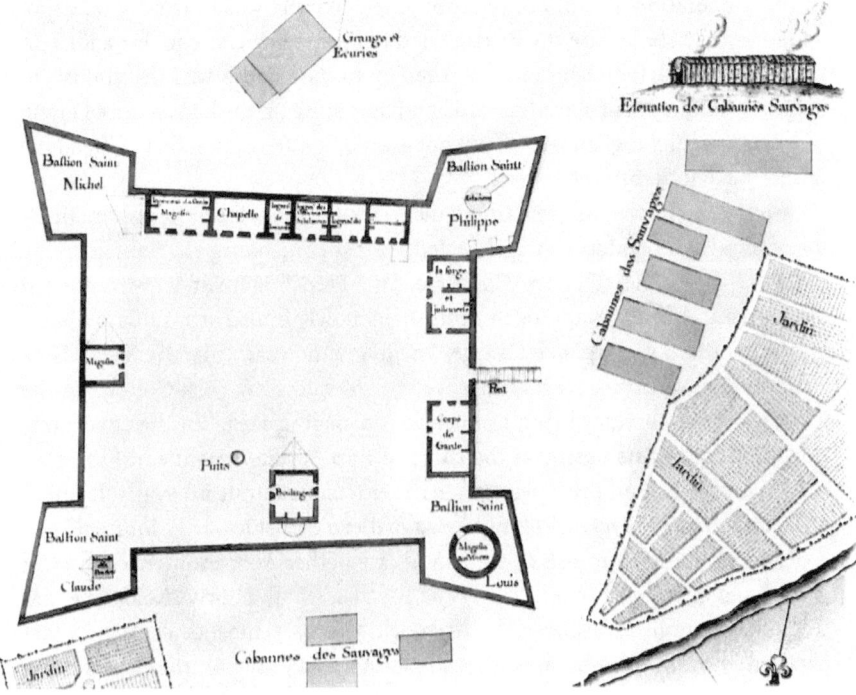

Royal Fort Frontenac, ca. 1740
Built in July 1673 at the mouth of the Cataraqui River, where Lake Ontario empties into the St Lawrence River. The original fort, a crude, wooden palisade structure, was originally called Fort Cataraqui but was renamed for Louis de Buade de Frontenac (1622–98), governor of New France. It was abandoned and razed in 1689, then rebuilt in 1695 completely of stone. This map shows the footprint of the fort with its well, gardens, outbuildings, stone kiln and ovens, and adjacent Indian longhouses (including a depiction of the latter). Courtesy of Boston Public Library.

state of defense, concluding prophetically: *if no improvements were made*, any enemy could take "it with the greatest of ease since they have no marches to make and can come with their bateaux and land on these shores in one night without being seen."[31]

Later the same year, after the destruction of the British fort at Oswego in August 1756, the French artillerist François le Mercier assessed that there was an acceptable risk of not improving Fort Frontenac's defenses as it did "not seem possible that the English could for a long time make an attempt on it since they no longer have Choueguen (Oswego)," despite its being "one of the worst posts" he had observed. In Le Mercier's opinion, the "works which have been made there to the present could not keep a company secure." He believed the only operational utility of retaining the aged fort was to use it as a depot and forward base in case the British tried to reestablish Oswego. He added an important caveat pointing out that the key to its defense was the ability "to keep our barques [ships] well-armed" and operating on the lake. André Doreil, Montcalm's chief logistician, would not even deign to call it a fort; instead, he pronounced it "a miserable shack."[32]

In 1757, the fort would remain a quiet backwater, with the British main effort under Lord Loudoun being directed against Louisbourg via Halifax on the main sea approach to Quebec. Conversely, the French main effort was directed on the central interior approach against the newly built Fort William Henry on the southern end of Lake George. The following year, 1758, the Marquis de Vaudreuil, governor of New France, wanted to raid New York Colony via the Mohawk River corridor using Frontenac as a staging area, but the concentration of a large British army at the ruins of Fort William Henry in June convinced him to call off this operation in order to concentrate all available forces at Ticonderoga to block this dangerous northern thrust toward Montreal.

The key question to ask at this point is whether Fort Frontenac was still considered a strategic objective in 1758. It was a small, poorly sited stone and wooden fort built to overawe the Iroquois in the seventeenth century, a fact apparently overlooked by most British planners. Plainly put, the post was ascribed capabilities it simply did not have. By the early eighteenth century, its place as a strategic stronghold and interface on the extreme frontier of New France with Indian nations had been replaced by Fort Niagara, built in 1726 at the southwest end of Lake Ontario, and Fort Detroit, on the west bank of the Detroit River between Lake Erie and Lake Huron.

In reality, by the time of Bradstreet's raid in August 1758, Fort Frontenac was no more than a transshipment depot manned by a skeletal garrison of invalids and commanded by a sexagenarian commandant. The latter was well-liked Pierre-Jacques Payen de Noyan, sixty-three, a long-serving veteran of the colonial regular troops, a seigneur, and the king's lieutenant at Trois-Rivières. His father, Bruno-Pierre Payen de Noyan, had been a colonial regular before him and had married Catherine-Jeanne Le Moyne de Longueuil et de Châteauguay, the sister of the celebrated Charles Le Moyne. Ironically, at the outset of his career, Pierre-Jacques had served briefly as commandant of Fort Frontenac while a twenty-six-year-old ensign.[33]

An active and intelligent man with a knack for speaking Indian languages, the Sieur de Courville described Pierre-Jacques Payen de Noyan as a bon vivant. De Noyan had held important command appointments during his career at Detroit and Fort St. Frédéric, where his influence with the Haudenosaunee saw him adopted as a brother of the Onondaga. In May 1749, he was made town major of Montreal; and by March 1756, the King's Lieutenant at Trois-Rivières. From 1744 onward, de Noyan attended most of the conferences held between the governor and the Six Nations. At a council held at Cataraqui in 1756, the Haudenosaunee asked Vaudreuil to "be so good as to give us our son, Monsieur de Noyan, as Commandant of Fort Frontenac." The following year the governor reassigned the sexagenarian captain with his several infirmities back to Fort Frontenac. De Noyan relieved the senior captain of the *troupes de la colonie*, M. de la Valtrie, on 22 May 1757, his ability to conduct diplomacy with the Six Nations considered more important than his cushy post as lieutenant governor in Trois-Rivières. The appointment to a frontier supply depot was a demotion in most people's eyes, though de Noyan was allowed to retain his sinecure as King's Lieutenant, causing Bradstreet in postraid letters and commentary to grandiosely style him as "the third in command of New France." With the appointment, Governor Vaudreuil actually believed he was doing the Sieur de Noyan a favor because of his outstanding debts. The lucrative opportunities of the post were well known, and, as the Sieur de Courville noted in his *Memoires*: "He had been given this command, which was far below his pay grade, in order to put his business affairs in order."[34]

De Noyan's troops numbered a grand total of fifty-seven aged and infirm officers, noncommissioned officers, and soldiers drawn from twenty-seven different companies of the colonial marines. All able and "fit to serve" soldiers had been sent to Montcalm's army at Fort Carillon on Lake Champlain in anticipation of the large northward thrust by Abercromby's army. The remainder of the tiny fort's complement included twenty-three women and children, one surgeon, twenty-seven voyageurs, two storekeepers, and seventeen laborers including an armorer, a blacksmith, a cowherd, coopers, carpenters, and shipwrights (see appendixes A and B).[35]

Weak and inadequately garrisoned, Fort Frontenac still had some strategic value for the French. It was a place for transshipment and storing Indian trade goods used to secure the loyalty of the tribes of the pays d'en haut. It served a similar purpose for munitions and provisions destined for the forts and defensive outposts of New France. Most importantly, it was the base for nine French ships, the entire naval strength of the French on the Lake, used primarily to transport materials across the lake. This tiny fleet comprised four French-built ships and five captured British vessels from Oswego (see appendix C). However, at the time of Bradstreet's raid, only two were armed and rigged for sailing. Naval "control" of Lake Ontario by this "fleet" of two, however, was chimerical at best given the lake's size and unpredictable weather. The two operable ships, it will be shown, were totally ineffective in preventing Bradstreet from making his coup. No one had paid heed to Le Mercier's advice that the true key to the fort's survival was maintaining an active and vigilant fleet on the lake, or Chevalier de la Pause's recommendations that the fort's defenses needed a serious overhaul. Both were significant oversights and failures that aided and abetted the able and audacious Bradstreet.

"No person in America is more capable of conducting an Inland Expedition in these parts"

Bradstreet was a consummate planner and ably performed the duties as one of the key logisticians for several successive campaigns mounted out of Albany during the Seven Years' War. While refining and developing a fledgling, then burgeoning, riverine operational capability for the British forces in this capacity, Bradstreet was knowingly and simultaneously honing a core of experts he could then utilize to execute his own pet project and, in the larger scheme of things, to perform his duties as DQMG for his respective commanders. This one activity in and of itself is Bradstreet's true legacy of the war and the one great accomplishment that guarantees him a place of the pantheon of British-American commanders. A pragmatic professional who did not suffer fools gladly was always destined to rub people the wrong way, but this trait was perhaps essential in conducting large armies through the wilderness. Bradstreet was also committed to consistently gathering intelligence, by both his own private means and a network of Albany traders (some former smugglers), of conditions at Niagara, Cataraqui, and down the St. Lawrence River to La Galette.[36]

His primary goals, if his sole biographer, Canadian historian William Godfrey, is to be believed, were entirely personal—promotion, profit, and preferment—rather than strategic. Godfrey suggests that Bradstreet's fixation with the raid stemmed from his steely focus on "the land and furs within the Great Lakes empire of the west . . . not fortresses at Quebec and Louisbourg." Fortresses and sugar islands were typical bargaining chips in European peace negotiations and could be ceded or returned by the diplomats in the wink of an eye. However, possession of the vaguely defined Great Lakes empire and a total restructuring of Indian alliances and trade patterns promised tangible gains to the colonies that the French would have difficulty countering even if the territory itself was eventually bartered away by Whitehall.[37]

With each successive commander from 1755 to 1758—Shirley, Lord Loudoun, and Abercromby—Bradstreet was relentless in his quest to persuade the local leadership and the political masters back "home" of the raid's importance and his unique qualifications to lead it. In the process, he was constantly forced to stress the perceived operational or strategic advantages to be achieved by such an operation—advantages that would justify the large expenditure of effort and resources necessary. In late 1757, Sir Richard Lyttleton, a regular recipient of Bradstreet's schemes and proposals in London, received a detailed analysis of the American situation from Bradstreet, who was blunt as to which person should benefit from his insights and recommendations.

"Should your friend Mr. Pitt be in the Administration, be pleas'd to lay this before him and assure him it is wrote prematurely but well digested and founded upon much experience," Bradstreet penned. He added that if Pitt was not in power, his friend was to use the submission as he thought fit; but Bradstreet hoped his "name is not mention'd lest umbrage might be taken at a person of so little consequence giving his thoughts so freely or medling at any rate with matters of so much importance." But the original plan to take Fort Frontenac, and the attendant reasons for doing so, were not Bradstreet's initially.[38]

As noted above, the idea originated with his superior Gen. William Shirley in September 1755. Unable to attack Fort Frontenac at that time because it was clearly a fort on French soil, Shirley wrote to the then secretary of state, Sir Thomas Robinson, after hostilities broke out in Nova Scotia and western Pennsylvania, stating that he could not move against Niagara the following year without undertaking "the Reduction of Fort Frontenac in the first place (which must be the work of but a few Days if attack'd early in the Spring with 4 or 5000 Men, and a proper Train of Artillery)." He believed the post to be strategic because it allegedly guarded "the only Entrance which the French have from Canada into the Lake Ontario with Vessells or any kind of Boats" and concluded that "Fort Frontenac is as much the Key of the Lake to the French, as Oswego is the Key of it to the English."[39]

In fact, Frontenac, as already stated by various professional French observers and landlords, did not control anything. Its true importance was as a naval base, for the real key to the dominion of the lake lay in naval mastery. In an enclosure to his letter, Shirley identified the real key terrain that needed to be taken or controlled to prevent French shipping from operating on Lake Ontario: La Galette, later replaced by Fort de la Présentation on the opposite south shore of the St. Lawrence River (near present-day Ogdensburg, New York) was located some sixty miles downriver northeast of Fort Frontenac in the Thousand Islands situated at the head of the first major set of rapids falling down to Montreal. He noted that the sixty-mile stretch of the St. Lawrence running from Fort Frontenac to La Galette was completely "navigable for Vessels of Force" and argued somewhat presciently that a robust British fort should be built "where Fort La Gallette now stands, or some Island conveniently situated for that Purpose in the River Iroquois near it, to secure that pass, from whence the Navigation of the River, near as far down as Montreal itself, might on Occasion be commanded by small Craft sent from thence, whilst the Fort would prevent the French from building any Vessells of Force at Oswegochi for the Navigation of the Lake."[40]

The only problem with seizing La Galette, as some members of Shirley's council pointed out, was its distance from Oswego and "the difficulty of supporting it against the strong Force, with which it must be expected, the French would, upon Favourable Opportunities attack it from Montreal; especially if there is a practicable road to it from Montreal by Land for transporting Artillery and Stores, as it is said." One might add that that such a move would have made the Haudenosaunee nervous, possibly angering them, and thus making the balancing act between the British and French more difficult for the Six Nations. As it was, by the mid-eighteenth century, the Mohawks were establishing a village at Akwesasne and the Onondagas at Oswegatchie, astride the western approach to the heart of New France.[41]

Shirley thus admitted that Frontenac was *not* really the key to naval control of the lake, but he went on in the same letter to confirm that he was "fully determin'd to begin Operations upon Lake Ontario by an Attack of Fort Frontenac alias Cadaraqui: unless I shall receive his Majesty's Orders to the Contrary."[42] His correspondence with Secretary Robinson thus concluded, Shirley told his subordinate Bradstreet that he could start planning the Frontenac strike over the winter of 1755-56 as he would be the principal candidate for command. But, as we have seen, the plans of the erstwhile governor of Massachusetts were foiled by Montcalm's preemptive strike against Oswego in the summer of 1756, and Shirley's replacement by Lord Loudoun.

Having been given the responsibility for the initial project, Bradstreet took complete ownership of the expedition plans and never let them go, despite the disheartening loss of Oswego in 1756. Indeed, by 1757, he was lobbying influential persons back in England and claiming that he was the ideal candidate to lead any expedition against Canada going by way of Lake Ontario. He bragged to his friend Sir Richard Lyttleton that "were it not owned by all degrees of People that no person in America is more capable of conducting an Inland Expedition in these parts than I am, I would by no means be so presumptious as to offer Myself as a Candidate for the Command of that part of the Forces which should go by the way of Oswego as I now do to You should the Scheme be approved of."[43]

However, in early 1757, with the forward operating base at Oswego gone, a strike against Frontenac was not even considered by Loudoun as a key element in the year's campaign design. Upon the Scottish earl's return from the aborted Louisbourg expedition, it was only Bradstreet's constant persistence to be allowed to execute the small boat raid that finally wore Loudoun down. While sorting through the political, administrative, and military muddles caused by the unfortunate loss of Fort William Henry in his absence, Loudoun read Bradstreet's detailed memorandum dated 4 January 1758 in which the latter offered to save the Crown some money and finance the entire Frontenac expedition, should it fail, out of his own pocket (and probably some of his Albany trading cronies' pockets as well).[44]

Loudoun agreed to let the raid proceed, but on the condition Bradstreet did not neglect the construction of all the bateaux required for the next campaign. The actual scope and intent of the raid from Lord Loudoun's perspective were laid out in as follows in his February 1758 letter to Pitt:

> Bradstreet . . . proposes to collect [batteau] Men early, and with Eight Hundred, (such as he can raise at his own Expence, and who will remain in the Batteau Service after this is over) to make an Attack on Cadaraqui, which he thinks, he can carry as soon as the Ice breaks up, or at least, to bring off or destroy, all the Vessels they now have on that Lake; and if he Succeeds, to be repaid his Expences, and be recommended to the King's Ministers, For their Favor and such Reward, as they may think fit his Services deserve. I am to furnish him with Boats and Provisions.[45]

Just as the plans for the raid appeared to be progressing, they were put on hold by Lord Loudoun's recall in March 1758. A new set of "strategic" instructions issued by William Pitt arrived for Bradstreet's new superior, Major General Abercromby, and once the latter had digested his new remit, he was unwilling to detach Bradstreet on his cross-lake foray in the spring when the ice broke up, especially given Pitt's very definite and prescriptive directives on the campaign at hand.

Bradstreet's biographer states that the frustrated logistician had felt obliged to have his plan reapproved and endorsed by the new commander for the upcoming campaign. To that end, he claims that a council of war was convened in March 1758 at Albany at Bradstreet's insistence. But the historical record does not bear this out. Official British documents, various journals of key officers, and diaries for the month of March, including Abercromby's personal correspondence, make no mention of any such council. The only document on which Godfrey bases this assertion is the first page of Bradstreet's own *Impartial Account*, published a year after the fact, and a somewhat dubious nineteenth-century biography of Philip Schuyler by one Benson J. Lossing, a self-taught editor, engraver, writer, and amateur historian, whose work has been characterized as "precariously located somewhere between serious scholarship and 'popular scribbling.'"[46]

Maj. Gen. James Abercromby reported to Prime Minister Pitt on 16 March 1758 from New York that he only received news of his new appointment as

"The Idol of the Army"
Brig. Gen. George Augustus, Viscount Howe (1725–58), was the de facto tactical commander of the British army in 1758. In this drawing, Lord Howe (*left, looking up*) is depicted leading by example: his lordship's hair is cropped short, his tricorn trimmed into a round hat, and all lace and colored facings and coattails are removed from his regimental jacket to make it as light as possible. Muskets of the men have been cut down to make them lighter and more manageable in the woods, while their barrels have been blackened to prevent sun glint. *The Renovated 55th*, courtesy of the artist, Gary Zaboly.

commander in chief with Pitt's new campaign instructions at Albany on 7 March. Upon receipt, he quickly gave Lord Howe "the necessary Orders relative to this Command; and immediately set out for this place, which from the depth of the snow, then beginning to melt, rendered the roads so difficult, that I was not able to reach it, till the 13th at noon."[47] He said nothing of a raid directed at Fort Frontenac.

"The Idol of the Army"

Strangely, Bradstreet's own correspondence to his agent Charles Gould and other patrons during this pre-Ticonderoga campaign period make no mention of a council of war. If there was a "council" convened in March 1758 to discuss Bradstreet's scheme as per biographer Godfrey's assertion (as alluded to in Bradstreet's *Impartial Account*), then it would have had to have occurred before

7 March while Abercromby was still at Albany. This author is of the strong opinion that Bradstreet's pre-Ticonderoga council is a fiction and that the story of Lord Howe's alleged removal of "every objection" to Bradstreet's scheme was used by him to embellish his account and shamelessly to take advantage of the popularity of the dead hero.

It is a perfect example of eighteenth-century self-serving propaganda done in bad taste and goes a long way toward explaining the complete silence and indifference that greeted Bradstreet's *Impartial Account*, published in London several months after the raid. The self-promoting colonel stated that early "in the spring of the year 1758, when the plan of operations for the then ensuing campaign was the subject of deliberation in our military councils it was [Howe] who judg'd an attempt upon Fort Frontenac (whilst the whole force of Canada was employ'd in opposing our incursion into their country on the side of Lake George) to be attended with the utmost probability of success." Surprisingly, Bradstreet makes no mention of his previous commanders' involvement in the plan, nor does he make any mention of the defeated James Abercromby, except in generic terms such as "commander in chief" or "general." The only inference one can draw from Bradstreet's one-sided account was that he, and he alone, was the sole progenitor and advocate of the daring—but more importantly, successful—plan.[48]

Cunningly, his 1759 *Impartial Account* played up unnamed mysterious naysayers who objected to his 1758 raid, noting that, from the outset, many "objections were started, and many difficulties rais'd against it, as an unfeasible plan." More important was the identity of the white knight who rescued his plan, the beloved George Augustus, Viscount Howe—who was tragically killed before the Battle of Ticonderoga the previous summer. Howe, a champion who "excell'd in penetration and judgement . . . highly approv'd of the scheme," stepped forward, "remov'd every objection, and obtained the assent of the general, to its being carried into execution as soon as our army had made an establishment on the north side of the Lake George."[49]

Bradstreet's savior was thus a personage carefully selected to capture the attention of all who picked up his privately printed, "Anonymous" pamphlet, and his selection was gauged to convince the meanest of skeptics of Bradstreet's obvious merit and ingenuity. With Howe conveniently dead, and thus unable to dispute the details of what transpired prior to the disaster at Ticonderoga, the message in the pamphlet was unequivocally clear: the sainted hero had given Bradstreet's plan a resounding stamp of approval when no others would.[50]

To say that the aristocrat was as beloved in death as he was in life would be an understatement. Brig. Gen. Howe had been the *de facto* commander of the Ticonderoga expedition, much admired by both provincial and regular soldiers alike for his no-nonsense approach to soldiering. The oldest of three brothers, Prime Minister Pitt described Lord Howe as "a character of ancient times; a complete model of military virtue." Some historians have gone so far as to say that if Howe had survived the Seven Years' War and become the commander in chief of North America instead of Thomas Gage, there would have been no American Revolution. He had once admonished his regimental officers for criticizing provincial soldiers saying, "Every gentleman officer will find his equal in every regiment of Americans," and he claimed to know them very well. "Beware how you underestimate their abilities and feelings, civil, social and military."[51]

A Massachusetts soldier assigned to the Ticonderoga expedition was moved to write in his journal:

> Lord How was the Idol of the Army, in him they placed the utmost confidence, from the few days I had to observe of his method of conducting, it was not very extravagant to supose that every Soldier in the army had a personal attachment to him, he frequently came among the Carpenters, and his manner was so easy and fermiller, that you loost all that constraint and diffidence we feele when addressed by our Superiors, whose manners are forbidding.

Another provincial, though not a raid participant, also closely witnessed firsthand Bradstreet's "method of conducting" but dismissed him as "the furious Bradstreet hated by all the Army."[52]

Bradstreet and Howe form an interesting contrast. The first was a tireless results-oriented workaholic with a giant chip on his shoulder, embarrassed of his perceived lower social standing because he was an American regular officer who had advanced in rank further than any other native-born soldier. The second was a charismatic aristocrat and natural-born leader, comfortable in his own skin. In private correspondence at the end of May 1758, Bradstreet bragged about his herculean efforts in the quartermaster's department, claiming his conduct had gained "much credit with all degrees of people in America that are Free from Envy." His successes naturally brought detractors, but confident that he had the backing of Howe, Bradstreet openly gloated, "I am sensible I am an object of their attention and in which I glory as much as I despise them and lose no opportunity of making them sensible of it." He perhaps might have been a little less arrogant and forthright in his behavior around headquarters had he known that Howe's days on earth were numbered.

The psychological rout of the army started with Howe's demise on 7 July, the day *before* the day of battle, which affected everyone in the army from

Abercromby down to the enlisted ranks. Sgt. Garret Albertson of the New Jersey Blues confessed, "I do not remember ever to have felt greater distress of mind than I did that night. I thought the hand of Providence was turned against us in a lonely wilderness." Bradstreet would also find himself alone in a wilderness after Ticonderoga, but a metaphorical one of his own making. He would need to muster every ally, bend many arms, and call in every favor owed him before he could land his long-sought-after prize—an independent command.[53]

Eyes and ears

Forty-two Haudenosaunee warriors accompanied Brother Bradstreet on his raid as scouts and pilots. Their participation provided diplomatic cover and intelligence for the respective Haudenosaunee nations at the operational level while the presence of their warriors guaranteed the physical security and tactical safety of Bradstreet's force on its travels through disputed lands and waters. *Life and Death*, courtesy of the artist, Robert Griffing, Paramount Press.

CHAPTER 2

Assembly

Defences, musters, preparations, should be maintain'd, assembled and collected.

—*Shakespeare,* Henry V

The raid started and ended at the Great Carrying Place. Known to the Haudenosaunee as *Deo-wahne sta*, "the place where canoes are carried from one stream to another," it was vigilantly guarded by the Oneida nation. Throughout the early years of the eighteenth century, the Five Nations (later Six, with the addition of the Tuscarora in 1722), whose land stretched west from the Hudson River to Niagara Falls, had tried through diplomacy to establish a policy that no more forts would be built without their consent on their territory as the French had done at Fort Frontenac on Lake Ontario. They did, however, tolerate the French building a trading post at Niagara as early as 1679, followed fifty years later by the English building a rival post at Oswego.[1]

Faced with two powerful European colonial powers, the Haudenosaunee developed three parties, defined by historians according to their "foreign policy": neutral, pro-English, and pro-French. Each had its supporters among the various members of the Confederacy. The neutralist party, or Keepers of the Fire—who favored the most independent stance possible, and were drawn heavily from the Onondaga—kept their council at the central village named Onondaga near present-day Syracuse. The Anglophile party was clearly and loudly led by the Mohawk, who previously had been allied with the Dutch and who began what came to be known as the "Covenant Chain alliance." In the west, nearest to Fort Niagara, were the Seneca, who broadly favored the French. The other members of the Confederacy set their course according to their assessment of the discussions between these three. The result of the neutralist councils and the annual conferences at Albany and Montreal was a careful elaborate interplay of positions toward the two colonial powers neighboring the lands of the Haudenosaunee and their indigenous allies beyond. The political debate reached a crescendo at the end of the seventeenth century as the Confederacy endeavored to respond to an increasingly devastating war with French and indigenous enemies. The Great Peace of Montreal of 1701 basically set neutrality as the agreed-upon Haudenosaunee stance in any future wars between European colonial powers.[2]

As early as 1724, two years after the establishment of a British post at Oswego, New York, merchants had recognized the importance of the Great Carrying Place. This portage between the Mohawk River and Wood Creek became a critical node in the main eighteenth-century trade route between the Atlantic seaboard of North America and interior of the continent. The actual "carry" or portage road went up from the Mohawk over a plain connecting the two rivers where they approached within a mile and a half of each other in their respective watersheds. At this point, both waterways were still deep enough for bateaux and their cargoes to negotiate. Stockade forts were erected at either end of the portage to protect the troops as well as docks to facilitate the loading and unloading of stores and provisions. The only other significant waterway connecting the Atlantic Ocean to the Great Lakes was the St. Lawrence River.

The Oneida tribe benefited greatly from this arrangement, earning cash as navvies loading and unloading boats, and by supplying carts and sleds with which they hauled the boats' cargoes over the portage. Many of them became experienced "battoemen" themselves. The distance the cargo had to be carried depended on the water levels on each side of the portage. Both rivers were usually high in the spring from snows melting in the Adirondacks that made for a short carry, but much lower in the summer months during times of drought or little rain, making for a longer carry.[3] The latter problem was solved on the western end by building an ingenious dam system, similar to a lock system, but with larger ponds or basins in which the boats could first be loaded. They were then floated down the creek by opening a sluice gate in the dam to temporarily raise the levels of water in the creek below until the next pond and dam farther down was encountered and the step-down process was repeated.

From Albany, New York, on the Hudson River, cargo would first be transported overland the approximately twenty miles to Schenectady, located on the Mohawk River. Supplies were then carried upstream on the Mohawk using bateaux. The vessels varied in size depending on whether they were being used on rivers, or on wide-open spaces like lakes; those used on lakes needed their sides built higher to account for wind and choppy conditions. Sturdy,

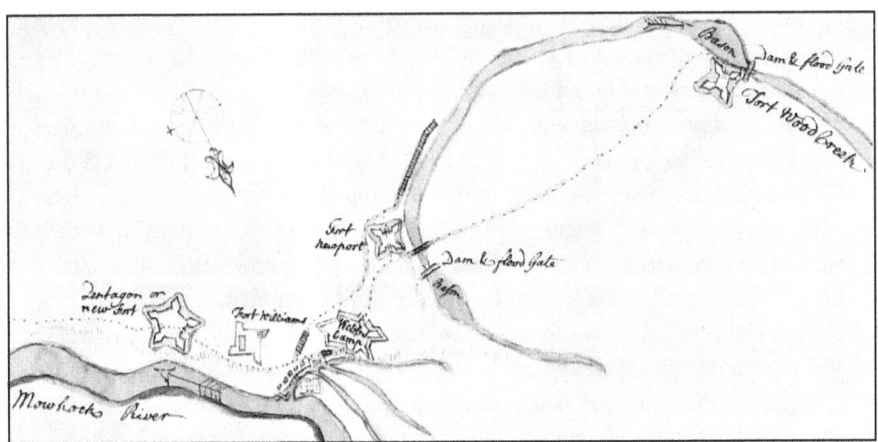

The Oneida Carrying Place, 1756

A contemporary ink sketch map of the Carry showing the 1756 encampment of Gen. Daniel Webb where the new Fort Stanwix was constructed in the fall and winter of 1758 on the eastern, or Mohawk River, side. John Bradstreet launched his force against Fort Frontenac on Lake Ontario from here on 16 August 1758, but first cleared the jammed four-mile section of the creek between Forts Newport and Wood Creek that General Webb had ordered blocked after destroying all the forts and buildings at the Carry. Courtesy of the *Rome Sentinel*.

clinker-built, and flat-bottomed, each bateau could carry a cargo of one to two tons upstream against the current, and as much as five tons on the return trip. Two tons, on average, was equivalent to twenty-two men and eight barrels of flour. The bateaux quickly became an army's workhorses that could be used to enhance its capability in a riverine environment.[4]

After negotiating various rifts and rills in the river, as well as one major portage around the Little (or Mohawk) Falls just above Fort Herkimer, the bateaux would reach the Great Carrying Place, which is the location of modern-day Rome, New York. After relaunching into a new watershed at the western end of the portage, the boat followed the serpentine course of Wood Creek (appropriately named *Kah-ne-go-dick* by the Haudenosaunee, or "the place where one gets lost") to Lake Oneida. At the western end of the lake, one entered the Oswego River and ultimately traveled downstream to Lake Ontario at Oswego, the gateway to all the Great Lakes stretching for another thousand miles inland.

The cost to the British of losing control of the Great Carrying Place became clear not long after the destruction of Fort Bull and the subsequent capture of Fort Oswego in 1756 by Montcalm. This sad truth was first hammered home by two attacks on the German settlers who lived on the westernmost edge of

German Flatts. The first bloody raid occurred on 12 November 1757, at three in the morning, when a mixed Canadien-Oswegatchie force of three hundred colonial regulars and Onondaga warriors attacked the north side of the river, burned sixty-five houses and farms, killed 40 men, women, and children and took another 140 captive to Montreal. Although the friendly Oneida had warned their German neighbors of the pending attack for weeks, the settlers, who thought they had an understanding with Governor Vaudreuil that they were to be considered neutral, had made no defensive preparations. Four and a half months later, it was followed by smaller and swifter attack on 31 April 1758, this time directed at the south side of the river around Fort Herkimer. One of Sir William Johnson's officers wrote to him that the Palatines were "in the utmost Consternation, . . . determined to abandon the River." Soon an exodus of frightened families was flowing down the valley to Schenectady and points south.[5]

"Press'd or otherwise employ'd"

For these and other reasons, the ever-cautious General Abercromby was keen to retake the strategic height of land that controlled the portage to and from Oswego on his western flank. One of his first measures was to authorize the raising of a new ranger company under officers and men of the Indian Service familiar with the country. Sir William Johnson was grateful for the money to raise the rangers, which had actually been his recommendation. He found that he could provide capable officers to lead the new company, but men to fill the ranks in such a specialized scouting unit were few and far between. Johnson reported to Abercromby in May that his Indian officers had only managed to recruit twenty men. Most men had already been snapped up as battoemen, wagoners, and provincial soldiers.[6]

The leadership of the new ranger company was solid. Hendrick Wendell, the captain; his lieutenant, William Hare; and ensign Jacob Snell were all wood-wise locals, but they were unable to recruit "the Best Men" because they had already "been press'd or otherwise employed."[7] Thus Wendell and his recruiting sergeants were forced to recruit further afield, principally New York City. Not surprisingly, they got the leftovers and dregs from a shrinking colonial manpower pool that had been drained by regular and provincial regiments and the Royal Navy. The rangers assigned to the Mohawk–Oswego corridor were, therefore, with a few exceptions, just as raw and inexperienced as their counterparts in the provincial regiments and probably even more likely to get lost in the woods.

The regulars of the 22nd and 17th Foot that had guarded the valley for the winter had marched off to Albany and taken ships to New York in April 1758 to take part in the Amherst expedition against Louisbourg and Cape Breton. They had been replaced by the first provincial companies that reported to Albany for duty and the four New York Independent Companies of the regular army, long stationed in the province. Abercromby's predecessor, Lord Loudoun, had struggled to sort out the latter upon his arrival in North America in 1756. The problems of the Independent Companies all stemmed from their initial establishment in the year 1700 and had remained unresolved for fifty-eight years. They were the poorest-paid British regulars in the army as 10 percent of the private men's pay was deducted to provide for their two surgeons and a chaplain. As the companies had no colonel or effective supervision from Britain, one might add the "most neglected" as well. They simply became a source of profit to unscrupulous officers who pocketed their men's subsistence money and were lax in recruiting to fill recurring company vacancies. Upon arrival, Loudoun found the Independent Companies to be at only 40–60 percent strength and badly trained, disciplined, and equipped as well. Loudoun weeded out commanders, cashiering one for embezzlement, and forcing another to resign under the threat of court-martial. These immediate actions improved discipline and accountability, but it was still hard for the new company officers to compete with other recruiters to fill out their ranks when almost every other

Frontier baronet

Sir William Johnson (ca. 1715–74) was appointed British superintendent of Indian affairs in 1756 for the Northern Department. Throughout his career, the Irish-born Johnson combined his personal business with official diplomacy, acquiring tens of thousands of acres of Native land and becoming very wealthy in the process. Johnson commanded Haudenosaunee, regular, and colonial forces during the French and Indian War. His victory at the Battle of Lake George in 1755 earned him a baronetcy, and his capture of Fort Niagara four years later brought him additional renown. Courtesy of Library and Archives Canada, Acc. No. 1989-407-1.

regiment, whether provincial or regular, could offer more pay. A veteran of the Battle of Monongahela and the senior Independent commander, Capt. Horatio Gates, while stationed at Fort Herkimer, became the senior British officer on the western frontier of New York.[8]

By 1 June, the intelligence picture on enemy movements toward Oswego and the Mohawk Valley had begun to coalesce. At Fort Johnson, about halfway between Schenectady and Fort Herkimer on the Mohawk River, Sir William informed Abercromby that he had just that day received a belt of wampum, "lodged with the Oneidas" several weeks earlier with the explicit instruction that it was "not to be sent [back] unless the Intelligence of the Enemy's approach was certain." George Croghan, Sir William's right-hand man and deputy, also sent intelligence by courier that arrived the same day as the wampum. After a visit to the principal Oneida village near the lake of the same name, Croghan reported that he had been told by trusted members of that nation "that a body of French & Indians would soon come to the carrying place from Sweegatchie by Land, that at the same time there would come another body by Oswego with artillery." When all had rendezvoused at the Great Carrying Place, they would then "proceed down this river as far as they could & destroy every place they came."[9]

This intelligence was a very accurate description of the spoiling attack ordered earlier in the year by the governor of New France. It was still very much in the offing in mid-June, with preparations at Montreal, Oswegatchie, and Fort Frontenac well underway. Vaudreuil's plan called for Brigadier General Levis, seconded by the governor-general's brother, François-Pierre de Rigaud de Vaudreuil, to take an elite force of 2,500 men and threaten the exposed western flank of Abercromby's area of operations. The hope was that such a raid would disrupt the assembling British-provincial army located at Fort Edward. The French force would comprise 400 regulars drawn from the pickets, or light infantry companies, of Montcalm's regular regiments; 400 colonial regulars; 800 Canadien militia; and approximately 800–900 native warriors, including 500 Ottawas, Abenakis, and Mission Haudenosaunee drawn from Oswegatchie, Kahnawake, and the Lake of Two Mountains.[10]

The French raid was the pet project of Vaudreuil and one he was loath to abort. The regulars under Montcalm had deemed it "Don Quixotry" in the light of the overwhelming evidence that a British-American army outnumbering Montcalm's army by three to one was coming in force up the Lake Champlain corridor. By the last week of June, Vaudreuil reluctantly redirected Levis's raiding force to rejoin the regular battalions with Montcalm already posted at Ticonderoga, where they were feverishly establishing a defensive blocking position. A senior British officer would later observe that timing had been the most critical factor in all the operations conducted during the 1758 campaign.

Maj. James Robertson of the Royal Americans, a Scot serving as Abercromby's DQMG in New York City, remarked to the Earl of Morton at the end of the campaign year that they had lost invaluable time "by laying aside Lord Loudoun's [plan] which was Calculated to improve every Advantage, that Climate, Situation and Numbers could give us over the Enemy."

Loudoun's plan had called for a small army, composed principally of regulars, "at Ticonderoga by the end of May, and before the Enemy could have brought together a Thousand Men to oppose him." Instead, great strains were placed on the colonial mobilization system, with Abercromby its principal victim, unable "to get the Provincial Troops in motion till late in the Season." Because of the large provincial contingent, the army "had double the Number of Battoes to build and Provisions to carry, could not arrive at Ticonderoga till the 8th of July, and there found the Enemy's entire force entrenched, the greatest part of it which had only been able to get there a few Days before General Abercrombie." One might add some logistical shortcomings: not enough muskets to go around, nor tents to go over their heads. In Robertson's assessment, the pick and shovel work at Louisbourg would have been more suited to 8,000 New Englanders, "every labouring man worth two soldiers" and easily supplied by the Royal Navy. By contrast at Ticonderoga, the blunt Scottish logistician thought that "every man *but a good soldier* [was] an unsupportable Burthen."[11]

"Yankee Doodle came to town"

The fifty-year-old doctor leaned back against the stone wall of a well, just outside the Dutch house known locally as "Fort Crailo" where he was staying with Col. John Van Rensselaer's family. The Crailo estate consisted of 1,500 acres in what is currently the city of Rensselaer, New York, plus another 60,000 acres in and around the village of Claverack, which by the mid-eighteenth century had come to be known as "Greenbush." The owners, a branch of the powerful Van Rensselaer family, were prosperous, ambitious, and very much involved in the military and civic affairs of Albany County and the colony of New York.

Richard Shuckburgh, a London-trained surgeon, had first come to New York in 1737 to take up a commission as one of the two surgeons to the four New York Independent Companies now in garrison along the Hudson–Mohawk corridor. He had become a close friend of Sir William Johnson, and through this social connection, he moonlighted as the surgeon to the Mohawks and learned their language. The affable and witty doctor soon married a local Dutch woman, dabbled in land speculation, and quickly became a fixture in Albany society. On his death in August 1773 at Schenectady, a New York newspaper would describe him as "a gentleman of a very genteel family, and of infinite jest and humour."[12]

The sketch he was preparing of the house would be a small personal thank-you gift for his gracious hosts who had accommodated him on such short notice on his way to Albany. The afternoon sun shone brightly on the western walls of the brick house, highlighting the small high windows above ground level that had served as makeshift loopholes in earlier times against Indian raiders. Fort Crailo's location on the eastern bank of the Hudson with its flat alluvial farmlands, orchards, mills, a store, and a ferry crossing to Albany on the western bank, made it an ideal mustering point and encampment for the provincial regiments marching westward from Connecticut and Massachusetts to soldier on the New York frontier.

As Dr. Shuckburgh finished off his drawing, a body of troops came tramping down the road, their officers mounted, raising clouds of dust. He was struck by the plainness of their brown jackets of varying shades but enchanted by their solemn sense of purpose, every man including the officers with a jaunty chicken feather stuck in his tricorn hat. An old melody from a child's nursery rhyme drifted up from a forgotten recess of his mind as the Connecticut provincials proudly marched past. Words to a little ditty quickly took shape on one of his sketchbook pages, the first four stanzas destined for history:

Yankee Doodle came to town
Riding on a pony
Stuck a feather in his hat
And called it Macaroni.

The reaction of his Dutch hosts to this tongue-in-cheek but affectionate parody of the serious New Englanders (probably sung by Shuckburgh after dinner) is unrecorded, but it no doubt brought a chuckle or two. There was no love lost between the Dutch Yorkers and the New Englander Yankees. It was certainly a tradition in the Van Rensselaer family that "Yankee Doodle" originated at Crailo, though the derisory song's true origins have been the subject of inordinate musical scholarship and debate since. It would become a popular song for the remainder of the war with many verses added, some of a very ribald nature. It would only be proudly reclaimed and sanitized by the New Englanders as a marching song in the next major war, with many more patriotic verses added.[13]

Shuckburgh was an old hand at campaigning. He was a veteran of the Monongahela battle and very much involved in dealing with the medical aftermath of the fighting at Fort William Henry. He tried to stay out of Albany proper as much as possible, since smallpox still lingered there after three years of constant troop movements back and forth through British North America's largest inland city. Every spring of the war, the permanent population of the

Pearl Street, Albany

Artist's reconstruction of what eighteenth-century Albany might have looked like to the Rev. Daniel Shute and other provincial soldiers passing through: a bustling port and trading center, located at the head of the navigable Hudson River. Note the strong Dutch architectural influence. Postcard of painting by James Eights (1798–1882), courtesy of Library of Congress.

small city would swell from 3,000 souls to over 10,000 at any given time, with infusions of troops assembling to draw all the paraphernalia needed for waging war on the frontier, the nearest French fort being a mere one hundred miles away. At the end of campaigns, the hospitals and private homes would be filled with the wounded and dying.

Located at the head of the navigable Hudson River, Albany was a bustling port and trading center, and, almost a century after its capture from the Dutch by the English, it still retained the largest non-English-speaking population of any British colonial city. Petr Kalm, the famous Swedish botanist who passed through town in 1749, did not speak from any preconceived bias when he recorded his first impressions of its citizens:

> The inhabitants of Albany and its environs are almost all Dutchmen. They speak Dutch, have Dutch preachers, and the divine service is performed in that language. Their manners are likewise quite Dutch; their dress is however like that of

the English.... The avarice, selfishness and immeasurable love of money of the inhabitants of Albany are very well known throughout all North America, by the French and even by the Dutch in the lower part of New York province... I was here obliged to pay for everything twice, thrice and four times as much as in any part of North America which I have passed through. If I wanted their assistance, I was obliged to pay them very well for it, and when I wanted to purchase anything or be helped in some case or other, I could at once see what kind of blood ran in their veins, for they either fixed exorbitant prices for their services or were very reluctant to assist me. Such was the people in general. However, there were some among them who equalled any in North America or anywhere else, in politeness, equity, goodness, and readiness to serve and to oblige; but their number fell far short of that of the former.[14]

The outbreak of the "French war" gave the merchants of Albany and New York City easy opportunities to reap vast profits from the prodigious amount of provisions and stores needed upriver to victual the army. Money was also to be made by transporting regiments of regular and provincial troops on their sloops and brigs to and from their campaigns. Major landowners in and around Albany and points north cashed in as well, making their estates available for use as encampments, complete with stables, wells, ovens, forage, cartage, and other services for regiments starting on campaign.

The first provincial regiment to be fully armed, accoutred, and allocated their bateaux and carts in 1758 was Oliver Delancey's New York Regiment. It was a three-battalion unit that drew its recruits from all the counties stretching from Albany County on the frontier in the north down the Hudson River valley to the eastern tip of Long Island. As these Yorker soldiers were the first skilled laborers to assemble at Albany in May, they were immediately targeted and canvassed by Bradstreet and others to be the specialists urgently needed to kick-start the massive logistical machine that would feed, house, and transport the largest army ever to have been assembled in North America to this date. Carpenters, stonemasons, and bricklayers were needed to build and maintain the forts and blockhouses along the lines of communications. Battoemen were urgently needed to move supplies and troops up and down the rivers, shipwrights to build and maintain the bateaux and whalers, and wagoners to convey the tons of cargo from the wharves in Albany to the loading docks at Schenectady, or further upstream on the Hudson and Mohawk Rivers. As both these rivers had large falls and rills blocking the river navigation, these major chokepoints necessitated transshipment of large cargoes to wagons plying the portage roads or trails built to bypass the obstacles. The cargoes would then be reloaded into other battoes or scows waiting above or below to carry the cargoes forward or downward on the next stretch of the respective river.

The case of Capt. Goose Van Schaik's company of the 3rd Battalion, New Yorkers, reveals the impact of placing men on detached service to address critical logistical needs. The unit was stationed at Nistiguana (Niskayuna) on the Mohawk River just east of Schenectady as of 24 May 1758, his company of 102 men of all ranks had withered away to just 35, a weak platoon. One officer, four NCOs, and 42 men were detached on the "Battoe Service," and another 21 were detached to serve as wagoners. All of them were working for Bradstreet.[15]

Thousands of provincial soldiers were headed to Albany. Some came by water, as one New York newspaper reported in early June: "several vessels have passed this City on their way to Albany, having on board some of the Connecticut, Rhode-Island and other Eastern Government forces who are to act in the present Campaign to the Northward." The *New American Magazine* reported on 5 June 1758 that "the New Jersey Forces of between 11[00] and 1200 of the likeliest well-set men for the Purpose [and] perhaps, turned out on any Campaign, passed by this place for Albany." They were the Jersey Blues under Col. John Johnston, "all in high Spirits; their Uniform blue, faced with red, grey Stockings and Buckskin Breeches."[16] The rest, mostly Massachusetts troops and some from Connecticut and New Hampshire, came by land. Traditionally, the Bay Colony troops mustered at Worcester and used the western post road to march to the border of the colony via Springfield. Most regiments preferred this route as it went through inhabited villages with taverns, wells, stables, and large dry, warm barns to sleep in at night.

"A way so bad that it is become a Proverb"

Not all regiments used the post road. There was a shorter, supposedly faster, route farther north, reached by branching north off the main route at Brookfield then marching to Northampton and Hatfield. From the latter town it was only a five-day march west to the Hudson, albeit on a twenty-mile trail traversing some of the most unforgiving wilderness in western Massachusetts. "The greater part of the way our Troops marched from Hatfield to Greenbush is *inexpressibly* bad," wrote Daniel Shute, a young Massachusetts minister, after his arrival at the Van Rensselaer estates, "and the greater part of the Regiment, at present, what with the badness of the way . . . appear to be unfit for duty."[17] Dr. Caleb Rea, the surgeon of Colonel Bagley's regiment, which had preceded Shute's regiment by just a few days, could not restrain himself from writing down what was on everyone's minds: "I can't but remark here the universal complaint there was among all the Bay Regiments of their being march'd thro' these woods . . . a way so bad that it is become a Proverb. No one need pass muster or any other Proof of their Fittness for a Campain but to march thro' these woods." Rea went even further, hinting darkly that a cabal of provincial colonels was responsible for inflicting unnecessary casualties on his men such as "broken shins, spraint joints, bruised feet and other accidental wounds by falling over stones & stumps into quagmires &c."[18]

While most of the soldiers' campaign diaries and journals that have survived from 1758 are simple chronicles recording the daily weather or distances traveled, the Reverend Shute's is very revealing. Shute, a thirty-three-year-old Harvard-trained minister from Malden, Massachusetts, was one of many young chaplains stepping forward for their first campaign. He had joined his regiment at Hatfield just before it marched into the wilderness. Ordained at twenty-four as the pastor of Second Church in Hingham, Shute carried in his pocket his commission that charged him to "carefully and diligently discharge the Duty of a Chaplain" with "Loyalty, Piety and Learning" in "a Regiment of Foot commanded by Colonel Joseph Williams."[19] His chatty journal is full of observations on meeting interesting people along the way, including many fellow ministers, civilian and military, whose services he would attend. He also wrote compassionately of the conditions encountered by the private soldiers and their welfare, his own fearful obsession regarding smallpox and other diseases, his worries about his personal expenses on the campaign, and the vexing loss of his horse from Van Rensselaer's pasture in Greenbush. But of most interest are his asides on the leadership of his regiment and the army writ large.

His entries also reveal something of what motivated the men in his regiment. His Sunday sermon on 18 June was drawn from Genesis 28:20–21: "Then Jacob made a vow, saying, 'If God will be with me and will watch over me on this journey I am taking and will give me food to eat and clothes to wear so that I return safely to my father's household, then the Lord will be my God.'" He was preaching to officers and men—most of them born during the Great Awakening—who had been told from an early age they were part of God's divine purpose.[20] Descendants of men and woman who had fled religious persecution in the Old World with their Bibles and their copies of Foxe's *Book of Martyrs*, they had also brought with them to the New an unshakable conviction as to the truth of their religion and the righteousness of their cause. At the core of this still-Puritan outlook was a vision of a godly society, founded on a national covenant between God and his chosen people. Shute was reminding his flock that their benefactor was watching over them and that if they honored their covenant or "vow" to him, God would see them all safely returned to their "Father's household."

Returns detailing the arrivals of provincial regiments indicate that they were trickling in as late as mid-June, predominantly from New England. Daniel Shute's regiment was one of the last to arrive. —the first 436 of all ranks arriving on 13 June, and the second division, 443 strong, coming in the following day. Their weapons and tents were brought over to Albany Flatts and issued on 15 June 1758. Their "fractious" commanding officer, Joseph Williams of Roxbury, Massachusetts, spent his days in Albany, constantly bickering with staff over arms, tentage, provisions, and other kit to which he felt entitled.[21] John Appy, secretary to General Abercromby, was frustrated by the slow pace at which provincial colonels in Albany were moving their units up the line to participate in the campaign and complained to William Pitt's undersecretary on 2 July 1758. "Their dilatoriness and the constant trifling demands they make of sundries not provided by His Majesty," Appy believed, were motivated by "no other view than Cloaking their tardiness, . . . almost incredible to those who have not been an Eye Witness to it."[22]

When Colonel Williams and his regiment finally got underway and marched north to Fort Edward on 21 June 1758, news of his troublesome behavior and the rawness of his troops preceded him. It was decided that he was persona non grata in the main army and was therefore ordered to turn his men around at Half-Moon and return to Schenectady to relieve Colonel Bagley's Massachusetts regiment. One regiment's disorganization was another's reprieve. Dr. Caleb Rea reported in his journal on 23 July that his unit was ordered "to March to Fort Edward, and Col° Jos. Williams to take our station this way." The switch of regiments took place, Rea explained, because "our Regiment had been recommended to the General as better for a Martial Enterprise than Col. Will^ms." Rea's colleague, the Rev. John Cleaveland, added that Bagley's regiment breathed a collective sigh of relief, "the officers and soldiers [now] pleased with the thot of Joining the Army." By contrast, Daniel Shute confided in his journal that the change of assignment had given "great uneasiness" to his regiment, "and not less to ye Officers than to ye Privates."[23]

On 1 July 1758, Gen. John Stanwix, the senior officer tasked by Abercromby to build the new fort, confirmed to Colonel Williams that "he must in a few days march his Regt up the Mohawk River, to ye great carrying place, about 60 miles above the German Flatts." Stanwix, a sixty-five-year-old late bloomer, was colonel-commandant of the 1st Battalion, Royal Americans, and was the perfect choice for the job. The newly promoted brigadier was well liked, and he had extensive logistical experience as a deputy quartermaster general like his subordinate Bradstreet.[24]

The Massachusetts men were to carry "two months provisions, artillery & ammunition in Battoes prepared for ye purpose." Not only did this order effectively shut the door on any hopes that Williams's provincials would be part of the Ticonderoga expedition; it constituted a very public and humiliating slap in the face for their self-important colonel. Not surprisingly, Shute's commanding officer traveled personally "to Albany to wait upon General Stanwix for redress of some difficulties," but Williams's plea to get out of the newly assigned mission fell on deaf ears. His regiment would be the second provincial regiment to march to the Great Carrying Place.[25]

A week earlier, on 14 June, the muster master for Albany and the New York Regiment, Sir William Johnson, had received a letter from one of the Yorker captains sent up the Mohawk Valley earlier in the summer whose troops were now garrisoning one of the settlements vacated by the regulars. Capt. Elias Hand, commanding a company of 2nd Battalion men posted at Stone Arabia, complained that another Yorker captain, Samuel Badgely of the 3rd Battalion, was pulling seniority on him and trying to order him and his men around. Johnson, not really in the chain of command, referred the matter immediately to Oliver Delancey, their colonel in chief, and General Abercromby at Fort Edward. This discord, plus the latest intelligence from Sir William—that all the Six Nations were now agreed on the likelihood of a large French force coming to raid the Mohawk settlements—finally stirred Abercromby into action. Ironically, his decision coincided with the same moment that his French counterpart was forced to stand down his long-awaited and much-touted raid and instead send the proposed strike force under Levis south to Carillon to reinforce Montcalm's small army.

But in the meantime, a firm paternal hand was needed up the valley to command and control the disparate units of rangers, regulars, and provincials, while the remainder of the army moved northward to Ticonderoga—someone who could prepare the way for a new fort to rise in the wilderness. They found the ideal man.[26]

"It gave me great Concern"

A tall, white-haired man stood in the darkened upper story of a fortified house built in 1739 by Hendrick Frey and looked south over the Mohawk River. The stone house, shutters loopholed for defense, had a feel of permanence, though it was relatively new, having replaced the old palisaded log trading post known as Fort Frey during Queen Anne's War (1701–13). Lt. Col. Charles Clinton had arrived there the previous Sunday afternoon, 25 June, from Jellis Fonda's house downstream and turned in early. He awoke at dawn from a peculiar dream, so vivid that he felt compelled to record it in his journal: "Dreamt that my Father was Dead and Laid in his coffin. that my mother was by & it was to be Closed, but I said it should not till I would Strow over him some sweet herbs Georg had Gather'd for that purpose and Left in the Coffin, which herbs I thought I shaked over him and [then] waked. it gave me great Concern as I Expect it Relates to some death in my family."[27] The strict Presbyterian elder had apparently fallen back on his earlier Irish upbringing steeped in the myth and superstitions of the countryfolk. His immediate feeling was one of distress.

Clinton was certainly no stranger to death, having already lost two family members earlier that year to smallpox. Both his eldest son, Dr. Alexander Clinton, and his new daughter-in-law, Marij Keen, had died at Shawangunk, New York. Over thirty years before, another son, James, three, and a one-year-old daughter, Mary, had predeceased him as well, dying from measles on the voyage over from Ireland to America in 1729. His daughter Catherine was the only Clinton child to survive the trip. The George mentioned in the dream was his third-oldest living son, then sixteen and serving aboard the privateer *Defiance* out of Providence. The twenty-two-year-old namesake of his dead son James, James Clinton II, his second-oldest son, was marching upriver with a company from Ulster County to join him. Clinton's oldest living son, Charles Jr., was a Princeton-trained doctor practicing back in Ulster County.

Could it be that the milestone event depicted so vividly in Clinton's dream was triggered by the anxiety and concern he felt now as a military commander? His father, James Clinton Sr., had been dead for forty-one years, and his mother, Elizabeth Denniston, for nearly thirty, the latter having died at the family farm in Corboy, County Longford, before the family came to America. Charles Clinton had been an only son when his father died in 1717. The realization then that he was assuming the mantle as head of a military "family" with great responsibilities must have been daunting at the time—the flashback to the coffin lid waiting to be closed symbolic of one door shutting on his life and another opening.

And now he stood in a darkened room in the Frey House at the Palatine Bridge with his new command responsibilities and another enormous task ahead of him. The sexagenarian surveyor, gentleman farmer, slave owner, scientist, and muster master of Ulster County had never truly been to war before—except, that is, for the skirmishing with the Delaware who had been active around his home at Little Britain since he first settled there in 1730 with several other Irish Presbyterian families. The New York frontier had shifted westward in the last twenty-eight years, but he had remained in the militia and was now, on Surveyor General Cadwallader Colden's recommendation, the lieutenant colonel of the 2nd Battalion of Col. Oliver Delancey's New York Regiment.[28]

Upon arrival at Fort Herkimer, Clinton took command of a polyglot force consisting of six companies of his own regiment, Delancey's New Yorkers; two regular companies of the New York Independents; as well as a company of rangers and various detachments of battoemen. He would be responsible for the lives of some 1,000 men in the midst of the wilderness. And it was here Clinton, and his small command perched on the left flank, would learn the news of Abercromby's decisive defeat at Ticonderoga and his subsequent retreat to camp at Lake George.

"The best part of the army is unhinged"

Lt. Col. John Bradstreet was furious. He wrote after the 8 July battle to his agent in London:

> I must now tell you that after my having transported & conveyed an Army of 16000 Men full of helths & Spirits with every requisit for War and driving 1100 Men from an advanced Guard and one of 1200 from another and the whole Army assembll'd within a mile of the Enemy, the want of knowledge in the Commander-in-Chief has sacrifis'd about 2000 men killed and wounded and shamefully deserted with the remainder that night.[29]

Bradstreet's casualty figures are almost exactly on the mark, the final total for Abercromby's four-day debacle at Ticonderoga being 1,967 killed, wounded, or missing out of a British-American force of 17,550 men in all ranks—an 11.2 percent casualty rate. The French, by contrast, had a total of 554 (all ranks) killed or wounded out of 4,236 officers and men over a three-day period—a casualty rate of 13 percent. This anomaly suggests the standard historical conclusion—that the British were slaughtered and the French behind their breastworks suffered very light casualties—are misinformed.[30] And it raises the question why Abercromby did not use his much larger army to mount another assault or undertake a siege of the French fort. Of the two armies, the one that could least afford an equal or higher casualty rate was the French army, and this simple fact is one of the key reasons why Montcalm's troops remained in their defensive positions long after Abercromby's army had fled down the lake on 9 July 1758. It should also be noted that the French were down to their last day of rations, though the next few days would see the hungry French battalions rejoice to find that the British, in their haste, had left behind hundreds of barrels of provisions, which they soon put to good use. That the British withdrawal was disorderly is confirmed by Capt. William Hervey of the 44th Foot in his journal: "9th. This morning the whole army moved off in great confusion, and regulars, Provincials, Artillery and sick sailed mixed together, not stopping till they came to the end of the Lake, the general among the first." The report of the battle offered to the British public by way of the *Gentleman's Magazine* openly recited the commander's blunders and oversights. It spoke of "pannic at the headquarters," bad intelligence and ignorance concerning the enemy's breastworks, lack of artillery to support frontal assaults of infantry that persisted for most of the day, and the somewhat hasty abandonment of what still could have been a successful siege as an army of "near 14000 men" retreated "from an enemy not above 3000."[31]

Three days after the ignominious return of his army, Abercromby convened a council of war to try to determine what his next courses of action should be. Bradstreet now renewed his efforts to be allowed to launch his raid that had been scrubbed from Lord Loudoun's operational design for 1758. His select "Battoemen" were standing by, as well as a large contingent of provincials who had not really been employed yet on the costly campaign, which, he argued, could be very quickly deployed against Fort Frontenac. But, in his own words, he "was again oppos'd, and depriv'd of the aids of my Lord Howe (who unfortunate for these colonies, fell in the skirmish on the sixth of July) [and] in the greatest dilemma, least the influence of his opponents might occasion a rejection of his plan." He also claimed somewhat pompously that it was he who "desired a council of war, before whom he laid open his scheme, subjoining the strongest reasonings on the probability of success" and that the "many, after the warmest opposition, reluctantly approv'd, and finally by a majority it was carried in the affirmative, and a report drawn up in favour of the scheme."[32]

This well-documented council of war did take place on 13 July 1758 but was not, as Bradstreet claims, solely for the purpose of discussing his "scheme." Present at the council besides Bradstreet were Major General Abercromby; Brig. Gen. Thomas Gage; Sir William Johnson, superintendent of Indian affairs; and five commanding officers of the regular forces: Col. William Haviland (27th Foot), Col. Francis Grant (42nd Foot), Col. Frederick Haldimand (4th/60th Foot [Royal Americans]), Maj. Eyre Massey (46th Foot), and Maj. William Eyre (44th Foot). The two questions actually put to the council are shown below in their entirety, as they speak clearly to the intent of General Abercromby, rather than the subsequent "spin" presented in Bradstreet's *Impartial Account*:

> 1st . . . The Question being put whether under our Present Circumstances it is not advisable to detach a strong Reinforcement to the Mohawk River, to reinforce Brigr. Stanwix,—& that a fort be built at the Oneida, or what is commonly call'd the Great Carrying Place? It was unanimously agreed in the Affirmative.

> 2nd . . . Whether it is proper and adviseable to appear on Lake Ontario, and if possible, to attempt an Enterprize on that Quarter, in order to distress the Enemy, and to favour the Operations to the Southward, and if so, with what force?

The resolution of this second question was not so clear-cut as was the first item of business, and it probably generated the most-heated discussion of the council. It vaguely states that the purpose of the "Enterprize" is "to distress the Enemy" which would, in turn, have the effect of "favour[ing] the Operations to the Southward." The issue of what resources could be made available for such an "Enterprize" was also on the table for discussion. In the end it was "agreed in the Affirmative, provided there is no Apparent reason to the contrary, [that] when the Troops assemble at the Great Carrying Place:—& that the N. Yorkers, New Jerseys, Dotys Massachusetts & the Rhode Islanders be destined for this Service [i.e., the "Enterprize"], leaving always 2000 Men at the Great Carrying Place, for Carrying on the Fort."[33]

What is most surprising is that none of the provincial commanding officers, whose regiments were being tasked to accompany Bradstreet and Stanwix to the Oneida Carrying Place, were consulted or even present at the council. This was no oversight. It was a deliberate decision on the part of the regulars to keep the proposed "Enterprize" secret until the force had been completely assembled at the Great Carrying Place. This decision to keep a key part of the chain of command in the dark, however, would lead to several major problems, not the least of which were mass desertion and heated disputes over the leadership of the expedition.

The same day the council met and approved the enterprise, Abercromby wrote out Bradstreet's orders, which gave some more-specific direction as to "this Service"—the raid's objectives. It stressed, first and foremost, that "a strong reinforcement should be detached to the Mohawk River to strengthen Brigadier Stanwix and to build a Fort at the Oneida or Great Carrying Place." If there was no perceived French attack pending in that quarter, then, and only then, would Bradstreet be allocated 3,000 troops by Stanwix "to advance to Lake Ontario, to watch the Motions of the Enemy and, by giving them Battle, if adviseable prevent their intended Inroad on the Mohawk River; or otherwise, if found practicable, to attempt the reduction of Fort Frontenac, and destroy the Shipping at Cataraqui." This latter action was intended "to render the Retreat of the Enemy, sent this Spring to the Ohio, as difficult as possible."[34]

Bradstreet's instructions, then, were very clear. There were several conditions to be met before he could launch his pet project. Abercromby's intelligence assessment reflected a realistic analysis of the situation in the Lake Ontario sector designed to provide immediate defense of the area against a possible attack. Bradstreet, rather than proceeding triumphantly from the council of war with his long-sought-after and much coveted independent command, was told he was still very much the DQMG of the army with a serious job to do until he got to the Oneida Carrying Place. With Bradstreet still responsible for forwarding all the forces and matériel destined for the priority task—fort building at the Carrying Place—it was in his best interest to move them as quickly and efficiently as his "Battoe Service" could convey them. Every extra day spent east of the Carry was one less day for him on the west side to conduct his coveted operation. When all troops, artillery, provisions, and tools had been deposited at the Carry, it would then be determined by his superior John Stanwix (based yet again on the latest intelligence available) whether Bradstreet could launch his "diversion" or not.

In essence, the raid became a dangling carrot to ensure the feisty logistician did his best for his immediate superior. Within hours of a war council breaking up at Lake George on 13 July, the provincial regiments placed under Stanwix's command started marching southward. As they did, rumors were rife as to their destination. The assembly point given out in orders to provincials and regulars alike was one that occasioned much dismay, just as it had for Williams's Massachusetts regiment two weeks earlier. The patrician Col. Melancthon Taylor Woolsey, whose New Yorker battalion had been left out of battle and tasked as baggage guards for the army at Lake George, wrote bitterly to his brother: "We are now under Marching orders . . . for the Onida Carrying Place as 'tis said to Build a Fort for some General Webb to destroy hereafter."[35]

The men, already discouraged and dismayed at the performance of their leaders after the shambolic assault at Ticonderoga, were demoralized. Front-row witnesses to an "injudicious and wanton Sacrefise of men" by an incompetent British commander, another provincial colonel summed it up for his brother: "In one word, what with fatigue, want of sleep, exercise of mind, and leaving the place we went to capture, the best part of the army is unhinged." Col. Henry Babcock of the Rhode Islanders concurred, claiming that after the retreat from Ticonderoga, regulars and provincials alike became "a confused rabble."[36]

Now provincial soldiers were told they were expected to march into an inhospitable wilderness on the most dangerous frontier ostensibly to build forts and perform other manual and menial tasks. They balked. Angry soldiers shouldered packs, clubbed their firelocks, and marched off in large and small groups, or melted way in ones and twos by night. Just nine days later, Massachusetts troops bound for the Great Carrying Place finished packing their tents and camp baggage into wagons and were forming up in marching order near a small hamlet called Half-Moon. Their encampment, situated strategically near the confluence of the Mohawk and Hudson Rivers, about nine miles north of Albany, was the proverbial fork in the road: southward lay home; to the west and beyond, up the Mohawk Valley, was the unknown.

"Sickness, Discontent, Disertion, Reluctance and Want of Spirit"

At 10:00 a.m. on 22 July in the Half-Moon encampment, an astonished Pvt. Abner Barrow of Capt. Benjamin Pratt's company watched as "about three score men belonging to [our] Regiment Clobed their fier locks and [went] marching off, two Sergt headed them." Their outraged commanding officer, Col. Thomas Doty, ordered the rest of his drawn-up regiment

> to Load their fier locks Emediately and fix their bayonets. then we were ord to march. We march'd round them. Our Colo & adjutant took their armes from them. Putt all under Guard their. They were kept about two howers, then the Ringleaders of them wair took and pinioned. Six of them were sent down to be Putt in the prison at Albany. The about fifty or so men that wair put under guard for same crime wair Released by making Good Promises for the future &c.[37]

But this was just the start of the hemorrhaging. Another 140 soldiers of Doty's would desert before the unit reached Fort Herkimer, thirty miles east of their final objective. Desertion in broad daylight was not restricted just to Doty's regiment. It snowballed to become one of the largest mass desertions by provincial troops from any campaign during the entire Seven Years' War.

By 6 August, a tally of the "immence desertion" from provincial regiments compiled by General Stanwix at Fort Herkimer was approaching some 500 men. It included 250 men from Johnston's Jersey Blues, 190 from Doty's, 52 New Yorkers, and 50 from Babcock's Rhode Islanders. With Stanwix bringing up the rear of the army with the train of artillery was a grim-faced Bradstreet, who reported to Abercromby that they had been dogged the entire way from Schenectady by "Sickness, Discontent, Disertion, Reluctance and Want of Spirit" permeating "throughout the whole of the Provincial Troops ordered to serve this way." Still, he fully intended to attempt his mission, even if his force was reduced to a mere 1,000 men. After all he had been fully prepared back in the spring to make the attempt with only 800.[38]

Bradstreet seems to have been oblivious of the major trade-off he was making in not telling the provincials that they were being sent on an important offensive operation to regain the honor of the army. On the one hand, with desertion rates high, this move was perhaps good for keeping the expedition secret for as long as possible. On the other hand, the decision had disastrous consequences. It hastened the early onset of a breakdown in discipline and loss of "the will to fight" of the provincial corps. Most believed that they had signed on only for the invasion of Canada, not to serve the remainder of the campaign as laborers on the bloodiest frontier.

However, a year later Bradstreet would proudly boast in his *Impartial Account* that he had made the right decision, as there "never was . . . an expedition undertaken, the destination of which, the individuals who compos'd the army, were more profoundly ignorant of; even the commanding officers of the corps were uncertain, at leaving the Oneida station, whether they were to be led against Niagara, Oswegatchie or Cadaraqui."[39] While this claim may have been inserted to provide a chuckle or two at the expense of the "profoundly ignorant" provincial commanding officers for Bradstreet's London audience, it was just not true. Even officers left out of battle knew the destination. Melancthon Taylor Woolsey, commanding officer of the 2nd battalion of the Yorkers, who fell ill with the fever and flux at the Great Carrying Place and was evacuated downriver to Schenectady, informed his brother: "Two days before I left the army [August 13] there was a detachment from the several Regts . . . under the command of Colo Bradstreet who are gone down Wood Creek into the Oneida Lake to surprise, Take and Destroy Cadroque, a fort on the Lake where the French keep their shiping and craft of all kinds."

The myth of total surprise is one of several stories repeated about the raid that bears closer examination. Bradstreet would maintain long after the raid, and even in light of evidence to the contrary, that all his precautions and efforts toward maintaining the strictest security were a complete success. Because of this achievement, the Sieur de Noyan and his tiny garrison at Frontenac were supposedly completely unaware of the raiding force's approach until a mere day and a half before Bradstreet's forces landed. This claim was first salted into the *Impartial Account* and several of the letters that were sent to London newspapers after the event by some of Bradstreet's cronies. It is still perpetuated by the historians who have taken Bradstreet at his word.[40]

Remarkably, a number of disparate people surmised the concentration of troops at the Carrying Place was more than just a fort-building exercise from the number of bateaux and whaleboats being sent up the river. Even a neophyte such as Ens. Moses Dorr could not fail to be impressed by the volume of traffic streaming through Schenectady and westward up the Mohawk. The nineteen-year-old native of Roxbury, Massachusetts, faithfully recorded the endless parade of troops, ox-carts, "battoes," and artillery pieces in his diary and mused: "There Seams to be Great Preparations to go up the Mohawk River this Year." The next day the bulk of his regiment was ordered to join the procession upriver to the Carry, and he would conclude upon his arrival: "Great Preparations for an Expedition Secret to us."[41]

Others much further afield had known of the raid from its inception and could easily guess what was about to happen. General Forbes on the southern expedition to take Fort Duquesne had been the adjutant general and close confidant of Lord Loudoun in January 1758 when "Captain Bradstreet" had pitched his hit-and-run raid plan to the then commander. Forbes reminded Abercromby at the end of July, after receiving the details of his nominal superior's defeat at Ticonderoga, that "Lt Colo Bradstreet's [Frontenac] proposal last winter was a Chimera. But might have been attended with some advantages that made my Lord [Loudoun] agree to it in some measure." He concluded by lecturing his current commander that he was always of the opinion [that] the building of a fort at the Oneida Carrying Place . . . ought to have been the first thing sett about" on their return from Halifax the previous fall. Forbes had even drafted a set of orders (never issued) for Bradstreet to assemble his proposed force of eight hundred handpicked battoemen "at Chenactady the 1st week of March [1758] . . . ready to sett out upon the first order."[42]

Forbes's close friend and fellow Scot, Cadwallader Colden, was also pretty sure of Bradstreet's destination. In a letter dated 29 July, the surveyor general of New York told a friend back in Britain that the 4,000 provincials dispatched westward to the Carry earlier in the month were meant to ostensibly "secure our frontiers from an irruption with which they are threatened & to rebuild the Fort at the Oneyda carrying place which Gen. Web[b] ordered to be destroyed & for which he was greatly blamed." But he then hinted that he was "in greater expectations of greater advantages from this large Detachment as it will be very difficult for the French in Canada to guard against attacks in so many places. They may attack a French fort where the River St. Laurence issues from Lake Ontario, if a proper opportunity offers."[43]

Even the French were not long in figuring out what was afoot. After all, there were only two land approaches to Montreal. Louis Antoine de Bougainville wrote in his journal that all intelligence gathered by 24 July indicated that Sir William Johnson had "gone off with all his Indians [and] a body of three thousand men and five six-pounders [had] followed him toward the Mohawk River." Not only were these estimates of British guns and troops accurate, Bougainville correctly guessed their destination, then speculated as to the reasons why such a large force was making its way westward: "Perhaps they fear lest we wish to take up again today the secret expedition of Sceneactady? Perhaps also, for the rest of the campaign they will offer us a demonstration of an offensive in order to force us to hold forces here and during this time, the body which marched towards the Mohawk River will make, without opposition, dispositions for the re-establishment of Oswego." Four weeks later, Bougainville's musings were finally confirmed by a British deserter from Lake George, who revealed during interrogation on 24 August (a mere three days before the fort's fall) that Stanwix's forces had cleaned up the blocked navigation in Wood Creek some weeks past "in order to go and besiege a French fort in Lake Ontario which can be only Frontenac."[44]

"Should wear a petticoat, go home and make sugar"

Ounewaterika, also known as Capt. Charles Lee, of the 44th Foot, was mending slowly from broken ribs, an injury received at the Battle of Ticonderoga caused by a spent musket ball. He was under the tender care of a Seneca woman who was his wife, according to Haudenosaunee custom. An adopted member of the Bear clan of the Mohawks, Lee would observe after the battle that the large host of "Mohocks and River Indians" that had accompanied Sir William Johnson to fight with the British ("the greatest number than ever we cou'd assemble before") chose not to remain with the army for future operations. "The Indians will not go with us," the British regular wrote to his sister. "They told the General that the English Army has very fine limbs but no head. That he was an Old Squah that he should wear a petticoat, go home and make sugar."[45]

After the defeat, Sir William, try as he might, was able by personal persuasion, calling in favors, and by the unrelenting endeavors of his Indian officers to assemble only 150 warriors at the Great Carrying Place to hear what the British intended to do next. At a preliminary Indian council held outside at Fort Johnson on 22 July 1758, with "some of each of the Six Nations, Except the Cayyougas" present, Johnson, also known as Warraghiyagey to the Haudenosaunee, had given a fiery speech. He reminded them of General Abercromby's speech made two weeks earlier at Lake George and his promise that "a Number of Troops were assembling in order to take Post at the Great Carrying Place" to build a new fort. The new fort would enable the British "to guard [their] part of the Country by any attempts which the Enemy might make, of whose designs against the Mohock River you have lately given repeated Informations." Not only would the new fort protect them "from the Insults of the Enemy," but it would also provide a safe meeting place "for carrying on an Advantageous Trade for & with your People."

Then Sir William cut to the chase. General Stanwix was coming up the river from Schenectady and

> with him comes Colonel Bradstreet known to most of you. In consequence hereof, I desire that your young Men will make themselves ready to join our troops at the German Flatts & proceed with them to the Oneida Carrying Place where your Brother Col. Bradstreet will acquaint you with the Service you are wanted upon & have some Talk with you, and he will also settle every thing with you to your Satisfaction. I shall send Capt. Thomas Butler to receive his orders & take Care of you.[46]

Johnson emphasized for them that the new fort to be built was one they had "frequently & earnestly requested," and that he, Warraghiyagey, expected them all now to "Show your readiness to aid & Effect these good Purposes by attending & assisting our Operations & accompanying your Brother Col. Bradstreet who will take care that whoever he employs shall be kindly used & duly rewarded for their Services."[47]

A week later, twenty-two young Mohawk warriors arrived at Fort Johnson, sent to help escort and guard General Stanwix up to the Oneida Carrying Place. Their chief, Abraham, made it perfectly clear that as the intended fort would directly benefit the western Haudenosaunee nations, he did not doubt that "the Oneida &c will take care to act like Brothers in Scouting &c." In other words, the Mohawks who had provided the lion's share of warriors in the Ticonderoga expedition would sit this one out, and his warriors would return home "after our Young Men have seen the General safe there." The general's Mohawk escort joined his entourage as he passed Fort Johnson, as well as some of the other nations that had been present at Johnson's council and had indicated their willingness to assemble at the Great Carrying Place to hear what "Brother" Bradstreet had to say. On reaching Fort Herkimer on 6 August, Sir William took time before turning back for Fort Johnson to impress upon his senior Indian Service officer Thomas Butler, an adopted member of the Oneida tribe, that he was to use "his utmost Endeavours & Influence to get as many Indians of the Six Nations as you possibly can to join Col. Bradstreet in the present Enterprize."[48]

While the superintendent was wooing the less than impressed Six Nations and as Stanwix's small army assembled at the Carrying Place, the French already began to respond to the British activity and alter their own plans. Governor Vaudreuil had sent one of his most trusted diplomats and interpreters to the Seneca in early July to explain the reasons for the delay of the proposed French raid. He also sought to reassure those upper nations (Seneca, Cayuga, and Onondaga) of the French interest in executing the long-planned secret expedition to attack and sweep the British once and for all from the Mohawk Valley. To this end, a French force of sixty Canadien militiamen and three dozen Oswegatchie warriors arrived at Oswego in mid-July under Paul-Joseph Le Moyne de Longueuil, laden with many presents. He met with Haudenosaunee representatives who warned him to go no farther up the Oswego River "without running great risks," as the British were rebuilding Fort Bull (also known as Fort Wood Creek, or Eagle) and another larger new fort overlooking the eastern end of the Carry with some 5,000 men. They would not accompany him there now nor assure his safety but agreed publicly they would send deputies to Montreal to confer with Vaudreuil in twenty days' time.[49]

Longueuil, armed with this intelligence and greatly unsettled by his reception among the Seneca, usually the most friendly and pro-French of the Haudenosaunee nations, returned to Montreal on 10 August. En route, he stopped off at Cataraqui to pass on his concerns to his first cousin, the commandant of Fort Frontenac, Sieur Payen de Noyan. The Sieur de Courville would later write that the worried Longueuil had warned de Noyan in early August of "several

"Yankee Doodle"
This jaunty provincial ranger and others like him were the inspiration for the song "Yankee Doodle" composed by Dr. Richard Shuckburgh, who accompanied Bradstreet's raid. Lord Howe's 1758 much-needed clothing and equipment reforms for the bushfight are in evidence: cut-down hat, cut-down coat, cut-down musket, Indian leggings and moccasins, a wooden canteen, and a bearskin bedroll. Courtesy of the artist, Gary Zaboly.

indications that the English were assembling a considerable force at Fort Bull, [and] concluded that they were coming to take Frontenac." He then "promised him he would advise M. de Vaudreuil to send him help." Thus, as early as the first week of August 1758, the Sieur de Noyan knew the British were coming and from what direction, but not the size of their actual force or when. The suspense would be short-lived.[50]

"It was my tour of Duty"

The troops who embarked on the raid under Bradstreet's command were in relatively good health, as only the fittest, most able, and "those accustomed to working on water" were selected for the expedition (see appendix D for the order of battle). In the provincial officer corps, many of the officers wounded at Ticonderoga in July, such as Capt. Timothy Parker of the Massachusetts troops and Capt. Goose Van Schaik and Capt. Jonathan Ogden of the New Yorkers, made light of their injuries and persisted in leading their respective companies on the expedition. Another officer who could have easily sat out the raid was Lt. Col. Charles Clinton, who, at sixty-eight years of age, was feeling under the weather as the army assembled at the Great Carrying Place.

As the most senior provincial officer commanding the largest provincial detachment, Clinton was stubbornly determined to set an example for his men. "The General and Col. Delancey knowing I had for some time before, kept my Bed with the Dysenteria of flux and was not yet Well, sent for me and would not have me go," he wrote on 13 August after the final review of troops by Bradstreet and Stanwix. But when Clinton awoke the following day, his iron constitution kicked in and he found himself "better [and] at noon I went to the Gen. and told him as it was my tour of Duty, I would go." By contrast, his superior, Col. Melancthon Taylor Woolsey, commanding the 2nd Battalion of the Yorkers—twenty-seven years his junior and suffering from the same ailments—was evacuated down the line of communications to Schenectady and died shortly thereafter.[51]

Stanwix convened a council of war on the evening of 11 August, and understandably, the provincial colonels, kept in the dark until then as to the scope of the expedition, were said to have balked when told they would serve under a regular lieutenant colonel on an overland amphibious operation. They refused to serve under Bradstreet's command because, as a result of Pitt's new directive on regular officers' and provincial officers' seniority, they all outranked him. Stanwix reported to Abercromby after the council that the irascible Lieutenant Colonel Bradstreet "seem'd not a little offend'd that the provincial Colonels would not go upon his Enterprise under his Command, the King having given all these Rank of Colonels which no provincial Colonels ever had before." The general solved the problem by ordering "detachments" of each regiment to go, each to be commanded by their respective lieutenant colonels or majors, rank based on their total numbers going.[52]

If one is to believe the Rev. Daniel Shute of Williams's Massachusetts regiment, it was his own "fractious" colonel who led the cabal against Bradstreet's commanding the raiding force. The minister's journal entries reveal a subtle, but distinct disenchantment with his argumentative colonel, and several entries record instances of the man's arrogance, penny-pinching parsimony, and boastfulness during the campaign. "Notwithstanding ye opposition made chiefly by Col Williams," the clergyman recorded dryly, "a Detachment [was] made from ye several Regts to go forward under the command of Col Bradstreet, where is not disclosed, supposed to be Cataraugue, alias Frontinack."[53]

Joseph Williams's contrariness is easily explained. An overbearing and physically imposing man, a member of the Massachusetts Provincial Council used to getting his own way, Williams was still burning from the public humiliation he had received at the hands of the army commander less than four weeks ago. An exasperated General Abercromby had singled out his tardy, unequipped regiment and sent it back to the Mohawk Valley before it could reach the army at Fort Edward. It had been replaced by another more prepared Massachusetts regiment. To add insult to injury, he learned from Stanwix upon his arrival at the Carrying Place that his green regiment had not been assigned to the raid and would essentially act as a fatigue battalion at the fort construction site.

Whether Williams was motivated to volunteer his regiment because otherwise he would miss out on the glory of any success (and thus a share of the plunder and spoils), or because he might have had pretensions of taking nominal command of the expedition over Bradstreet's head, is unclear. But he immediately lobbied Stanwix upon his arrival that his regiment should be included in the fighting force. His key arguments were that his regiment was fresh, well-rested, and healthy, but more importantly, their desertion rate was negligible when compared to the other Massachusetts regiment (Doty's) as well as the Rhode Islanders and Jerseymen who were actually slated to go. Somewhat alarmed by the "immence desertion" experienced in the past couple of weeks, Stanwix quickly acquiesced.

The provincial colonels were given a day to sort out their detachments and choose their respective commanders. Orderly books show that the following day was one of extreme preparation. So great was the level of activity that the New Englanders had to forgo their divine service in the bustle to get ready. Individual regimental parades for the issue of axes, paddles, setting poles, tools, ropes, ammunition, and provisions occupied the waking hours of the day, until the appointed hour. The men formed up late afternoon on 12 August 1758 under the eagle-eye of the raid's adjutant, Lt. Archie Brown of the Independents. The twenty-three-year-old Englishman was a stickler for details, but his affable manner gave him the patience to sort it all out before the reviewing party of General Stanwix and Lieutenant Colonel Bradstreet, with the ever-present Provincial colonels in tow, arrived.

The parade was simple. No marching was involved, the men had formed up in three ranks ready for inspection, and each detachment stood in line arranged by order of seniority from right to left (see appendix D for order of battle). The rangers and some battoemen were excused from the parade, having already departed on scouts westward to Lake Oneida and onward to Oswego. The remainder of the battoemen were still hard at work on the westward side of the Carry where Bradstreet had spent most of the day pushing his men to have all the battoes ready for loading on the morrow.

The gloaming of the day brought a golden haze to the sky, the long line of troops formed facing westward, their backs to the Mohawk River. The setting sun shone directly into the eyes of those in the front ranks as well as their officers causing many to squint or pull their cut-down round hats lower over their eyes. To Lieutenant Browne, the 2,700 men formed up on the dusty general parade were the largest group of soldiers he had ever paraded in his life: a long, living, shifting, coughing line of color. On the far right, one could see the blue coats, red-faced, of the artillerymen, followed by the drab greenish-brown field uniforms of the regulars and the New Yorkers, the latter by far the largest block of men on parade with a frontage of three hundred soldiers. Green then gave away again to the crisp blue and red-faced uniforms of the Massachusetts troops and Jerseymen, and finally, the plain faded blue of the Rhode Islanders, who counted themselves lucky to have been provided with uniforms at all.

The parade adjutant had placed the most senior, but smallest detachment of the force—"The Train"—on the extreme right of the line. The artillery detachment—consisting of one captain, one surgeon, one lieutenant, one sergeant, and twenty-three gunners of the Royal Regiment of Artillery—was commanded by Capt.-Lt. James Stephens, the acting commander of the only artillery company assigned to Abercromby's army. Stephens's gunners were arrayed in two ranks behind the eight pieces of ordnance going on the raid, each mounted on its field carriage complete with all its accoutrements laid out. All of these men had loaded, stowed, and rowed their guns to and from Ticonderoga without firing a shot. Their presence now on the expedition trumpeted the fact that the destination of the raid was a stone fort. By process of elimination, anyone who knew anything about the Six Nations—which included virtually all the rangers and battoemen drawn from the valley, the Indian Service officers and interpreters, as well as the majority of the New York Regiment—the destination could only be Frontenac. Bradstreet's expedition did not have permission to go through Seneca territory to besiege Fort Niagara, the only other stone fort on the lake.[54]

Next to the gunners stood the only other British regulars in the raiding force, a composite company of 150 men drawn from the fittest soldiers of three of the four New York Independent Companies. They were commanded by one of the most experienced officers in the force, Capt. William Ogilvie, an American-born regular and the older brother of the Rev. John Ogilvie, chaplain to the Mohawks. Their deceased eldest brother, George, had served under Adm. Sir Peter Warren as a midshipman aboard the flagship *Launceston* and had died at sea in 1746. William's family had obtained his entrée into the British army with an ensigncy in Gooch's American Regiment, which was raised for special service under the command of Admiral Vernon in the unsuccessful 1740 expedition against the Spanish possession of Cartagena (Colombia). He had advanced in rank to full lieutenant by May 1741, as the British-American troops at the siege succumbed to yellow fever and died by the hundreds. When the peace came, Gooch's was disbanded effective Christmas Day 1742, and Ogilvie found himself on half-pay. He returned to active service as a lieutenant in the 19th Foot (Howard's) on 25 June 1744 and fought at Fontenoy, Rocoux, and Lauffeldt with the "Green Howards."

All the experience and expertise in the world of their commander, however, could not improve the quality of men he commanded. His regulars were old soldiers that Bradstreet "saw no Regularity in" and whom he pronounced to be "a Number of Plag[ue]y Rogues." They were dressed in black cropped hats, cut-down greenish-brown uniforms verging on khaki, with deerskin breeches and an odd assortment of *mitasses*, or leggings, ranging from green and blue to beaded buckskin.[55]

Next to them, also dressed in green, was Bradstreet's favorite provincial regiment, Oliver Delancey's New Yorkers. When the fiery Bradstreet would rant and rail about the "Disertion, Reluctance and Want of Spirit" of the provincials, he would always qualify his comments by adding, "except the Yorkers." The first colony to muster its regiment was also the one most decisively engaged with the enemy on its frontiers. The New York Regiment for 1758 was led by a cadre of officers who were semiprofessional in outlook and, who, for the last three years, had experienced firsthand the depredations and defeats inflicted on the families of the Mohawk Valley and points beyond. Many regimental officers were drawn from influential families of Albany County, such as the Schuylers, Fondas, Van Schaicks, Ten Broeks, and Stuyvesants.[56]

It was no mistake that the desertion-prone New Jersey Blues had been placed between Delancey's and Colonel Williams's Massachusetts men. The steady Yorkers had served as jailers and prison guards for 111 of the Jerseymen on the way up the valley, two deserters assigned per New York regimental bateaux, while the NCOs were placed in the New York officers' bateaux. This deliberate segregation of the Blues junior leadership from the rank and file involved in desertions was intentional and designed to bring them all back to their duty by association with other colonial colleagues.[57] A hard-luck regiment, the Blues had been taken prisoner en masse at the surrender of Oswego in 1756, along with their beloved colonel, Peter Schuyler. Reconstituted from scratch in 1757, the regiment was ravaged yet again the following year while conducting a reconnaissance in force on Lake George from the ill-fated Fort William Henry. Their new colonel, John Parker, was surprised leading a boat convoy of twenty-two bateaux just off Sabbath Day Point on 24 July 1757, where 160 men had been killed and many more wounded or captured.

Thus the regiment had no real core of veteran leadership that had built up over the first three years of the war as did other provincial regiments. Their late brave lieutenant colonel, John Shaw of Perth Amboy, had been shot down in the tangled abatis of Carillon, and Col. John Johnston's elderly major, Samuel Hunt, appears not to have stepped up after Shaw's death at Ticonderoga, nor attempted to stem the chronic desertion post-Ticonderoga. Colonel Johnston was a very capable commander, his family prominent in New Jersey affairs, but he was a relative unknown to his men then or to historians today. In his youth, he is said to have studied a year or two at Woolwich Academy in England as a private student before the war, in order to acquire a good knowledge of military engineering. It was an attainment put to good use the following year at the Siege of Niagara when he assumed the mantle of acting chief engineer after the supervising engineer was killed, until felled himself by a Canadien sharpshooter. The Woolwich training is a plausible theory as his colleague, Col. "Harry" Babcock of the Rhode Islanders, would do the same thing in 1764 after the war, perhaps inspired by his late provincial colleague's example.[58]

Given the regiment's history, Colonel Johnston needed a strong captain to lead the New Jersey contingent on the raid. His choice was Joseph Ellis, twenty-eight, who was born in Ellisburg, New Jersey, the son of prosperous Quaker farmers. A large man and a blacksmith by trade, Ellis had joined the county militia at an early age. When the call went out for the raising of a New Jersey regiment of 1,000 men in 1758, he secured a commission as a captain and raised a company of provincials drawn from his home county of Gloucester. This form of active military service, however, was the last straw for his Quaker family and neighbors, as it was in direct contravention of their pacifist beliefs. Ellis was disowned and expelled from the Society of Friends.[59]

Colonel Williams's and Colonel Doty's Bay Colony detachments stood next in line, dressed in their cut-down hats and cropped blue uniforms faced with red. The first detachment of 432 men was commanded by Maj. William Arbuthnot, a thirty-three-year-old Bostonian and a survivor of the Fort William Henry siege a year earlier. His men, as yet, had seen no action. The second, smaller detachment of 241 New Englanders was commanded by thirty-nine-year-old Maj. Richard Godfrey of Taunton, Massachusetts, and constituted the remnants of Doty's regiment that had been at Ticonderoga who were still fit to fight. Reverend Shute, on seeing these men from their sister regiment arriving at the camp for the first time on 11 August, wrote that his "heart was grieved to find ye men so greatly fatigued, and nothing comfortable to take. No Sutler, no Doctor, no Chaplain with them."[60]

Last but not least, Bradstreet and Stanwix reviewed the Rhode Island Regiment, commanded by Col. "Harry" Babcock. To date in the war, the regiments supplied by this parsimonious colony had been notoriously undermanned, far below allocated quotas, and never supplied with enough arms or tentage, if any.

Whenever questioned by successive British commanders on this inability to produce the required numbers of men and matériel, the colony cited many reasons, but its chief excuse was that its pool of competitive manpower was very small. The lure of lucrative privateering conducted out of the colony's ports and coastal towns was a siren's call for most able-bodied men. Rhode Islanders could make more money out on the ocean hunting French shipping than in the primeval woods of upstate New York being hunted. Because of the high proportion of men regularly working in maritime trades and because a significant number of Rhode Islanders held pacifist religious beliefs, only 56 percent of the colony's white men over the age of eighteen even served in the colony's militia, which appears to have been the lowest rate of militia service in the colonies outside of Delaware and Pennsylvania, both of which lacked militias.[61]

The Rhode Island colonel, the youngest regimental commander in North America, was noticeably absent. Babcock, twenty-two, had commanded a company of the Rhode Island Regiment at the Battle of Lake George at the age of nineteen under Sir William Johnson in 1755 and had finished the campaign as its major. By 1758, Babcock was the officially designated second-in-command of the Rhode Island Regiment for the campaign against Ticonderoga, but when his colonel, Godfrey Malbone Jr., resigned suddenly in May, Lieutenant Colonel Babcock was promoted on the spot to take his place.[62] Inexplicably, the experienced major below him, Daniel Wall, who should have replaced him as lieutenant colonel, was passed over for command. Babcock instead elevated Capt. Jonathan Potter Jr. to the vacancy, skipping the rank of major, no doubt a nod to the latter's powerful half brother, Stephen Potter, who sat on the Provincial Council's Committee of War. Wall's reaction is not recorded, but he could not have been happy to have been superseded by a junior officer with less experience. Potter appears occasionally in general orders as duty field officer for the day and would later command the Rhode Island detachment on the raid.

At Ticonderoga, Babcock soon had cause to regret his decision. Unhappy with the dynamic of his new leadership team, both officers would incur his wrath at Lake George by not arriving in time to help command and administer the battalion before it launched down Lake George on 3 July. On departure, an exasperated Babcock would write to the governor: "Neither Potter nor Wall have, as yet, joined me; and if they don't today, they had just as good be at home." Babcock and his regiment left without them.[63]

Potter and Wall arrived after the Battle of Ticonderoga, which saw 110 Rhode Islanders killed or wounded before the regiment's reassignment to join General Stanwix at the Oneida Carrying Place. Shot through the knee, Colonel Babcock was one of the casualties, and he would hand over the regiment to Potter to lead it westward to its new post up the Mohawk Valley. His men, however, would desert in droves, and, surprisingly, one of his captains. Caleb Hacker, who had been promoted from lieutenant to replace Potter in May, disappeared on the march south to Schenectady, forcing Babcock to send a request to the provincial war committee to apprehend the fugitive.[64]

After each unit was reviewed, it was dismissed, and the men fell out to continue with their preparations. The artillery train guarded by Ogilvie's Independents marched immediately for the far western end of the Carry, Fort Wood Creek. The site of the original Fort Bull Massacre in 1756, it held an almost lurid touristlike fascination for most provincial soldiers passing through the Carry, despite the fact that a new fort with a new name stood in its stead.[65] The 13th and 14th of August saw whaleboats, provisions, cannons, sieging tools, and shot as well as barrels of rum, flour, and gunpowder carried or carted over the portage. Troops were prepositioned along the banks of the creek between the two bateaux ponds and their respective forts to await the right moment to board their loaded boats and open the sluice gates.

By the evening of 14 August, everything was ready. An impatient Bradstreet down at the first pond at Fort Wood Creek, waiting for the bateaux, was raring to go. But one final ingredient was missing as Bradstreet subsequently reported. "The want of water in Wood Creek detained our boats all night, between Fort Newport and Bull's fort." Then after last light it started to pour. Orderly Sgt. Garret Albertson of the Jersey Blues remembered with some clarity the long, uncomfortable wait with his mates down at "Boll's Fort," all of them soaked to the skin in the much needed downpour:

> We made tents of our blankets and lay on the ground [when] that night there came on an exceeding heavy rain, and being fatigued we made a fire before our poor tent, slept sound awhile, but behold when we awoke, the water was running under us, two or three inches deep; we rose and passed the remainder of the night without sleep. Early in the morning, I went with my surgeon's mate, my corporal, and one man more, to a sutler and bought a pint of rum, in hopes it would elevate us in distress, but too late, I had taken a heavy cold, and had not one day's perfect health until I arrived home at my father's house.[66]

But the rain that flooded Albertson's tent also raised the water level in the creek.

"Glaring proof . . . of their general disaffection to our interest!"

The complex ethnic diversity of the force of young Native warriors that went on the raid and the different motives that fueled their participation deserve a more thorough and thoughtful study than they are usually given. Too often historians have assumed that the raid's Native contingent was homogenous, consisting entirely of Onondagas such as Red Head, or Oneidas, who lived near the Carrying Place, or, Mohawks recruited by William Johnson. In fact, all Six Nations of the Confederacy were represented on the raid.

Diverse motives produced this diverse force. The promise of plunder and captives certainly played a conspicuous part in motivating young warriors. Some of the individual warriors that went on the raid were young men who had not arrived in time to take part in the Ticonderoga expedition. For example, ten disappointed Seneca warriors were asked by Warraghiyagey at Fort Johnson to go with Bradstreet on his expedition, to which they readily agreed. No doubt some warriors accompanied their adopted brothers among the several Indian officers and rangers, influenced by their friendship and trust of "brothers" such as Hendrick Wendell (Oneidas), Thomas Butler (Oneidas), John Butler (Mohawks), and John Lotteridge (Onondagas).[67]

At the same time, there were other underlying calculations that explain why these Natives accompanied Brother Bradstreet. The member nations of the Confederacy were reassessing their neutral stance in the face of the ongoing conflict. Thomas Butler, traveling through Iroquoia in 1757, noted the impact on hunting and agriculture that resulted in widespread poverty: "I must acquaint you that Provisions amongst the Indians is very scarce and dear. . . . Several of the Oneidas . . . say they have nothing to eat at home and are come here to beg provisions. . . . I am plagued by them." When French-backed Oswegatchie warriors passed through Oneida territories to attack and murder their Palatine German tenants and friends over the 1757–58 winter, the Oneida were outraged. Their German Flatts neighbors had generously provided food aid to them earlier in the year, saving many from starvation. All of these efforts had slowly but steadily improved relations between the British and the Six Nations, but there was a worrisome lack of trade goods such as clothing and tools, dwindling food supplies because of bad harvests, and repeated threats from the French. At Oswegatchie in the north, families had been abandoning the St. Lawrence mission as early as 1757 because of food shortages and returning southward to their homeland.[68]

It was the impact of these developments on indigenous interests and the resulting assessments that determined the scale and character of the response and not appeals from the British per se. This was lost on Bradstreet, however. On the morning of 15 August, he met with "about one hundred and fifty fighting men from the different nations" and "inform'd them of his design" through a translator . He then handed over the assembly to Ononwarogo, also known as Red Head, an Onondaga warrior and son of the late, great Red Head the Elder. Red Head's beloved father, Kak8enthiony, had been a great sachem and Speaker of the Council Fire of the Haudenosaunee people. Bradstreet wrote of the son: "Red Head appeared a public advocate for the execution of the meditated scheme; and by a pathetic and animated harangue, influenced a party from each nation to grasp the hatchet and join Col. Bradstreet's army." But then bitterness creeps into Bradstreet's "impartial" recounting of events, as neither Red Head's "eloquence, nor his personal influence, both which he exerted on this occasion, could, however, prevail on more than forty-two heartily to join in the cause."[69]

That only forty-two warriors were willing to join Brother Bradstreet's raid as scouts was not an indication of any Six Nations perfidy or any intentional disloyalty. In fact, in the grander scheme of things, Six Nations participation was the point. Not only did it provide diplomatic cover and intelligence for the Haudenosaunee, the very presence of warriors from each of the nations guaranteed the physical security and safety of Bradstreet's troops on their travels through disputed lands and waters. Any pro-French Indians encountering Bradstreet's forces with their screen of Six Nations warriors would be forced to think twice before engaging. With one exception—the killing of the two white scouts by Natives from Oswegatchie at the outset of the raid—Haudenosaunee warriors allied with the French and Mississauga from Cataraqui appear to have given Bradstreet's forces a wide berth. His Native emissaries were not just there showing a token flag to their British allies, or, in operational terms, providing them with a scouting and guiding capability. They were the living certification to all outsiders that this was a Six Nations–sanctioned event.[70]

The remaining one hundred or so warriors who decided to forgo the raid and return to their respective castles were immediately branded as being hostiles by the diplomatically inept Bradstreet. Many warriors in attendance at the Carrying Place had been to Ticonderoga, but had politely listened to Bradstreet as they had been asked to do by Warraghiyagey. Now they wished to go home and start hunting and fishing for the upcoming winter. Bradstreet branded the entire Haudenosaunee Confederacy as being in cahoots with the French, dependent "on the magazines of Cadaraqui for their subsistence." Because of this reliance, he believed they were unwilling to assist in "the reduction of Fort Frontenac, under the specious pretext of the impracticability of [it] succeeding." Despite being written several months after the raid, Bradstreet's words still resonate with the immense pressure and the heavy weight of responsibility he must have felt before launching on his first independent command of the war.[71]

One does not need hindsight to see that this lack of overt enthusiastic support for Bradstreet's raid was completely understandable on the part of the Six Nations, given a recent British defeat at another French stone fort not too far distant. Their reluctance to repeat what they had already seen happen at Carillon was, in Bradstreet's naive view, "glaring proof . . . of their general disaffection to our interest!"[72] Bradstreet, by choosing to interpret the lukewarm response to his offer as a personal snub, illustrates how completely out of touch he was with how Haudenosaunee culture and people worked. He assumed that his success or prestige would be measured by how many warriors showed up for his raid, without realizing that it did not matter whether he had six or six hundred warriors, so long as each nation was represented. As far as the Six Nations were concerned, they had kept their word to Warraghiyagey (Sir William) to cooperate fully with Brother Bradstreet in the removal of a French fort from their traditional lands, but they had done so with minimal effort for maximum gain in advancing their own interests.

Notwithstanding the subtleties and nuances of Indian diplomacy that escaped a bull-headed commander who tended to view everything in a monochromatic light, Bradstreet's intent to attack Fort Frontenac was now fully in the open. He had to act swiftly as he knew he had just surrendered the advantage of tactical surprise. Only with a dash of maneuver and maximum effort would operational surprise at the next level be achievable. It was only a four-day trip north to Oswegatchie for any warriors inclined to warn their brethren living at the French mission and fort situated on the St. Lawrence. From there it was only another three days upriver to Cataraqui or three to four days downriver to Montreal.[73] Bradstreet's last letter to Abercromby, written the same day he got into the boats at the Oneida Carrying Place, was hopeful in tone but uncharacteristically subdued: "I wish our being so long upon the way may not give time to them to send Troops to Cadarque as the Onidas sent them notice of the First Troops which came here. . . .—as to Indians, the number I shall have is uncertain, as well as their behaviour, *tho some of all Nations have promis'd to go with me.*" To this, he added the intelligence that the French had brought presents to bribe the western tribes and that he was certain the latter had "kindly received the French," whose intention was "to invite the young men . . . to act upon this River, the truth of all which I hope to know soon as we have now everything over into Wood Creek, our dams made up and shall soon put off."[74]

Bradstreet's legacy

A detail from *A View of the Passage of the Army under the Command of his Excellency Major General Amherst down the Rapids of the Saint Lawrence River for the Reduction of Canada in the Year 1760*, executed by Lt. Thomas Davies (1737–1812), Royal Artillery, sometime between 1762 and 1765. It shows the newly acquired riverine capability of the British army as whaleboats shoot the rapids on the St. Lawrence accompanied by their indigenous allies, a scene no doubt similar to Bradstreet's force descending the turbulent Oswego River to Lake Ontario. Courtesy of Library and Archives Canada, Acc. No. 1948-13-1.

CHAPTER 3

Approach

Perils did abound, as thick as thought could make 'em.
And appear in forms more horrid,—yet my duty,
as doth a rock against the chiding flood,
should the approach of this wild river break
and stand unshaken

—Shakespeare, Henry VIII

One can imagine a sharp-eyed eagle flying low and west over the forts and dams of the Oneida Carrying Place on the gray dawn of 16 August 1758. The sight below through the rain would have been intriguing—the smell, noxious. Intriguing—for there was a never-ending line of bateaux stretching away for four miles alongside the banks of Wood Creek until it disappeared into the mists rising from Canada Creek. Noxious—because on the immediate banks below, the smell of 3,000 unwashed men in wet clothing performing their last ablutions and dousing their campfires wafted up from their muddy campsites.

The drums had started beating "The Generale," the signal to embark, a mere fifteen minutes after reveille had sounded, but most of the men were already awake after spending an uncomfortable rainy night huddled by their boats, their tents already aboard, ready to leave on a moment's notice. But there was no time for morning prayers or psalm-singing, just the profane provosts rousing the last of the drunks or malingerers with the tip of their boot. Everyone was soaked but excited. The much needed rain had raised the water levels in each of the head ponds during the night so they could now easily float the heavily loaded bateaux and propel them downstream with the current.

The creek stepped down three levels, with the first dam and pond at Fort Newport being the highest point and entry to the system. It was also the closest portage fort to the eastern end of the Carry. The next stretch below its dam and sluice gates was the newly cleared section full of boats. It hooked sharply westward for four miles to Bull's Fort, which guarded a second head pond full of boats stretching back to the first. Below the second dam, the last level stretched west to Canada Creek where another dam was built across that northern tributary to help flood the lower reaches of Wood Creek and give the lead boats of the huge convoy clearance over the shallow waters and the heavy deadfall that littered the creek bed. In some cases, entire trees, deliberately felled two years before to block the passage of a French invasion force that had never materialized, were still sticking up out of the chocolate brown mire.

The process of getting the huge elongated snake of boats floated, untangled, and underway would be the opening of the Canada Creek dam at the far western end. The whaleboats in the vanguard, manned by the battoemen and ax detachments from the provincials, would lead the way downriver to Lake Oneida. They would be followed by the train, guarded and ably assisted by Williams's Massachusetts men commanded by the thirty-two-year-old Maj. William Arbuthnot. The Boston native had served as a captain with Frye's regiment at Fort William Henry in 1757 and was a survivor of the so-called massacre. The day before, the major, feeling his mortality, informed the regimental chaplain, Mr. Shute, that "he had left some money and other things in the hands of Mr Camel, or Campbell, merchant in Schenectada. His Paper, Orders, &c with H. Arbuthnot; and, in case he sho'd not return, to inform his wife." The good reverend does not appear to have traveled down to see the major and the rest of his flock off, but others of the regiment did.[1]

A wistful young ensign of Williams's watched as his company commander, Timothy Parker, a twenty-four-year-old innkeeper, gave some instructions to Lt. Benjamin Bass, the company's second-in-command. Youngest of the four company commanders in Williams's Massachusetts Regiment, Timothy Parker Jr. was of "unusual size, possessing prominent and striking features" in addition to "an exemplary moral and Christian character." At the Battle of Lake George in 1755, he had served as a young second lieutenant in Colonel Gridley's regiment; in November of the same year, Parker had been promoted to captain for exceptional bravery and leadership. His men would follow him anywhere.[2] His sergeants, John Dinsdill and William Bosson, were inspecting the packs, weapons, and ammunition of their fifty-six privates before they loaded them into five of the assigned bateaux of their company, eighteen men per boat with eight barrels of provisions. Another fifty men of Capt. David White's company had been attached to Parker's command (see appendix E). These men under "Capt. Parker brot up the Rear of the Whole."³

Ens. Moses Dorr of Williams's regiment was not happy at being left in camp to supervise work parties and mount guard. His entry for 16 August was uncharacteristically morose, almost abrupt in describing his closest friends disappearing downriver without him. The nineteen-year-old simply noted, "This Morning the whole Army sot off, the Flood gate histed and it floted the Battoes off very Well"—the New England twang hardwired into his quaint phonetic spelling. Not only had "the Whole Army sot off" without Ensign Dorr to fight at Ticonderoga earlier in the summer, but now the "the Whole Army" was leaving him behind again, despite the 2,000-man brigade in situ, now commencing the construction of Fort Stanwix. In later life, an older and wiser Moses Dorr, Esq., married with children, a wealthy flour merchant and town selectman, probably changed his tune whenever called on to recount his 1758 campaign adventures in mixed company or with a minister present. Surely, God had been watching over him, just like the Reverend Shute had promised them weeks before they had marched off into harm's way. It is quite possible that Moses Dorr saw his safe return home as a sure sign that his service had been godly and that he had upheld his end of the covenant. Certainly, the 1758 campaign year had been the worst to date in the war in terms of British-American casualties—both civilian and military—from combat, sickness, malnutrition, and disease. Particularly in Dorr's case, one is prompted to use the adjective "lucky" rather than "blessed by God's divine providence." By missing the Ticonderoga battle, where two out of every five men were casualties, and Bradstreet's Raid, where every third man was a casualty, Dorr had done well to beat the odds.⁴

By evening, the head of the convoy had only progressed about five miles past the entrance of Canada Creek, so that the tail end of the convoy with the New Yorkers and Parker's rearguard spent the night in and around the dam where Bradstreet and the whaleboats had started in the morning. Bradstreet blamed the delay on "meeting with the utmost obstruction from the trees, which had fallen cross the creek and, in many places, entirely block'd up its passage." Bradstreet led from the front with his battoemen and, assisted by crews of experienced axmen drawn from the detachments, removed the logjams "to make an opening for our boats . . . with the greatest difficulty."⁵

With the advantage of hindsight, one wonders why no advance working parties were sent ahead in weeks prior to clear this unnavigable section of the route before launching the raid. After all, the expedition required maximum speed and mobility to achieve its mission in a timely fashion. The only explanation is that Bradstreet probably feared that such activity would tip his hand and reveal his true intentions to watching eyes.

The advance was also slowed by the condition of the troops. Men bringing bateaux down from Fort Newport had developed a virulent form of "trench foot" as they had worked standing nonstop in the water and mud of Wood Creek for two days. Many "had the skin entirely taken from their feet," Bradstreet observed," in which a very high inflammation was raised." Another medical issue that had a severe impact on the welfare of his men right from the outset was the bad drinking water and its "malignant effects." Bradstreet demonstrated, after the fact, in a rather apologetic, self-serving section of his *Impartial Account* that he knew full well that "the very extraordinary sickness which afterwards prevailed in our troops was probably in great measure owing to the bad quality of the waters they drank." He explained for his London audience how "Indian traders who frequented this route on their way to Oswego" circumvented this hazard by taking "a keg of water in each of their batteaus at the springs rising from the high grounds near the head of it which they used with such oeconomy as to make it last till they reached the Oneida River, where fresh supplies could be had."[6]

Surprisingly, though, Bradstreet the commander did not explain why *he* had failed to take the same precautions with his own men. There is not a single entry in any of the several surviving orderly books that indicate Bradstreet was concerned for the health of his men prior to the commencement of the raid. While there were no explicit instructions issued ordering the detachments to include a barrel of clean fresh drinking water in each boat, plenty of other mundane administrative missives of lesser import abound. Simply stating later that the sickness (which could have been largely prevented) was "extraordinary" was disingenuous at best. For a professional logistician and a veteran traveler on this stretch of the Oswego–Albany corridor, there is simply no excuse for this negligence. Equally disturbing is Bradstreet's unwillingness to shoulder the blame for any "extraordinary sickness which afterwards prevailed" or the casualties that ensued.

On the second day of the approach march, the convoy made good time, covering some twenty miles. The head of the convoy managed to reach Lake Oneida after a long, serpentine meander through low, swampy woodland. Sgt. Garret Albertson and his fellow Jerseymen rowed for three miles around one large hairpin turn in the creek and were told by some of the accompanying battoemen who were "well acquainted with the creek, that we had not gained ahead more than twenty rods, so crooked did the creek run." Colonel Clinton of the Yorkers, a surveyor by profession, left us a more detailed description using a creek in his home county of Ulster as a reference point. Wood Creek was "about the width of the Otterkill but Deeper and very much Crooked much resembleing in that respect the Mahawk River but not so Large till within two

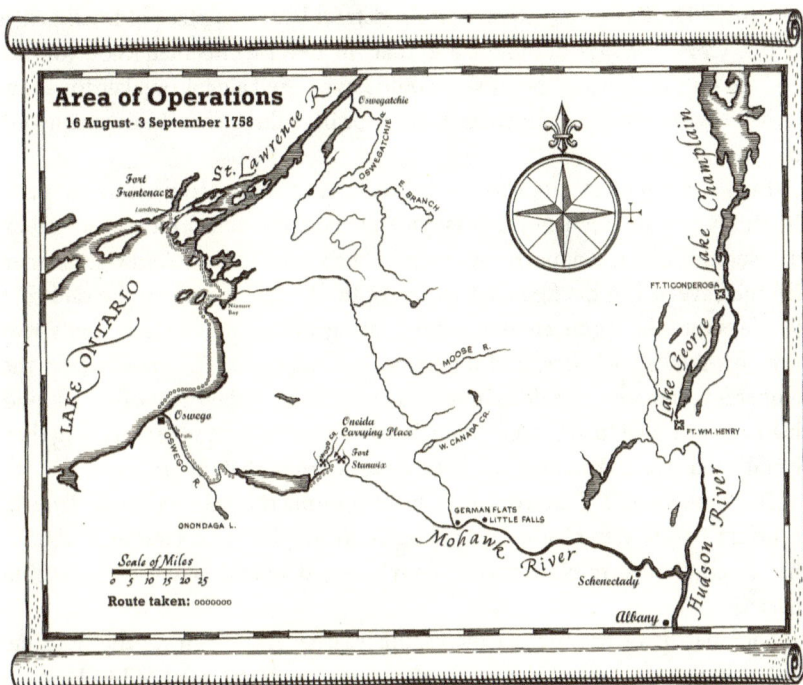

Map 2. Cartography by Ian McCulloch.

miles of the Onida Lake where it is very much wider and very Deep. Some Short turns in both of these Creeks where you sail near two-mile you turn almost back to where you Were and Can throw a Stone across the point of Land." For Clinton, no river in America had "finer land on it, nor so Large a Quantity" than the Mohawk, while Wood Creek, by comparison, was "Cold and Swampey, no Equal to the Other."[7]

Upon arrival at the eastern end of the lake, Garret Albertson of the Jersey Blues was fascinated by the Oneida Indians whom he met in person as they congregated around the night encampment. He informed his family, for whom his *Memoirs* were primarily written, that there was still some trepidation in the small army that not all Indians they would encounter would be friendly. The Oneidas, he explained, "would neither fight for, nor against us, but would trade with us; which they did in abundance, with dried eels and roasting ears of corn, for our beef, pork, and biscuits."[8] Bradstreet, for his part, was highly suspicious of the Oneida and would tell listeners after the raid that, as he was setting out, he had it "from good authority that some of ye Mohawk Tribes intended on his retreat, in case he did not Succede, to waylay him and cutt off all his army." Dr. Caleb Rea noted that Bradstreet kept this piece of intelligence to himself for the sake of morale and that "he never let his men know [of this plot] 'til on their return" because it could have posed a deal-breaker for some of the provincials and dampened their ardor in making their best "endeavour to prosecute their design."[9]

The morning of 18 August, before Bradstreet's small army set off to make the thirty-two-mile journey across Lake Oneida, the detachments took stock of casualties and the opportunity to send men back to Fort Stanwix. Charles Clinton revealed in his finalized return of the Yorkers going on the raid that two days into the approach march, his contingent had already lost twenty-two men to injuries, sickness, and desertion (see appendix F). Once out on the temperamental lake, the detachments were able to shake themselves out and the men were able to get some practice rowing on open water, something they would soon face on reaching the Lake Ontario leg of their approach.[10]

The Oneida and Tuscarora that lived around the lake called it *Tsioqui*, meaning "white water," a direct reference to the dangerous summer squalls that could transform New York Colony's largest inland lake into a seething maelstrom.

Fortunately for Bradstreet's forces, the weather stayed fair for the crossing. Still, the convoy hugged the north shore in case it was required to land on short notice. By 5:00 p.m., they were exiting the western end, where they encountered a rift of rocks and a stone fishing weir extending across the channel. They also found "an Indian encampment and a party catching fish and eels." As his convoy passed, Bradstreet took the time to question the Oneidas, only to discover that "a party of seven Oswegatchie Indians had been with them the previous day." Disturbed, Bradstreet learned the pro-French Indians had "gone forwards to Cadaraqui, but we could not learn [if] they had any intelligence of our approach." Confirmation would come the following day.[11]

"What is it that makes this officer so afraid?"

On the evening of 18 August, Native allies of the French saw the light of a bright fire winking at them from a small island located above the Oswego Falls over a mile away. As they closed the distance in their canoes, they became wary of the large fire. They had landed quietly on the south side of the island in dead ground, where they could not be seen, then crept forward through the darkness to a vantage point. After waiting, watching, and listening for an hour, they could see only two figures around the fire. Finally, they went forward in a loud gust of wind that rattled the leaves, tomahawks drawn.

When Capt. Thomas Butler commanding Bradstreet's reconnaissance party went down the Oswego River to scout as far as Lake Ontario on 16 August, he had left two "lads" with the officers' boat and baggage on a small island midriver above Oswego Falls and the rapids. They were to wait there hidden until Bradstreet's advance elements moved up to them, after which they could rejoin the main body. Despite instructions to light no fires, "the two boys left their boat laying in the stream uncovered, and kindled up a fire," Sgt. Garret Albertson wrote in his *Memoirs*. "The Indians discovered them, came on the island tomahawked and scalped them both; which we saw next morning, and buried them on the island."[12]

One aspect of the incident that resonated with the rank and file was a psychological one. That Natives lurked and hovered on the periphery of their camps was no longer in doubt. Albertson's unsympathetic comments linking the fate of the "two boys" directly to disobedience, not to mention their unstated conceit in not even bothering to try to conceal themselves in the wilderness, stemmed from a strong belief that the hand of Providence did not guard against stupidity.

A concerned Bradstreet viewing the dismal scene the following day was quick to note that the enemy warriors "had been in extream haste, as they never stripp'd the people, nor took away any of the stores." This absence of looting was a clear indication that the enemy were scouts on the prowl for information, and would now be on their way back to share that intelligence with their French allies. Unbeknownst to Bradstreet, this chance encounter between members of his raiding force and the enemy scouts was *not* just an unfortunate tactical mishap as he later portrayed in his *Impartial Account*. It constituted a major breach of operational security: more had been lost than the element of surprise.

For some inexplicable reason, Capt. Thomas Butler had left behind documents on the island, including a copy of his scouting instructions (see appendix G) and a handwritten copy of the General Orders of 11 August giving the detailed breakdown of Bradstreet's forces going against Frontenac, including the presence of artillery. These documents were taken by the Oswegatchie scouting party back to their settlement as quickly as possible. Five days later, on 22 August just as Bradstreet's forces were leaving Oswego, the documents were hand-delivered by an Oswegatchie chieftain to the commander at Fort Frontenac, Capt. Payen de Noyan.

Three weeks earlier, when Sieur de Longueuil had warned his cousin Payen de Noyan that a major British expedition was coming against him, the fort commandant had done his best to convince Governor Vaudreuil that he should be reinforced as soon as possible. He had also sent out scouting parties southward. The captured documents were read and digested at Fort Frontenac, then sent immediately downriver by express to Montreal to back up de Noyan's claims of a major force coming against him. The governor had ignored

Longueuil's earlier warnings and de Noyan's pleas up until now, complacent in his unshakable belief that the lack of a forward base at Oswego, the British fear of his little fleet and of his Amerindian allies, not to mention the unforgiving terrain, were strong deterrents for any such attempt. He is alleged to have contemptuously dismissed de Noyan's early requests for reinforcement with the words: "Qu'il falloit que cette Officier eût peur?" (What is it that makes this officer so afraid?)[13]

Vaudreuil, the Canadian-born governor, had failed to grasp that the old operating environment on the Lakes had changed significantly in the past three years. The transformation was due almost entirely to the new riverine capability honed and developed by Bradstreet. This development neatly dispensed with the need for a forward operating base and gave British troops the ability to maneuver on river and lake systems and to strike quickly over long distances. The same capabilities would be on display the following year for the siege and capture of Niagara, and again in 1760 during Gen. Jeffery Amherst's successful descent of the St. Lawrence River to reach Montreal.

With first blood to the enemy, Bradstreet's forces, as of 19 August 1758, were on high alert. After traveling twenty-six miles down the Oneida River to the Oswego Falls, the convoy arrived at the usual landing place of the portage, "a small cove into which the batteaus are brought in order to be drawn across." However, to cover and secure his landing, Bradstreet took the precaution of landing his entire army ("except four men in each boat") a half mile above the falls, where it formed up and then advanced on foot to the only major chokepoint and obstacle on the river. The men "advanced about a mile along the river," wrote Bradstreet, "whilst others were order'd to scour the woods: but on discovering no traces, or appearances of any enemy, they return'd and join'd their respective corps."[14] That evening, the entire army encamped on the open grounds opposite the Falls on the east bank of the river and the men slept on their arms.

The falls of the Oswego are located twelve miles upstream from the mouth of the river at Lake Ontario and, at their steepest point, cascade eleven feet to a jumble of rocks and white water. Sergeant Albertson remarked that the falls were "so high, and pitched over so rapid, that I saw our Mohawk Indians go under the pitch of water with long spears and fetch out a number of salmon." Bradstreet was well acquainted with the spot from his first days on the job in 1755, supplying the doomed forts at Oswego. From personal experience, he knew that it "is impossible to be pass'd with any degree of safety, by any boats whatever."[15]

Two years before, Bradstreet had witnessed an ill-advised attempt to go over the falls. Stephen Cross, a young carpenter from Newburyport, Massachusetts, on his way to Oswego to build ships, witnessed an exchange between Bradstreet and a boasting battoeman. The latter proclaimed there was "no Danger in going over the Steep Part of the Falls, and that much time was Unnecessarily lost in haling the Boats by land when they might go over." He then offered to find a crew and prove it to Bradstreet "for a small Sum." An intrigued Bradstreet, "on hearing this, offered the Sum he Proposed, and [the battoeman] soon found 3 others to joyn him." Cross and his fellow carpenters watched with amazement as the man and his colleagues "went over in the Whailboat [which] Plunged wholly underwater, Men and all, and Continued under Some time, the Water soaring upon her." His account continues:

> The Man who first proposed it was Steersman, which was with an oar [and] as the force of water fell on the blade of the oar & the other end being Under his arm, threw him A considerable distance below, where was a tree fallen over into the River. A man went [out] on the limbs which were above water and Catched him and saved his life. The other 3 kept hold of the Boat as she Drifted, Sometimes above water and Sometimes underwater. At length 2 of them lost their hold and was Drounded or Jamed to Pieces by the Rocks, one kept his hold until taken from her below the Rapids.[16]

After this failed experiment, a chastened Cross and his mates "did not Choos to trust our Baggage and tools by water as some others had done and lost them, but Carry them by land on our backs to the foot of the rapids where our Boat was taken to us by the Pilots who went over in them."[17]

It would take one and half days to get the entire army and all boats around the falls and through "the river below, full of rocks and a succession of rifts for near a mile in length which makes the navigation both difficult and hazardous." At this point, the battoemen came into their own, acting as pilots and shepherding the entire convoy down through the seething white water. The bateaux and whaleboats, still fully loaded, were first rolled on logs for a hundred yards, mostly downhill, to a section below the falls where "the force of the water which descends the precipice is somewhat abated." Garret Albertson noted that then "one person had to stand at the bow of the boat when launching, with a handspike or paddle to strike and break the wave at first entering." That was the job of the battoemen, who crewed each laden bateau with a steersman assisted by three pole-setters who then "convey'd [them] down the rifts to a small cove where the water is still and smooth."[18]

Bradstreet added that only experienced steersmen could "keep the channel and avoid touching the rocks," a rollicking passage lasting a brief three minutes, "which is proof of the great rapidity of the current."[19] He admitted that a shortage of such pilots on the expedition meant that several bateaux ended up "driven against the rocks [and] fill'd with water instantly, others by the violence of the force, were split asunder and sunk." During the first day of portaging and shooting the rapids, Capt. James Stephens and his gunners standing onshore were horrified to see a bateau carrying one of their howitzers and a twelve-pounder gun stoved in on the rocks and left hanging midstream in the flood. Bradstreet sent some battoemen and gunners down in an empty boat "and with great labour, the artillery was raised out of the water and put on board which arrived safe at the landing place."[20] Still, no fatalities were reported, but certainly some limbs were broken and egos bruised when the upended crews dragged themselves on shore, only to repeat the process.

As every surviving boat nosed its way into the sanctuary of a small cove below the rapids, it was handed back over to its respective detachment, which had marched down using the road. The battoemen then hiked a mile back upstream to pick up their next charge and do it all over again. Boats were quickly unloaded at the landing place by their owners and checked for damage or leaks before being reloaded and placed back in the river. The pervasive smell of hot pitch clogged everyone's nostrils for the next day and a half. Many boats needed to be recaulked, while others saw carpenters busily replacing stoved-in planks. The bateaux with their strong oak bottoms could take a lot of punishment underneath, but their clinker-built sides were vulnerable, made of softwoods like white pine to compensate for the weight of the oak.

Finally, on the afternoon of 21 August, the convoy was on the move downstream to Oswego on Lake Ontario, a twelve-mile voyage that took only an hour and a half. The site had been secured days earlier by Capt. Thomas Butler and the scouting company. Bradstreet's forces encamped on the level grounds on the west side of the river where the walls of the old Trading House were still visible. Also standing were the walls of several roofless stone houses "which had been the residences of the traders," wrote Bradstreet, "but there was scarce the appearance of there ever having been a fort or any place of defence."[21] After taking the fort in 1756, the French had burned everything in sight, including a half-finished sloop still in its cradle. However, upon the height of land across the river where Montcalm's army had first approached Oswego to put it under siege, the French had raised a large wooden cross to commemorate their triumph. On this cross, they had inscribed in Latin: *"In Hoc Signo Vincunt"* (In this sign, we were victorious).[22] Captain Butler's Haudenosaunee warriors cut the large cross down for amusement, chopped it into pieces, and then lit a large bonfire for all below to see.

The evening was taken up with more unloading and reloading of boats. Bateaux had to be repaired and caulked; three days' worth of provisions had to be cooked; all weapons and equipment needed to checked; and other provisions had to be stockpiled and cached for the return leg of the journey. A gill of

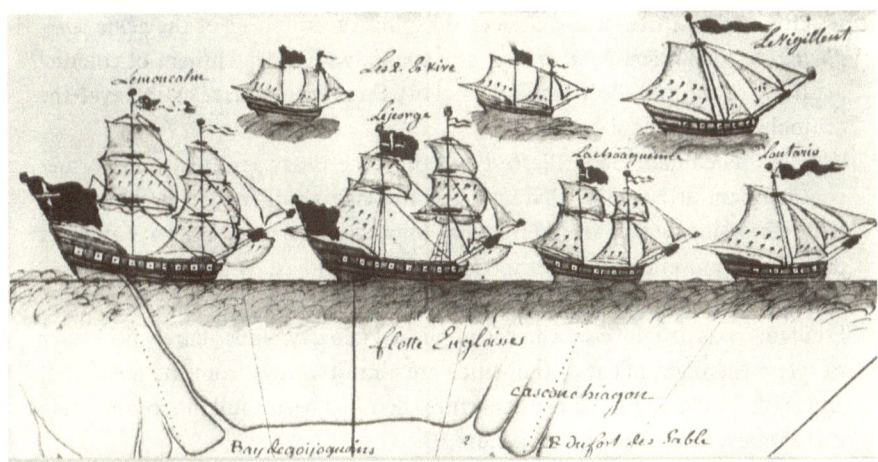

"La flotte Anglois."

This 1757 French drawing by artist-cartographer Capt. Joseph Boucher, Sieur de la Broquerie (1732–1802), a detail from a larger French map, shows the British squadron in full sail, complete with each boat's rig, size, and number of guns. This small fleet was captured in its entirety by Montcalm's forces at Oswego in 1756. The largest of the captured British brigs, the eighteen-gun *London*, was renamed the *Montcalm* and given to Sieur de la Broquerie to command. All of these ships, which represented a significant operational advantage to whoever maintained them on Lake Ontario, were burned by Bradstreet in the 1758 raid. Courtesy of the Toronto Public Library.

rum had been issued to all ranks in the encampments as a well-earned reward for the soldiers' backbreaking work at the falls. All men fit to fight were leaving for Cataraqui the next day, weather permitting. Ironically, the day of their departure for the final leg of their approach by water coincided with the day Montcalm's army had left Oswego a smoking ruin two years earlier—22 August 1756—bound for the same destination.

"The beautiful lake"

The French square-rigged schooner would have made a fine sight as it ran east-southeast before a faint but consistent lake breeze, all of its sails fully set, following the low-lying northern coastline of Lake Ontario. On a routine run, the *Marquise de Vaudreuil* was bound for Fort Frontenac having left Niagara around noon the previous day, 21 July, her hold and decks packed with bales of furs, the annual haul from the hinterland on its way down to Montreal and European markets beyond. She would have spent a toilsome afternoon beating northward across the lake against strong northeast headwinds until striking landfall at the bluffs just east of Fort Rouillé (Toronto). The only unusual cargo was the twenty-three-year-old Sieur d'Espinassy, an officer of the *2ème compagnie du canonniers-bombardiers du Canada* with a detachment of colonial artillery, come to collect stone from Fort Frontenac's quarries to revet the crumbling fort walls at Niagara.[23]

One Frenchman, Capt. Pierre Pouchot of the Bearn regiment, the former commandant at Niagara, characterized the lake weather as volatile, noting that "a crossing by ship from Frontenac to Niagara normally lasts 4, 6 or eight days unless one encounters a wind from the North East, which normally only blows during the phases of the moon." By contrast, the run from Niagara to Frontenac was usually easy and accomplished in a day, ships "barely necessary to spend the night afloat as the winds are almost always from the Southwest and brisk."[24] Two nights before departure there had been a full moon, and there was a robust headwind (see Appendix H).

The *Marquise de Vaudreuil*, named for Jeanne-Charlotte de Fleury Deschambault, the wife of the governor of New France, was the largest and most powerful ship on Lake Ontario. Built at Cataraqui shipyard in 1756 and rigged as a schooner, she was pierced for sixteen guns and had eight swivels mounted along her waist and quarterdeck taffrails. The latter armament was designed to repel boarders, shred an opponent's rigging, or rake small craft such as vulnerable boat convoys. But the French had been undisputed masters of the lake for the last two years since capturing the entire British fleet of five ships at the fall of Oswego in 1756. Now, the fast, sleek corsair was no more than an armed supply ship based out of Cataraqui, making its monthly rounds of the Lake Ontario forts at Toronto and Niagara.[25]

The captain of the *Marquise* on reaching the north shore would have changed course eastward for Cataraqui, close-hauled and heading back out into the lake. He would have maintained a respectful distance from the shore, as sudden violent storms were notorious this time of year and could erupt without warning on the lake that the Haudenosaunee had named *Oni-tario* ("the beautiful lake").[26]

The thirty-year-old captain, René-Hippolyte Pepin, Sieur de Laforce, had intimate knowledge of the tricky winds and unpredictable currents of the lake. He had even attempted to chart Lake Ontario with its numerous hidden underwater rocky shelves, as well as the tiny islands and unmarked sandbars that dotted the final approach through the Bay of Cataraqui.[27] He would have checked everything carefully before making his final approach, noting any wind changes and checking the low-lying islands that were starting to coast by on either side. To the port side, about a league distant he would have seen the Île de Tonti (Amherst Island), named for an Italian officer who had served with the explorer the Sieur de La Salle over a hundred years before. Looming up ten points off the starboard bow he would have seen another large, well-treed island, aptly named Île de Foret (Simcoe Island), though actually named for another long-dead officer.

Laforce had spent the first eleven years of his life at Fort Niagara, where his father, Pierre Pepin, a civil servant and surveyor, had held the lucrative post of king's storekeeper. Since a young boy, Laforce had shown an aptitude for sailing and had crewed on the sloops and barks of Lake Ontario that had run between his birthplace and Fort Frontenac. He was sent away at the age of twelve to Quebec, where he apprenticed to learn all aspects of seafaring. Having a ship's captain in the family was good for business, especially as his father and brothers were involved in illegal trading with the Dutch at Albany and Oswego until the latter's demise, as well as shipping their private consignments of furs and trade goods with impunity on the king's vessels. Laforce's older brothers, Michel and François Pepin, had both kept their feet on solid ground. Michel, an Indian interpreter and an officer in the colonial regulars, had been captured by George Washington at Jumonville Glen in 1755 and remained a prisoner of the British at Williamsburg, Virginia. François was the current clerk of the king's stores at Fort Frontenac. This brother was also an interpreter and had led the Mississauga contingent at Fort William Henry the year before.[28]

By the age of twenty-three, Laforce was commanding his own ship and engaged in coastal trading and privateering between Quebec and Louisbourg and points south. A well-connected local man who knew the vagaries of Lake Ontario, Laforce was the perfect choice for command of the newly built sloop the *Marquise de Vaudreuil*, in 1756. In addition to the plum appointment, Laforce was given overall command of the other naval forces on Lake Ontario by Governor Vaudreuil. In this role, he made naval history in 1756 by commanding a squadron in the first—and last—freshwater battle in North America between the French and British. He captured the smallest British sloop in the engagement. The remainder of the newly built British warships were added to Laforce's tiny flotilla at the surrender of Oswego in August, and all were taken back to Fort Frontenac as prizes (see list in appendix C).[29]

Since then, with no British maritime presence to disturb French lines of communication, only two warships were required for cruising on the lake and transshipping men, matériel, Indian goods, furs, and communiqués to and from the other trading posts at Fort Niagara and Fort Rouillé. In addition to his ship, Laforce had refitted the largest of the captured British brigs, the eighteen-gun *London*, renamed it the *Montcalm*, and placed it under the command of fellow seigneur and erstwhile cartographer Joseph Boucher, Sieur de la Broquerie. The other seven vessels of Laforce's so-called Lake Ontario squadron were now all sitting and rotting at anchor in Cataraqui, stripped of their cannons, completely unrigged, and used for overflow storage from the warehouses. The diplomatic Bougainville noted in his journal that this situation was yet another example of *"La Friponne"*—that is, The Big Cheat—hinting that perhaps the sails and cordage had been removed by Michel-Jean-Hugues Péan, a crony of the intendant, François Bigot, to rig and outfit his schooner fleet operating out of Quebec City and plying the routes from Quebec to Louisbourg and Acadia. Capt. Pierre Pouchot of the Bearn regiment was blunter: "Péan and his company had commandeered all the rigging for the vessels and had sold it for profit."[30]

The wind held and the *Marquise* glided into the inner harbor at Cataraqui around 5:00 p.m. Laforce dropped anchor within hailing distance of the fort, which seemed inordinately busy for so late in the day. Within five minutes, the captain and his crew learned why the fort appeared to be in upheaval: the British were coming over the lake in force to attack the fort and his ship, he was told, would be vital for its defense. The newly arrived artillery detachment's task to collect revetting stone for Niagara was immediately forgotten, and the Sieur d'Espinassy and his men were put to work by Payen de Noyan preparing the guns on the ramparts to receive the enemy. Laforce probably would have proposed taking the *Marquise* and de la Broquerie's *Montcalm* back out and down to Choueguen to see *if* he could intercept the force that must be coming in small boats.

Logically, the experienced gunners of the two crews and the two ships' combined firepower were essential to any credible defense of the fort. *If* they left the harbor, there was a chance the wind would not be favorable for them getting back in. Moreover, the morale of the garrison was already fragile with the news of the British approach. Payen de Noyan no doubt feared that *if* he sent his warships out, there was no guarantee his garrison would stay put *if* they witnessed their only salvation fleeing to fight another day. The ships with their guns staying in situ were the old soldier's best option to hold off *les Anglais*. If they could delay their enemy for at least three days, there was a good chance of reinforcement and relief coming up the St. Lawrence from La Présentation. There were a lot of "*ifs*."

La Présentation was a Six Nations mission village seventy-five miles downriver, located at the junction of the Oswegatchie River and the St. Lawrence. Approximately halfway between Montreal and Fort Frontenac, it was known more commonly as Oswegatchie from the river that bisected the community. Inaugurated just six years previously by Father François Picquet, it was home to some five hundred Christian Indians, mostly Onondaga and Oneida. Besides Catholicism, the other major attractions for the Haudenosaunee were that it was "dry" and "family friendly." The pernicious and debauching effects of the demon rum were conspicuously absent at the mission settlement. Also, the mission provided refuge to families from Iroquoia suffering encroachments and other unwelcome pressures of British colonists moving onto their lands and tapping out the traditional hunting grounds that lay to the south.[31]

Because it was located just above the Long Sault rapids on the St. Lawrence, Oswegatchie was part of the Lake Ontario supply system. It was the farthest point downriver that sloops making their way from Cataraqui and Niagara could travel. Used as a way station for the shipment of trade goods to the pays d'en haut from Montreal, it also had been fortified to protect the storehouses. But Oswegatchie was more than this. It became an ideal operating base for mounting raids against the Mohawk Valley, much akin to the most notorious of indigenous settlements on the eastern frontier—St. Francis, or Odanak—the scourge of New England.

The Oswegatchie chieftain, who may have been Oquandageghte, promised to return in three days with 150 warriors, who could be useful in harassing the enemy's siege camps. As he returned downriver in the twilight, he was accompanied by many Mississauga women and children clutching their belongings, all evicted from their houses just immediately south of the fort that were in the process of being torn down to improve the fort's fields of fire. Their menfolk were already gone, sent out southward in small scouting parties by Laforce's brother François, who had told them to merely observe and report back when they sighted the enemy.

The *Montcalm* had been stationed as a floating battery just a stone's throw off the northwestern bastion of the fort. From there, its guns covered the northern and western approaches to the fort. Now the *Marquise* would take up her position. By 10:00 p.m., Laforce had cleared his gundeck of fur bales and warped his ship around to block the entrance to the harbor, anchors set fore and aft. As he looked out over the shimmering waters southward, Bradstreet's forces were already moving north, making good time on the calm and quiet moonlit lake, riding the same current that hours earlier had been an impediment to Laforce.

"Looks More like a Sea than freshwater Lake"

It took Bradstreet's army three days to get to Fort Frontenac. Half of the journey was accomplished on the first day. Lt. Benjamin Bass recorded in his journal for 22 August 1758: "This Day Sot Sail from Oswago to go over the Lake Ontarioe towards Caterogua," the large flotilla of 123 bateaux and 95 whaleboats launching at 11:00 a.m., though the night before they had been ordered to be ready to leave by 8:00 a.m.[32] Weather on the lake did not respect Bradstreet's preferred time of departure. It was not until midmorning that the scouting company of rangers and Haudenosaunee warriors in whaleboats finally launched under the command of Capt. Thomas Butler, setting out a half hour earlier than the main body to provide a protective forward screen.

An officer of the New Yorkers detailed the order of the flotilla in his orderly book, noting that the force was "to keep as near as possible allowing a Small Distance between each Corps." First was the vanguard composed of Bradstreet's battoemen and whaleboat detachments of handpicked men from the provincial regiments commanded by Maj. Nathaniel Woodhull of the Yorkers. A gentleman farmer hailing from Long Island, Woodhull was a competent militia officer and muster master for Suffolk County. He had joined the New York provincial regiment with the rank of major in April 1758. To date in the campaign, Woodhull had served as second-in-command of the 2nd Battalion of Yorkers at Lake George, where they had acted as baggage guards while the regiment's other two battalions participated in the Battle of Ticonderoga.[33]

They were followed by the Independents, the bulk of the Yorkers, and the artillery with their precious guns, guarded on one flank by the detachment of Williams's Massachusetts Regiment and on the other by four companies of Yorkers. Behind them were Doty's Massachusetts men and the Rhode Islanders. Bringing up the rear were the reliable Yorkers in thirteen whaleboats commanded by the recently promoted Lt. Col. Isaac Corsa. The young major had stepped up after the Battle of Ticonderoga when the regiment's lieutenant colonel, Bartholomew Roux, commanding the 1st Battalion of the Yorkers, was seriously wounded. Corsa was also newly married, a bilingual Huguenot merchant who had started his military career as a captain in 1755 leading a company of Queens County men. A veteran of the siege of Fort William Henry, Corsa was described as being "small in stature and juvenile in appearance, though an intrepid officer," and he proved to be a stalwart and enthusiastic supporter of Bradstreet throughout the raid.[34]

People seeing Lake Ontario for the first time always marvel at its size. This reaction was the case even for experienced travelers such as Bougainville and Bradstreet who had traversed the North Atlantic. Most of the provincials behind the oars had been on Lake George, a comforting idyllic body of water bracketed with forested hills and landmarks that made it impossible to get lost, even in the fog. Immigrant Charles Clinton, who had had a particularly difficult Atlantic crossing from Ireland some thirty years before, recorded: "This Lake . . . Looks More like a Sea than freshwater Lake."[35] After traversing the lake with Montcalm in 1756, the scientist in Bougainville reported that "the navigation of Lake Ontario is quite dangerous and difficult [because] the least wind makes it rough, the waves are short and frequent, and in heavy weather, one gets more weary than on the open sea." He added that "there are almost no harbours or sheltered places." The eastern coastline was, in fact, a highly dangerous lee shore, much of which was shelved with rocky outcroppings.[36]

Bradstreet concurred writing that "on the least rise of wind, the swell is very great." This "obliged us to keep along the shore, that we might land, and draw up our boats, whenever the wind heightened."[37] The "swell" Bradstreet referred to is known today as a "seiche," a natural rhythmic motion in the lake as its waters slosh back and forth every eleven minutes. The effect is similar to a storm surge or tsunami caused by hurricanes or earthquakes along ocean coasts, but a seiche can cause oscillation back and forth across the lake for days at a time. This natural occurrence made it doubly important upon landing at night to draw one's boat as far up the beach as possible, and to tie them off or set grapnel lines.[38] Because all the waters of the other four Great Lakes flow down through Lake Ontario to the St. Lawrence, and on to the Atlantic Ocean, a counterclockwise current can also develop if winds die down on Lake Ontario. This current can propel a small boat without the aid of oars at speeds approaching two knots (2.5 miles per hour). Such a phenomenon appeared late morning on 22 August, and Bradstreet noted that the conditions on the lake "being calm and favourable, the opportunity of advancing was not to be neglected."[39]

Darkness must have been a cooling relief by the end of the first day, the men toiling at their oars with a waning full moon that rose at nine o'clock lighting their way. Whenever it became too cloudy and dark to see ahead, the flotilla's night navigation was enhanced, according to Sergeant Albertson of the Blues, by "a pilot called the commodore; who went ahead and flashed powder every few minutes, which light we followed." Masked lanterns may have been used as well.

Most mariners on the Great Lakes in the eighteenth century employed what was then known as coastal piloting or dead reckoning. Indigenous mariners relied on an intimate knowledge of the shoreline for navigation. To aid in navigating the lake, the Haudenosaunee made use of mnemonic devices by giving place-names to outstanding coastal features or prominent landmarks. For example, Oswego derives from the Haudenosaunee word *Osh-we-geh*, meaning "pouring-out place," especially as in a small river into a large lake.[40]

A freshwater pilot needed intimate knowledge and feel for the waters that were being traversed as well. Such an ability was far more important than the knowledge of how to take readings of the stars or sun. Part of that "feel" was understanding the vagaries of the wind, the lake currents, and the moon's influence on the wind and lake weather systems. That's not to say the indigenous people of Lake Ontario were ignorant of the North Star, and they would often rely on its constant alignment with the North Pole to help them navigate during their travels. The Haudenosaunee even oriented their longhouses according to the four cardinal directions so that the Sun would shine onto the entrance at dawn, and set in the direction of the exit.

On the first day, the British rowed a long time and covered a good distance. Charles Clinton wrote that they "sail'd till about 2 [a.m.] of the Clock at night then Came too At the Northeast shore in a Cove." Bradstreet called it "a fine bay." By counting the thirteen hours lapsed and calculating the approximately forty miles traveled, one can conclude that the landfall was at Niaoure, what is today called Henderson Bay, New York. Here Montcalm's army and bateaux had sheltered on their way south in 1756 to capture Oswego. Bradstreet gave his men five hours sleep and had them awake by 7:00 a.m. and back out on the lake by 8.[41]

Despite a good start, the weather threatened the army's progress on the second day. "We were Pretty far Advanced into the Lake," noted Clinton in his 23 August journal entry, but after an hour of rowing, "the Pilots observing the Wind likely to Blow which upon this Lake raises a very Great Sea, it was thought best to make into Shore and Stay to See what the weather Would do." The men, still bone-weary with fatigue from their herculean, adrenalin-fueled labors of the previous day and night, had another six hours of welcome rest. The location of their expedient rest halt, based on their time on the water, and the fact there was a northerly headwind, puts them at the entrance to Chaumont Bay, the next bay along the shoreline to the north. They stayed there until 3:00 p.m. The flotilla then rowed from three to ten o'clock that evening, managing a respectable leg of some fifteen miles before coming into a bay below Cape Vincent. The only excitement of the day was in the late afternoon when the scouts in the forward screen spotted "five Indian canoes near the land, which they pursued and fired upon," wrote Bradstreet; however, "the Indians putting into a creek made their escape."[42]

At 2:00 a.m. on 24 August, most members of the expedition were awoken from a deep slumber by gunfire. Bradstreet later noted that "the report of four discharges of cannon at Cadaraqui were distinctly heard, our distance from thence being about fifteen miles." It would later be revealed to Bradstreet that the guns were "fired to alarm the adjacent Indians" when the Mississauga scouts of the previous day had returned to Fort Frontenac and had "given information of our approach." Bradstreet seems to have assumed that this was the first time Sieur de Noyan and his garrison had become alerted to the presence of a large force coming against them. Unaware of the fact that he had been shadowed for most of the way from Oswego, he restated his belief after the event that until this point of his approach he had achieved total surprise.[43]

Later on the morning of 24 August, which was the expedition's third day on the lake, the wind worsened, forcing them to stay put for hours—an agony for any commander who knows he has been detected on his approach just miles short of his objective. The parallels with Braddock's march on Fort Duquesne three years earlier were not lost on Bradstreet, nor on others who had been on that ill-fated expedition, men like Capt. William Ogilvie and some of his Independents.

"One must take care not to get lost"

The Thousand Islands of the St. Lawrence River are still a navigational challenge today, but 250 years ago they were much more challenging. Even the French, who had plied the waters for nigh on 150 years and had acquired a wealth of knowledge on the lake's topography, meteorology, and hydrography could get easily confused by the Thousand Islands. A commandant at Fort Niagara noted: "They extend over at least three leagues [and] consist of an infinite number of little rocks covered with trees which in several places leave a wide enough channel to pass. In other places, vessels pass between two islands almost touching each shore. They are very safe. There is always deep water all away around each island & very little current. After three leagues, the islands begin to get larger. One must take care not to get lost."[44] Certainly, the Jesuits and other explorers such as Samuel de Champlain who had first passed through the area a hundred years before had drawn maps, but these were representational maps, with much of the detail being based on hearsay and not on accurate hydrographic surveys or precision drawings to scale. The creation of the first maps was more diplomatic than utilitarian: lines and borders proclaimed sovereignty and one's territory to the world.

For people sailing on the lake, such maps were useless, as they lacked any channel soundings, markings for safe anchorages with good bottoms, and most importantly, navigational hazards such as rocks, reefs, shoals, and sandbars to be avoided. That is, until 1757, when both French naval captains serving on the lake, the Sieurs Laforce and de la Broquerie, each prepared charts showing the entire lake. Their maps reflected the hard-won details of their shared experiences on the temperamental lake, and they made copies for their commanders for planning purposes. Joseph Boucher, the more artistic of the two mariners, filled in the white borders of his Lake Ontario map with the two opposing fleets in full sail, battle ensigns flying. As well as naming each French and British warship, he also depicted how they were rigged and the number of guns each carried. For a finishing touch, he inserted close-up drawings of each lake fort with their harbors and the detailed soundings in the corners. These two mid-eighteenth-century hand-drawn charts were the first real examples of military hydrographic mapping of Lake Ontario. Their discovery by the British aboard the captured ships abandoned by the French crews during the raid constituted perhaps the best intelligence coup of the 1758 campaign.

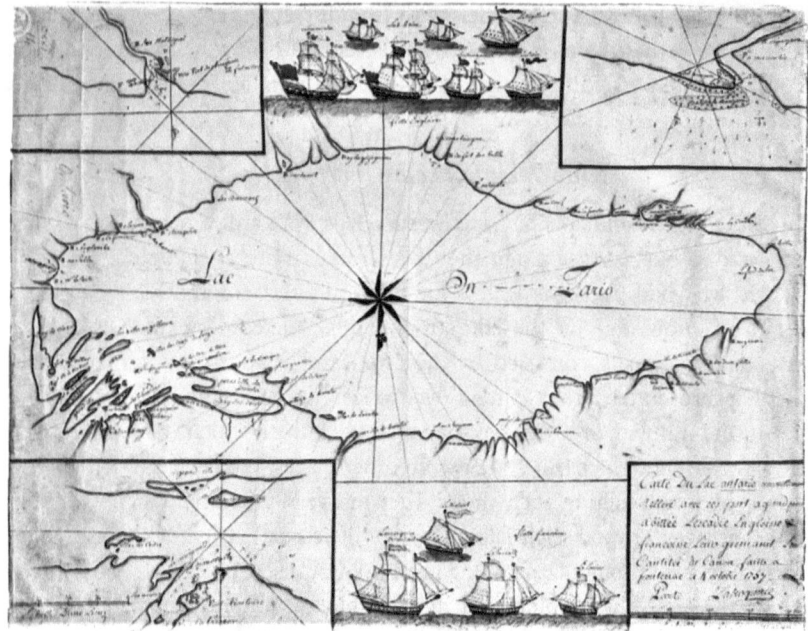

Captured French map

One of two captured French maps that constitute the first real examples of military hydrographic mapping of the Great Lakes showing harbor soundings, sand bars, and navigational hazards. Their discovery aboard the captured French ships at Fort Frontenac constituted perhaps the greatest intelligence coup of the 1758 campaign. Courtesy of the Toronto Public Library.

Thomas Sowers (1734–74), the engineer for the 1758 expedition, realized their worth immediately and took charge of them. Upon his return to Albany, he would churn out copies with the assistance of a junior engineer named Dietrich Brehm. Using the captured charts, Sowers was able personally to prepare a coastal route map from Oswego to Niagara for use by Generals Prideaux and Johnson in the 1759 expedition against Fort Niagara, as well as maps for Gen. Jeffery Amherst's 1760 expedition down the St. Lawrence via Oswegatchie to take Montreal.

But in 1758 Bradstreet had no such maps. Instead, he had to rely on the knowledge and experience of Ononwarogo (Red Head) and other Haudenosaunee warriors who were acting as pilots to guide him toward his objective. In the time spent waiting for favorable conditions on 24 August, Bradstreet may have quizzed Ononwarogo on the best route ahead. The Onondaga warrior, having made the lake trip many times while an original inhabitant of Oswegatchie, was an invaluable pilot and had some skills as an amateur cartographer as well. The following year, he would prepare a map for General Amherst with the assistance of Sir William's nephew, Guy Johnson, showing every Indian settlement around the lake as well as down the river to Montreal.[45]

The large island immediately to the north of Bradstreet's army across a choppy channel was *Ganounkouesnot*, meaning "long island standing up." The French called it simply Grand-Île, for if one went to the right in the channel, the big island stretched for nearly twenty miles downriver toward La Présentation and was, in parts, six miles wide. If one went to the left, skirting Grand-Île's sandy shores to the west, and then followed it around to the north side, one could row in behind two smaller islands. These islands would shield against northeast headwinds as well as any French warships that might swoop down across Cataraqui Bay.

On the morning of 25 August, the fourth day of the approach on the lake, Bradstreet awakened the men at five o'clock, but once again weather conditions caused a delay. Hoping to get some relief from the high winds and waves by hugging the southwestern shore of Grand-Île, they set off at 4:00 p.m. After a rough crossing of the channel, the raiders were forced to land at dusk on a smaller island called Île de Foret (Simcoe Island) just at the western tip of Grand-Île. By 8:00 p.m., the entire force was tucked in behind the Île aux Cochons (Garden Island, ON), "about three miles distant" from their target, Fort Frontenac. "The water in the bay being very rough prevented our crossing it at this time," wrote Bradstreet, who could now see his tantalizing objective. "We observed two vessels near it, equipped for their voyage, and several masts beyond it." The intelligence gleaned from this one view was significant. Only two ships of the French fleet were rigged for sailing, and thus posed potential trouble if they were to come out. But both had their sails furled and showed no intention of leaving their harbor.

Detailed orders were issued for an assault landing at midday on 25 August, including the disposition of forces for the run onto the beaches, fire discipline to be observed, signals for attacking, and tasks for the various troops once ashore (see appendix I). All were reminded that their Native allies would be well forward, and warned to prevent friendly fire incidents; Bradstreet told his men to take especial "Notice that our Indians have Red Gimp In their hair and to be extremely Careful not to fire upon them."[46] Midday came and went as the assault troops "lay in plain view of the French, until late in the afternoon." At this point, Garret Albertson and his compatriots "received orders to cook three days' provisions, and be in readiness to embark on board our boats, to cross the water and land on the French ground."[47] The Haudenosaunee burned some tobacco and white cornmeal to placate two particular wind spirits of Gaoh—the North wind, a great bear; and the East wind, a moose—believing both had conspired for the last two days to bar their progress.[48]

At 5:00 p.m., "the Whole immediately embark'd," Bradstreet having decided that the wind had died down enough to cross and that it was "practicable to land." Sergeant Albertson recalled the final run down to the beach: "the boats were to be drawn up in a line, within two hundred yards of the shore, and stand fast until a signal was given by the firing of a brass howitzer when the whole were to give three cheers, then every man immediately to his oar, and pull with resolution to land, which was soon accomplished."[49] As soon as the lead boats had nosed onto the long stony beach that stretched for a quarter-mile, the men jumped out and quickly "formed two Deep on the front of their Boats Except the Indians and Rangers who [were] to Scout Some Distance Round to See what they can Discover." Most had been apprehensive that the landing would be opposed, or that at least some war parties would snipe at them while they were at their most vulnerable out on the water. However, the landing went smoothly without any mishaps.

Onshore, Sergeant Albertson and his mates, as well as the other provincials, stood on guard for some time, waiting for "a detachment of our army . . . sent to reconnoitre the woods, lest a party of the French might be out of the fort in ambush" to return. They were stood down an hour later when some rangers returned to report they had "discovered no party out." Bradstreet ordered the night guards to mount and the remainder of the troops to lie on their arms, with no fires to be lit. The night was just getting started.[50]

CHAPTER 4

Assault

They may vex us with shot, or with assault.

—Shakespeare, Henry IV

The French gunners were crouching low, their six-pounder guns loaded with double grapeshot and run out, slow matches burning in their hands. The captain of the *Marquise de Vaudreuil* had anchored his sixteen-gun schooner in the entrance to the Cataraqui inner harbor. Laforce then had warped her around until her starboard battery of eight guns pointed directly out toward the outer harbor and Lake Ontario beyond.

A vast British flotilla had been observed crossing before last light from Île aux Cochons at around 6:00 p.m., but it had disappeared from view behind the Mississauga village on the point half a mile south of the fort. The Mississauga scouts, watching from the woods, told the French that the enemy had landed on a large shelving beach about a mile away, unobservable from the fort. It had been quiet since then, with just the lapping of the water and the occasional call of gulls or a lake bird, as the crew of the *Marquise* napped by their guns or talked quietly among themselves.

The sun had set at seven o'clock and it was now nine. A waning, but nearly full moon was not due for another four hours in the black-red sky (see appendix H). The French could just make out a long line of enemy whaleboats edging their way down the western shore of Point Montreal. The British were having a rough time of it, rowing, as it were, directly into a strong headwind. It is possible that Laforce was still disappointed that he and his fellow naval captain, the Sieur de la Broquerie, had been unable to convince their commander to utilize that favorable following wind for their ships (and cargoes) to exit the

Night Assault
This painting by marine artist Peter Rindlisbacher depicts Bradstreet's "cutting-out" attempt on the French warship the *Marquise de Vaudreuil* the night of their arrival, 25 August 1758. Thirty whaleboats manned by about two hundred provincials were foiled in their attempt by alert French gunners who dispersed them with well-aimed broadsides of grapeshot. Author's collection.

harbor and rain destruction upon the British flotilla at its most vulnerable—out on open water.

The British whaleboats on their final approach were spreading out into a line on the dark waters about thirty yards away. Laforce nodded to his 1st lieutenant to fire when ready. The entire brig shook from the simultaneous discharge, the broadside timed to wreak maximum havoc among the approaching boats packed with men. Screams of alarm and pain in the darkness confirmed that some of the guns had found their marks. Pandemonium ensued and Laforce's gunners quickly reloaded and kept firing into the cluster of milling boats. Then as quickly as they had appeared, the whaleboats withdrew under the cover of the French cannon smoke and darkness. Laforce's crew started to cheer, answered in kind by those manning the fort, their guns sending a few shots in the general direction of the retreating British for good measure.

Montcalm would later report in dispatches that "our two armed ships were attacked by about 30 whaleboats of English but these were repulsed with the loss of about 20 men on their part." Maj. Daniel Wall of the Rhode Islanders, writing to his governor after the raid, explained that the "cutting-out" expedition sent by Bradstreet against the ships moored beside the fort was "an attempt . . . to board the brigantine and schooner by whaleboats" but that it was quickly called off when "the ships warped in under the fort [and] it was thought impracticable to attempt it." Lt. Thomas Sowers, the engineer, was a little more precise in his report of the action to the board of ordnance. He wrote: "An attempt was made at Nine to Board the Vessels then in the Harbour but without Success."[1]

The British commander's first offensive move was in keeping with his character—bold and audacious, but also a wee bit arrogant. Bradstreet may have attributed the so-far passive defense of the French forces to timidity or indecision and, flushed with elation on having reached his objective unscathed and loath to relinquish the momentum he was thus enjoying, may have decided to make this first probe, underestimating the actual readiness of the French defenders.

Bradstreet's response to the failure of the attempt to cut out the French ships was to cut the incident out of his official reports and the *Impartial Account*. The "cutting-out" attempt and its dismal failure at the outset of the raid have never before featured in any historical accounts of Bradstreet's raid because he expunged any mention of it in his official reports and certainly did not mention it in his *Impartial Account*. Historians who have leaned heavily on his version of the raid, from Francis Parkman to Fred Anderson, have completely missed this first misstep of the raid owing to Bradstreet's deliberate omission. Still, French, provincial, and British regular accounts definitively confirm the failed "cutting-out" attempt occurred, although they ignore its losses.

It is unclear how many men were lost. The Sieur d'Espinassy estimated that at least twenty men in the thirty whaleboats must have been casualties, though how he arrived at this figure when the action took place in the dark is problematic. A definitive British casualty list for the raid does not survive because the officer who would have been responsible for collating such a return, the expedition's adjutant, Archie Montague Brown, was "bruiz'd a little in the breast with a small grapeshot," one of the two known officer casualties on the raid.[2] In his first official reporting on the raid's success to General Abercromby on 31 August, Bradstreet made no mention of any casualties but was happy to list the plunder he had taken: ships, cannons, provisions, Indian goods, and bales of furs. By 3 October 1758, however, Bradstreet was maintaining to anyone who would listen to him at the Lake George camp on his return "that he did not lose one man *in the action* [and that] 16 were wounded [and] two officers," for a total of eighteen wounded overall in the attack. Later, in his *Impartial Account*, he would admit that the French "only wounded eleven persons the whole night" on his *final approach* on the fort.[3]

Other participants offered various tallies. Maj. Daniel Wall's account of the campaign claimed that a total of only twelve men were casualties: "Lieut. Col. Corsa of the New York regiment wounded, an officer of the Independents [Lt. Archibald Montague Brown] and ten men of the different corps." Capt. Peter Jacquet, the senior battoeman, who was present on the flanking night march to establish one of the siege batteries, wrote that the enemy "fired mostly over our heads and only killed one man and wounded eight" for a total of nine casualties. Colonel Clinton, a credible witness, mentions another five wounded at the main battery, where he remained for the duration of the bombardment. Daniel de Normandie, also of the battoemen, offers what appears to be the highest total and most precise accounting. He wrote to Cadwallader Colden that the fort had been taken "with the Loss of Three men killed, and 17 wounded."[4]

What to make of all these discrepancies? Bradstreet and de Normandie suggest that a total of seventeen to eighteen were wounded in the action around Fort Frontenac. Taken together, the reports of Captain Jacquet and Colonel Clinton indicate that eight of them were wounded and one killed in the western flanking party and five more of them wounded at the main battery. These tallies are close to Bradstreet's statement that eleven were wounded in the "final approach" to the fort. However, a total of eleven to thirteen wounded still leaves five to seven wounded men unaccounted for, and possibly two more were killed according to de Normandie. These unaccounted-for casualties were likely sustained on Friday night in the attack on the *Marquise de Vaudreuil*. Such numbers are much lower than the French artillery lieutenant's estimate of at least twenty men but are a more accurate accounting of the attempt's significance and cost than Bradstreet's deliberate omission and silence.

After the initial repulse of the British whaleboats, the French guns warmed to their task, firing blindly at their maximum range in the general direction of the British camp a mile away for the remainder of the night, hoping to disrupt the troops they knew to be lurking to the south. "This night, the enemy discharged about fifty rounds of cannon shot at us," wrote Bradstreet, "but we were out of their reach, cover'd by a rising ground, between us and the fort."[5] What Bradstreet meant to say was that that the intervening hill protected them from direct "line of sight" artillery fire, thus they were in what was termed "dead ground."

Some of the French twelve-pounders could easily reach out a mile (1,760 yds), their maximum effective range being 1,960 yards, as one sergeant of the Jersey Blues attested.[6] Garret Albertson, who had stood an uneasy watch during the night, recalled that "when morning came the sun arose, I left my guard and went on board my bateau to take my breakfast." While he was "setting in the stern of my boat eating, the French sent a cannonball which just cleared the

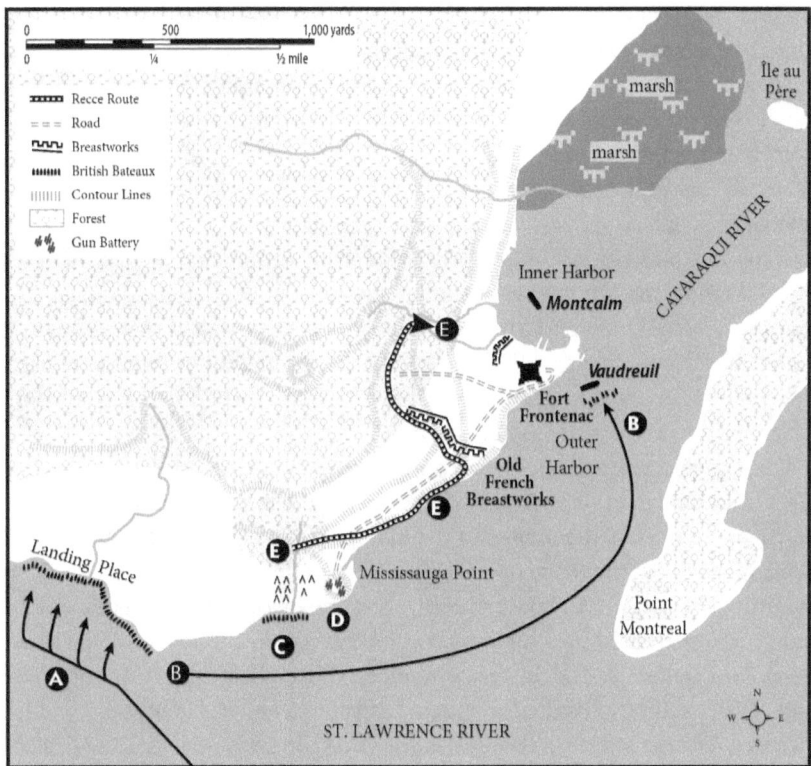

Map 3. Initial Deployment, 25–26 August 1758. Cartography by Mike Bechthold.

A. 6:00 p.m., 25 August 1758, Bradstreet's 3,000-man force lands.
B. 9:00 p.m., 25 August 1758, 30 British whaleboats repulsed attacking the *Marquise de Vaudreuil*.
C. 7:00 a.m., 26 August 1758, artillery boats moved to cove behind Mississauga Point.
D. 9:00 a.m., 26 August 1758, howitzer battery established behind crest of hill on Mississauga Point.
E. 7:00 a.m.–12:00 a.m., 26 August 1758, Bradstreet and engineer recce siege battery sites.

stern of the boat and went into the water, and cracked like a red-hot plowshare, dashing the water over us; my messmate put out a hard word, and said he would not stay there, for there was hot stuff."[7]

"A spot very advantageously situated"

Early on the morning of 26 August, orders came for all the artillery bateaux and those carrying shot and powder to move down the shoreline from their initial landing place (see map 3). They were brought into the cove directly behind the "rising ground" or ridge that ran down to Mississauga Point less than half a mile from the fort. There, all the guns were unloaded and checked over, and soon three howitzers were in action, two iron eight-pounders and one twelve-pounder Royal. A cross between a gun and a mortar, a howitzer was a large-caliber weapon designed to lob shells over walls using high trajectories, but they could also be used in a direct-fire role. Smaller and more mobile than a heavy mortar, the howitzer was cast with trunnions so it could be mounted on a wheeled field carriage. Stephens's gunners soon had them set up and ready, throwing "shells that did the enemy considerable damage, but our cannon could not make much impression on their wall at that distance."[8] The two eight-pounders, with their specific caliber of ammunition, were used sparingly throughout the day, maintaining a steady rate of fire to keep the fort occupied and in a constant state of alarm.

As a preliminary to his intended night operations, Bradstreet gave orders for three companies of Yorkers to flank west of the fort through the woods in daylight "to possess themselves of the high grounds on [that] side of the fort, which they did without any opposition." The remainder of the army, less those guarding the bateaux and the artillery, "were employed in making fascines and gabbeons, made of bushes, for fortifying an entrenchment," two essential items if one was contemplating the erection of a field-expedient battery on short notice. Then Bradstreet disappeared with his young engineer in tow, to conduct detailed reconnaissance of the area, guided by Red Head and with close protection provided by some of the Natives and battoemen.[9]

The woods rang with the sound of axes as the army gathered the materials required for the task at hand. A fascine was essentially a tightly bound bundle of straight, trimmed branches or pieces of wood, tied in several places to form an expedient lightweight log. These bundles could then be used to thicken up a wall's ability to absorb a round shot or to form a revetment wall against which dirt could be thrown to form an embankment. They could also be used as expedient logs to fill in a ditch obstacle. Typically, six men were employed in making a fascine: two to cut the boughs and trim them, two men to gather them, and the remaining two to bind them.[10]

Gabions required a little more finesse, being large, hollow, cylindrical tubes made with a mesh of woven wicker—or in this case, interlaced twigs. They could range in size from a large spherical garbage can to a forty-gallon oil drum. First placed upright, they would then be filled with dirt, like a sandbag, and placed to form an expedient wall. Extra dirt from a trench dug in front of them would be used to thicken the embankment in order to absorb any enemy shot or shell directed their way. A gun embrasure was made simply by leaving a gabion out of the wall. This would be the case for the fascine battery built to the west of the fort, but embrasures at the main battery would have to be dug through the existing old French breastworks.

Bradstreet and Sowers were out for most of the morning and returned at midday having formulated a plan based on a better knowledge of the terrain. Bradstreet ordered "the commanding officers of the corps . . . to appear at his tent" that afternoon in the main camp, where he told them he had "thoroughly reconnoitred the grounds surrounding the fort, and on the west side, discovered *a spot very advantageously situated*, at about 150 yards distant." Given that he had only a limited amount of ammunition ("only 70 rounds . . . for each piece of cannon") as well as a "scanty allowance of forty spades, and the like number of pickaxes and shovels," he told them bluntly it was impossible to contemplate "making any [siege] approaches at a great distance."[11]

Bradstreet's "advantageously situated spot" was a small hillock he had discovered on the western wood line overlooking the northwest bastion of the fort. This hill, he told his audience, was key terrain. He intended to haul two twelve-pounder guns with two ammo carts, four hundred fascines, an assortment of gabions, and entrenching tools through brush and woods over a distance of a mile and a half under the cover of darkness that evening. Upon arrival at the hillock, they would quickly dig an entrenchment and set up an earthwork battery fortified with fascines and gabions. Upon reflection, it was a noisy and dangerous proposition for any troops, whether regular or irregular, trained or untrained. Night operations are fraught with danger with friendly fire incidents or getting lost just two of the age-old results when tired and frightened troops are involved.

To carry out the investment of Fort Frontenac, Bradstreet's command would divide into three groups. The largest was a party of 1,400 men, almost half the force, detailed to remain at the beach to guard the boats, encampment, and provisions.

A second detachment of six hundred handpicked men, styled the "Investing Guard" in orders, would conduct a flanking march under cover of darkness and build the two-gun fascine battery on Bradstreet's chosen hillock. They would take under command a detachment of one hundred rangers and Indians under Capt. Thomas Butler, plus three additional New York companies already in situ on the approach to the objective, sent out earlier in the day by Bradstreet "to keep possession of the Hill" on which he intended to erect his fascine battery. These four hundred men, who had all seen the ground to be traversed in daylight, were tasked to blaze a trail and act as guides for the remainder of the "Investing Guard" after dark, as well as to picket the route to provide security. In addition to two gun crews for the twelve-pounders, it was "compos'd of one company of Regulars [under Capt. William Ogilvie], seven companies of the

New York regiment [under Lt. Col. Isaac Corsa] and a number of batteau men [under Capt. Peter Jacquet]," representing the best and most trusted men of Bradstreet's command. They would help transport the materials and guns to their destination as well as provide close protection against any sally made from the fort to disrupt its construction. The two twelve-pounder brass guns were to be commanded by Lt. John Wilson at the fascine battery, while his superior, Capt. James Stephens, would remain with the rest of the train setting up at the old French breastworks.

The third detachment, or "Main Guard," made up "principally of Rhode Island, Massachusetts and New Jersey troops" numbering some six hundred men, were the first to move out just after last light at approximately 8:00 p.m. The eight-pounder British howitzer battery at Mississauga Point stepped up its rate of fire to mask the noise of the forward movement of the two investing detachments and to distract the defenders. Bradstreet placed himself at the head of this force, which was "to take possession of the enemies old breastwork which was about 250 yards south from the fort." By "cutting embrazures for two pieces of cannon and three haubitzers [i.e., howitzers]," the breastworks would be transformed into a British siege battery. The digging activity involved in the process would also hopefully draw and distract the French garrison's attention "on this quarter." With the French distracted, the flanking force—"the Investing Guard"—could make its "silent" approach march to the west through the woods skirting five hundred acres cleared around the fort proper.[12]

Earlier in the day, Bradstreet and engineer Thomas Sowers had found the best-covered approach to the old French breastworks. By following the shoreline around at water level, hugging the limestone rock outcroppings and embankments, one could easily get into the breastworks without traveling over open ground in view of the fort.

A 1783 watercolor of Fort Frontenac clearly shows these river embankments before their disappearance under decades of city waterfront development. Sergeant Albertson of the Blues remembered that "under cover of a dark night, [we] marched under the bank of the lake and got into the French settlement near the fort in profound silence." His reference to "settlement" is an indication that the fort's fields of fire still contained some forty-odd outlying structures, probably belonging to the several families of farmers, workmen, and voyageurs that lived year-round at Cataraqui (see appendix B).

That it was "a dark night" is not in doubt, for the waning moon would not rise until 11:00 p.m., with last light occurring around seven o'clock that evening (see appendix C). We can also surmise it was a cloudy night, as Bradstreet claims the French only discovered his fascine battery on the western side "by the assistance of the moon, which rose about four o'clock." In fact, the moon

A view of Fort Frontenac
A 1783 view of the ruined fort by surveyor-artist James Peachey (ca. 1753–97) depicts the terrain around Fort Frontenac much as it would have looked twenty-two years earlier during the raid. The houses that have sprouted up around the ruined fort were erected by Loyalist settlers arriving after the Revolutionary War. One can see the high banks of the Cataraqui River shoreline that Bradstreet's force used as a covered approach to get into the old French breastworks, now obscured by modern waterfront. The treed high ground to the far rear is where Bradstreet erected a two-gun battery. Courtesy of the Toronto Public Library.

had been up already for five hours at 4:00 a.m. but was masked behind a heavy cloud cover. First light would be at 5:17 a.m. But was the moon the real culprit? Bradstreet would tell another story before going to press with his *Impartial Account* the following year. In October 1758, as Bradstreet "dined-out" and regaled audiences at Lake George with tales of his raid exploits at Frontenac, he told several provincial chaplains that his battery "was undiscovered till just as he had finished, when one of y' men accidentally discharged his Peice whereupon y' Enemy turn'd their Canon upon him with all fury."[13]

In his official account, however, it was a different story: "the noise and rustling which the fascines made among the brush" (and one might add, the six hundred heavily laden, swearing men carrying, in addition to two fascines each, other equipment such as spades and pickaxes or pulling gun carriages) caused the flanking force's detection en route to the hill by the fort's defenders. "As it was very dark," explained Bradstreet, "they only fired at the sound."[14]

The sound of shovels and picks clattering against the stony soil of the old French breastworks, a mere 250 yards away, soon alerted de Noyan's gunners as to the British presence south of the fort. "As soon as the enemy heard [us],"

Clinton recorded, "they fired constantly . . . with their cannon and their small arms." With an unlimited supply of shot and shell and a confirmed target, the French ships' batteries and the fort's guns created much noise and spectacle but inflicted little damage on the provincials snugly ensconced behind the substantial breastworks built by Montcalm's regulars in 1756. The men working on the embrasures were the most vulnerable, and "there were about five wounded at that place."[15]

Still, Bradstreet's bait had been set and taken, and so far, everything was going to plan. He left Clinton in charge at the French breastworks and returned to where the "Investing Guard" with two brass twelve-pounders waited for him and set off on his western flanking march, again personally at the head of the column. Bradstreet would later anonymously praise his own cleverness in his *Account* for turning the old French earthworks to his advantage. Stating the obvious that a day approach in the open ground "would have cost the lives of many," he instead "prudently made [his approach] within such a distance that every [British] ball might do execution" under the cover of darkness. These measures he unabashedly proclaimed to be "as daring and bold . . . a conduct is to be met with in the records of any military achievements of the most enterprising generals."[16] In reality, he was conducting an ordinary but abbreviated siege by following long-established practices.

The night flanking march was the part of Bradstreet's plan that involved the most risk, but it was necessary to force the French to surrender quickly before

Les Canonniers-Bombardiers

The French colonial artillery were the elite of the *troupes de la marine* and received higher pay than their counterparts. Here an officer instructs an NCO as a gun detachment trains with a twenty-four-pounder gun on a wooden platform. Artillery in New France was old and worn out, usually castoffs by the navy from decommissioned ships. Courtesy of René Chartrand, Company of Military Historians.

succor could arrive from Montreal. Bradstreet consciously decided to leave his least dependable troops to guard the boats, as well as to haul siege guns, dig embrasures, and provide security at the old French breastworks. For the most difficult phase, he would use his most dependable and disciplined troops.

"One could easily damage it with a sledge or pick"

A mortar belched a fiery roar and sent its bomb arcing high into the air, on a southward trajectory to fall upon some unsuspecting gun crew. Or, at least, that was the hope. The Sieur d'Espinassy, just twenty-three years old, was a lieutenant of the 2ème compagnie du canonniers-bombardiers du Canada of the colonial artillery. It was the newly minted officer's first siege and the greatest challenge of his short career to date. A trip to Fort Frontenac to obtain stones for construction at Niagara had suddenly changed into a life-and-death problem requiring every fiber of his being and training. He and his specialists were warmly welcomed by the Sieur de Noyan upon their fortuitous arrival, and then all were put to work.[17]

His gunners had spent the last three days feverishly overhauling and readying the ordnance of the fort for a siege, each trained regular worth his weight in gold. They became the gun captains, while the majority of the old colonial regulars and invalided soldiers garrisoning the fort were dragooned into service as their assistant gunners. All the voyageurs and civilian workmen were issued muskets, organized into watches, and assigned officers and fire positions on the ramparts. Because the Mississauga scouts had reported a Haudenosaunee contingent with the approaching force, all women and children had been brought into the fort and were sheltering in the stone chapel and in the commandant's house built into the north wall.

D'Espinassy and his men had surveyed every gun in the fort's inventory since their arrival on 22 August and the advent of the British the previous evening. In that precious fifty-hour window, many older guns were changed out, mounts were replaced and repaired, and powder and shot were brought up to the ramparts and bastions. But most of the guns were old iron, honeycombed artillery pieces that were obsolete castoffs from the French navy and ranged in caliber from four- to twelve-pounders. Most of those left outside the walls, row upon row, had already been spiked by the blacksmith and his assistants as a precaution against their capture. As Montcalm would later pointedly remark: "Why nearly eighty pieces of artillery taken at Oswego [in 1756] were still lying around at Frontenac is beyond comment. It is true we spiked them, but they are, none the less, lost to us."[18]

To a gunner, the fields of fire around the fort were poor to fair, the ground undulating with many spots in dead ground providing cover from observation.

Charles Clinton, an experienced surveyor, observed that the fort's "situation was bad for it Stood in a Low place. And Rising Ground N. West of it, and little Hollows by which we made our approaches with So Little Loss." The Mississauga and St. Lawrence Haudenosaunee families that earned their living by hunting and fishing for the garrison had been told to take down all their dwellings, which could provide cover for the enemy. Likewise, the voyageurs and the workmen were ordered to dismantle their shanties and cabins clustered up against the fort's walls. In 1755, Jean-Guillaume Plantavit de la Pause, Montcalm's adjutant general and chief of staff, noted that the trees had "been cut down within cannon-shot north and west and about two cannon-shots from the west to south."[19]

Once the fort was under attack, d'Espinassy's mortar crews engaged in counterbattery fire, dueling with the British howitzer battery tucked in just behind the rise on Mississauga Point. *Les Anglais* had been steadily lobbing eight-pound shells into and around the fort all day. Counterbattery work was a tricky business and required d'Espinassy to pay close attention to the fall or splash of his bombs so that he could adjust them if they fell too short or too long. He did this by physically adjusting the elevation of his mortars' barrels, as well as ordering the correct powder charge to propel the shell in a parabolic arc through the air to fall on the enemy from above. Wind conditions and air humidity also figured into his calculations.

There was only so much d'Espinassy could achieve with counterbattery fire given Fort Frontenac's fatal flaws. As an artillery professional, he had already logically deduced where the enemy would pop up next with their siege guns, the exact place that several of his predecessors like Malartic, La Pause, and Pouchot had all predicted as being problematic for the poorly sited fort—Bradstreet's "advantageous spot."

Siting was not the fort's only weakness. Every time one of the guns on the fort's bastions fired, the whole stone wall would shake, down to its foundations. The young lieutenant had taken to standing in the solid St. Louis Bastion on the southeast corner of the fort where he could see all approaches. The twenty-five-foot-high stone walls of Fort Frontenac were three feet thick at the base and tapered to two feet at the top. Around the interior of the fort, a wooden scaffolding provided access to the loopholes in the curtain walls and linked the bastions, except along the curtain wall on the north side where the commandant's two-story house, commissary office, officers' quarters, and chapel were located. This arrangement provided excellent cover from musket fire and was ideal for awing *les sauvages*.[20] But as one French officer had dryly observed three years earlier, the walls with their "poor foundations of small stones badly set and the lime [mortar] bad" did not need artillery to batter it down as "one could easily damage it with a sledge or pick."[21]

Even if the walls had been better built, they were useless against the direct fire of eighteenth-century artillery as they were uncovered with no encompassing dry ditch. Typically, earth was thrown up and banked to provide a sloping glacis in front of stone walls to deflect or absorb the shock of cannonballs. As it was, the terrain made it virtually impossible to mask Fort Frontenac's vulnerable walls from direct fire in such a manner, because one would hit bedrock after digging two to three feet down on the Cataraqui peninsula. "There is very little depth of earth in the neighbourhood of this fort," complained La Pause in 1755. "The place where it is most is on the north side where it is two, three and four feet deep, and often much less."[22]

D'Espinassy's British counterparts, John Wilson and James Stephens of the Royal Artillery, had had virtually no sleep since landing, supervising the unloading of the guns, siting the Mississauga Point battery, and overseeing the train's movement forward into its two expedient siege batteries: the fascine battery of two twelve-pounder brass guns commanded by Wilson and built from scratch on the northwest side of the fort at Bradstreet's "advantageous spot"; and the breaching battery in the old French breastworks pierced for five guns—the two remaining twelve-pounder brass guns, the two Royal Howitzers (12-pdr.), and one iron eight-pounder howitzer. Bradstreet had decreed that both batteries would commence firing at daybreak and that the cue would be the smaller battery on the hill unmasking and firing the opening salvos.

The fascine battery on the hill, which had been dug and constructed in darkness (except for the moonlight that emerged from the clouds around four o'clock), was largely the handiwork of the New York provincials under the able direction of Lt. George Coventry, late of Lord Howe's 55th Foot. A native of Glasserton, Scotland, the forty-eight-year-old Lowlander was an old soldier commissioned from the ranks, a sergeant with siege experience, who, according to his son, Dr. Alexander Coventry, was at the side of Lord Howe when he died in the woods of Ticonderoga.[23] Coventry had been recommended to Bradstreet personally by his lordship as "a proper person for an assistant deputy quartermaster, and more particularly as capable of being of great service on this expedition." Bradstreet was happy to praise the energetic Scot in his *Impartial Account* claiming that, of all the officers on the campaign, Coventry's "vigilance, activity, zeal for the service, indefatigable industry and distinguished bravery, all conspired to render him the idol of the officers and the admiration of the troops."[24] Strangely, none of the surviving officers' or other ranks' accounts makes any mention of "the idol," but he did get the difficult job done. As dawn started to glimmer around the edges of the horizon at five o'clock, Coventry ordered the trees that had been left in front of the fascine battery to conceal its position until the last minute, to be cut down and cleared away from the embrasures.

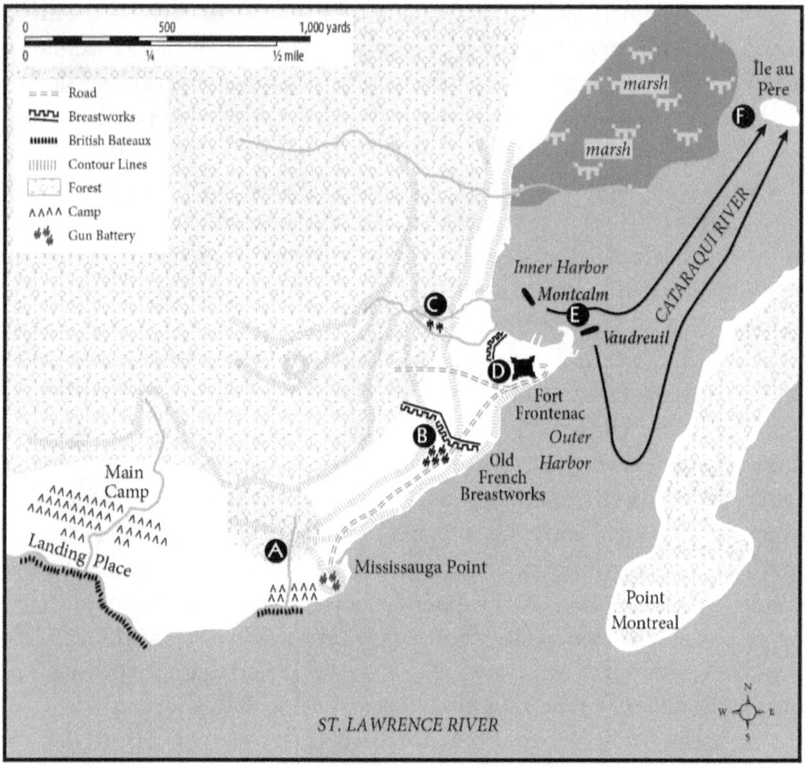

Map 4. Assault and Capture, 26–27 August 1758. Cartography by Mike Bechthold.

A. 9:00 p.m., 26 August. Troops commence marching in darkness to erect batteries at B & C.
B. 3:00 a.m., 27 August. A four-gun investing battery established.
C. 4:00 a.m., 27 August. A two-gun fascine battery established.
D. 6:00 a.m.–8:00 a.m., 27 August. Two-hour bombardment of fort commences from B & C.
E. 800 a.m., 27 August. *Montcalm* and *Marquise de Vaudreuil* weigh anchor to try to attack the main siege battery at B. Crews abandon ship due to heavy British counterfire. Ships drift back into inner harbor and run aground on Île au Pere at F.

John Wilson had personally laid both guns, one for the sixteen-gun brig that had been annoying them all night by spraying the woods with deadly grapeshot. The other he laid on the northwest bastion of the fort, which loomed from the murky dawn like the prow of some other ship. At a range of 200 yards for the actual ship and 150 yards for the stone bastion, he could not miss. At 5:15 a.m. he held up his arm, then let it fall to his side: "Fire!" The two twelve-pounders clanged almost simultaneously as the balls left the barrels and the

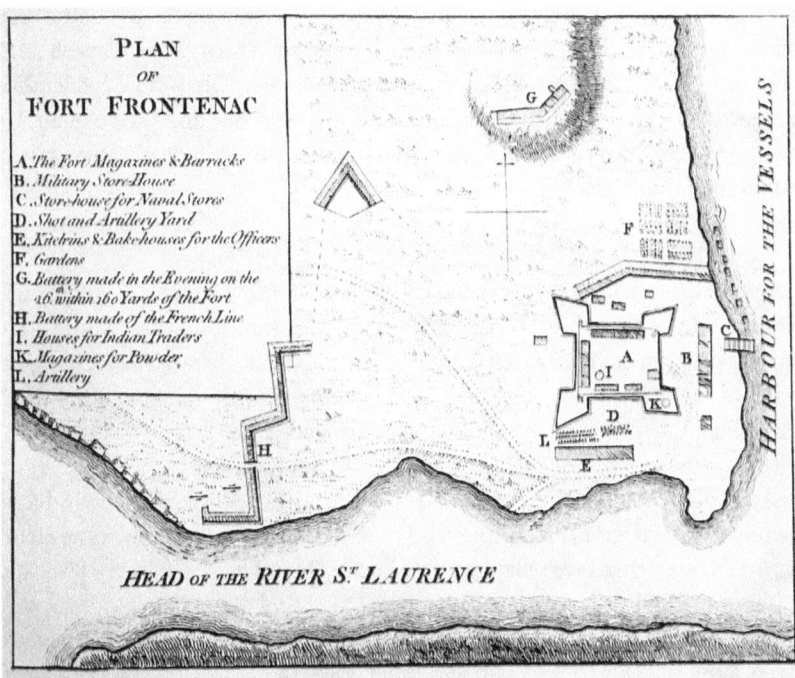

Sowers's siege map, 1758
The first British map of Fort Frontenac, drawn by the engineering officer on the raid, Lt. Thomas Sowers, clearly shows that the British believed Fort Frontenac was situated at the "Head of the St Lawrence"; the mouth of the Cataraqui River is thus mislabeled. The distances are rough, as Sowers would have only had time to pace them. Nor is the fort footprint oriented correctly to the land or lake. Courtesy of Toronto Public Library.

field carriages rolled back on their limbers. Seconds later, both shells crashed into their targets. The northwest bastion sentry box on the corner flew into a thousand pieces, and a portion of the stone wall fell inward onto the gundeck.

"We being now so near the fort, there was scarcely a shot but did execution," observed a delighted Sergeant Albertson. "[We] soon made a breach in the wall, beat down their sentry boxes on the corners of the fort, killed one sentry standing in one of the boxes, threw several bombs into the fort, and on their magazine." The other gun was also on target, sending its shot crashing through the forecastle of the *Montcalm*, producing a deadly shower of splinters, though fur bales had been deployed to shield the gunners as much as possible from enemy fire. The British gunners quickly sponged, reloaded, and ran the guns out again awaiting his next order to fire. On the southwest side of the fort, the main British battery at the old French breastworks opened up a few seconds later, lobbing bombs into the fort, its twelve-pounders joining the din of the battering of rotten walls. "Captain [Stephens] of the train . . . [t]hrew a number of shells into the fort with great success," noted Bradstreet. "They did considerable damage to the inner part and one burst near the magazine and fired a quantity of gunpowder which scorch'd some of the Indians almost to death, and greatly intimidated the garrison."[25]

"The Hereticks would take the place"

Early Sunday morning before dawn on 27 August, the frightened women and children of the French garrison were huddled in the stone chapel, kneeling and praying to a statue of the Virgin Mary. They had spent a sleepless night as the cannonading and musketry from the ramparts echoed around the tight confines of the little fort, the walls constantly shaking and the old rotten lime sifting down in clouds of choking dust.

A captured soldier of Wraxall's New York Independents, taken by Indians the previous year at Fort Herkimer and now an indentured servant of the Sieur de Noyan, was witness to what happened next: "In the height of their Devotion A Boom [bomb] Fell near the Place, Burst and Broke into the windows and without Any Regard to the Image Drove it in pieces off the table," he related to his colleagues. "This struck them with such terror they all Look'd up and Cryed Mon dieu! Mon dieu! All was Lost, the virgin Mary was Gone. The Hereticks would take the place!"[26]

The two British batteries firing at such close range could not miss, and Bradstreet commended Lt. John Wilson of the fascine battery publicly "in the management of his artillery" and display of "great judgement and skill." The heavy cannonade started at first light and was over by 8:00 a.m., though the major excitement for most of the raiding force who spent the bombardment as spectators was at 7:00 a.m. when the *Montcalm* and the *Marquise* made sail and moved toward the harbor mouth. Most British and American accounts assumed they were trying to escape, though the French official report stated they were merely repositioning to try to counter the devastating hail of fire that came from Captain Stephens and his five-gun battery at the former French breastworks. D'Espinassy reported to Montcalm that the "two ships attempted to leave the harbour to try to dislodge this battery by their fire but they were badly mauled which caused their crews to abandon ship."[27]

Maj. Daniel Wall of the Rhode Islanders, manning the main entrenchment at the old French breastworks, described it from the besieger's perspective: "At daybreak [we] began to throw shells which continued very warm till seven o'clock the enemy firing very smart, both with their cannon and small arms when we perceived them endeavouring to escape with the vessels. We immediately brought two twelve pounders to play on them which shattered them very much, and all the crew onboard took to their boats, and made off, and suffered the vessels to drive onshore."[28] When the two ships that had acted as critical floating batteries throughout the siege were put out of action, the Sieur de Noyan had no choice but to surrender. D'Espinassy summed up the situation in his report for Montcalm: "On Sunday morning, with a breech opened on one of the bastions and large enough for an assault, a number of the fort's guns blown up or dismounted, the powder magazine uncovered, the ships out of service and the garrison in no state to sustain an assault, M. de Noyan surrendered at 9 A.M."[29]

Lt. Benjamin Bass, a man of few words, recorded the event with some precision, accurately observing the length of the bombardment and the time of surrender: "At Day Brake We Began our fire from the New breast work on the fort and Continued about two howers and a half by this time the fort was Very warm and the white flage was struck and a Read Jacket imediately hoisted; this was done By Eight Oclock in the Morning." The European custom for initiating a surrender was to lower one's flag and to raise a flag the color of your opponent. In this case, the French garrison took down their plain white flag and, because they had no British flag, hoisted a red jacket as an indication that they wanted a parley.[30]

When the guns ceased firing on the appearance of the flags lowering andraising , the Sieur de Noyan sent out an officer with a drummer beating a chamade. "Mr Sowers, the engineer was sent to meet him and, by that officer, was conducted into the fort," wrote Bradstreet. He had instructed the young engineer to inform the commandant that "if he would instantly surrender, the garrison might keep their money and cloathing and should be carried prisoners of war to Albany, from thence to be exchang'd for an equal number of English as soon as possible, and that he would only wait ten minutes for an answer." The Sieur de Noyan readily agreed to the generous terms (see appendix J). However, Bradstreet immediately had second thoughts about trying to transport such a crowd of people back across the lake and up the Oswego–Albany corridor. They would slow his return to a snail's pace. He, therefore, decided to release them all on parole and send them down the St. Lawrence in their own bateaux. Two dozen of the captured civilians, who were hardened voyageurs that La Force had detained to bolster his numbers, could handle the boats (see appendix B).[31]

Bradstreet, eager for any intelligence of an approaching French relief force, was "inform'd that an army of four thousand Canadians and a thousand Indians were on the march from Montreal." The report was that they intended "to make an incursion into this province, on the side of the Mohocks River, and that they were to be join'd by all the Indians of the five nations." As "corroborative proof," the British "found the garrison had been employed in baking bread for this army, upwards of a fortnight."[32] This intelligence had, in fact, been overtaken by earlier events, referring outdatedly to the much anticipated Levis expedition that had been planned for earlier in the summer but placed on hold when Abercromby's army pushed up to invest Carillon at Ticonderoga. In Bradstreet's mind, however, it was still a real possibility and "the entire burthen of the event of the expedition" was now in the balance, making him "particularly cautious." The race was on to destroy the fort and its contents, load what plunder they could onto the two captured ships and bateaux, then return as quickly from whence they came.

CHAPTER 5

AGONY

Fetter strong madness in a silken thread,
Charm ache with air and agony with words.

—Shakespeare, Much Ado about Nothing

Garret Albertson watched with interest as a captured French sailor with "his leg shot off, was brought onshore and laid by the edge of the lake." Within seconds, the young New Jersey provincial was shocked as "one of our Mohawk Indians came along, took up a stone and dashing it on his head, killed him on the spot; poor creature clasped his hands, implored mercy, but found none."[1]

The Jerseyman can be excused for thinking it was a Mohawk warrior, as the subtleties of the differing Haudenosaunee tribes were lost upon provincials and regulars alike. But the killing remained imprinted on Albertson's memory for the rest of his life. Surprisingly, the culprit was none other than Red Head, Bradstreet's trusted Onondaga war chief and staunchest indigenous supporter. The act of a wounded and defenseless man being executed right in front of the French families who were frantically loading their possessions into bateaux to go downriver could have only increased their panic and haste. And while battlefield cruelty is a well-known phenomenon in the annals of military history, it would be appropriate to note that Woodland culture warriors gave the coup de grâce to those too badly wounded to survive, which might have been Red Head's actual intention. The French expression reveals that the practice was not unique to indigenous warriors and implies a certain element of honor: that is, it was still a warrior's death, especially if the coup de grâce was delivered by the enemy.

Chief of Scouts Thomas Butler was a little more laconic in his brief description of the incident. He reported to Sir William Johnson: "One of the enemy had his thigh shot off whom Red head scalped." Butler had seen far worse in 1755 at the Battle of Lake George, where his older brother Walter had been killed at the great Mohawk chieftain Hendrick's side, or the following year when he and his relief party had viewed the smoking ruins of Fort Bull, too late to help its mangled garrison.[2]

Ironically, Bradstreet would boast after the surrender that he had personally charged Red Head and his "ravenous beasts, full of expectations of satiating their blood-lust fury on the captives . . . in the strictest manner, not to injure or molest anyone of the prisoners." Their reaction, he reported, was one of dismay and "extreme concern" that they would be unable to collect the usual spoils of a victory—captives and scalps. According to Bradstreet, they argued and pleaded with him, imploring him to only "close his eyes and turn his back upon them agreeable to the practice of the French, but he, with some warmth, positively denied them, insisting on their strictly observing his orders."[3] Bradstreet's pronouncement to have restrained all his Indians from butchering the fort's inhabitants, besides being prominently reported in his *Impartial Account* published in England some months after the event, was also made upon his return to Lake George to his superior, James Abercromby.

The claim to have shown only the utmost mercy and humanity toward French captives was subsequently used by Abercromby to chide the French governor on his tardiness in respecting the terms of surrender agreed upon at Fort Frontenac at the end of August. Writing to the French governor on 1 October 1758, Abercromby included a sealed letter to the captive Col. Peter Schuyler that, he knew full well, would be opened and read by his French captors. In Schuyler's letter he opined: "From the good treatment and civility the French garrison had received from Colonel Broadstreet and the detachment under his orders, though composed of different Indian Nations (an evident proof that the latter can be restrained), I did, indeed, expect that you would have been ere this sent back with a like number of his Majesty's subjects of the like grade to those who were taken at Frontenac."[4] Abercromby could not resist playing up that British leadership was dictated by higher sentiments of humanity and civility, certainly more than was shown by the French at Fort William Henry the previous summer.

Vaudreuil's acerbic reply to Abercromby's self-righteous letter, which virtually ordered the French governor to execute the provisions of the capitulation without delay, was clear and to the point. He would honor the capitulation terms to the letter, but he could not resist informing Abercromby that his "generous" subordinate Bradstreet had not been completely open with him as to affairs surrounding the fort's surrender. The governor had received word of the incident involving Red Head and the wounded French sailor from members of the released French garrison who had witnessed the grisly event firsthand. His reply was rife with sarcastic double entendres. He informed the British general that he had been truly "penetrated" by the generosity of Colonel Bradstreet, but perhaps, just perhaps, the conquering hero of Frontenac was laboring under a troubled conscience since his raid? Vaudreuil professed tongue-in-cheek to being "fully convinced that that Colonel has been particularly affected by the cruelty of the small number of Indians he had with him, who cut the head off a wounded Frenchman and scalped him at the same time. I attribute this proceeding only to the ferocity of the Indians, whom it is impossible to restrain on those occasions."[5]

Abercromby's reaction to being informed by his opponent of an atrocity committed under the command of Bradstreet—who, it is fair to say, must have been aware of Red Head's overt disobedience of his wishes—is unrecorded. But Abercromby was more focused and fixated on negotiating a long-desired exchange of prisoners, an obsession that began long before he became commander in chief on Lord Loudoun's departure. His correspondence with Bradstreet after the raid confirms that the prisoner exchange weighed heavily on his mind, more so than anything else.[6] Earlier in the year, George II had become personally involved and interested in the plight of Col. Peter Schuyler, the original commander of the Jersey Blues, who had been captured at Oswego in 1756.

"We . . . have Rewarded them for their vilainey"

For the provincial participants of the raid, the defeat of the French, the destruction of Fort Frontenac, and the burning of Cataraqui village provided immense satisfaction. Col. Charles Clinton's tone of elation on viewing the scope of the desolation is unmistakable:

> We left that neat Hansom Garrison and Good Buildings (where the French lived well) in a heap of Rubbish. By this we paid them for the Demolishon of Osswego which they served the same way, with this difference: that we neither Insulted nor Injured any of the Prisoners but rather treated them with more Humanity than Ever that Perfiedious Bloody Nation deserv'd, whose Ambitions have Embroyl'd all Europe in war for many Years, and who have encouraged the savage Heathen to Murder and Butcher the Englis in a Horrid Manner And have Rewarded them for their vilainey.[7]

His evident satisfaction makes clear that revenge was a key motivation for the provincials who participated in the raid.

Several Boston newspapers, such as the *Evening-Post*, *News-Letter*, and *Weekly Advertiser*, had all reported Bradstreet's departure on a secret mission with considerable interest in mid-August, and all three now published the first news of the raiders' successful return, in the form of a much quoted letter by Capt. Peter Jacquet to his friend and fellow bateaux captain, Daniel de Normandie, dated 30 August 1758 from Oswego. The most interesting feature of this first published unofficial dispatch of the raid was that the correspondent had returned with "a brigantine . . . taken from us at Oswego two years ago," a theme all three papers immediately developed. To them, the implications were clear. The tide was turning. Victories in Europe and at Louisbourg, taken in tandem with Frontenac, proved that Providence once more shone down upon British arms. Jacquet's dispatch did not mention that the British brig, triumphantly returned to the fold, was quickly unloaded and ignominiously sunk in flames twenty-four hours later.[8]

One hour after the capitulation on the 27th, Bradstreet and several other officers who spoke French were still busy supervising the loading of the French prisoners of war—men, women, and children with their baggage—into their bateaux for their four-day journey down to Montreal. It was a top priority for Bradstreet, who was impatient that all the captives be gone so his Haudenosaunee warriors would not be tempted to violate the capitulation. The tension was palpable according to Sergeant Albertson, who had already witnessed the murder of one of the French sailors brought ashore from one of the captured ships. The Jerseyman noted that once the French garrison was finally loaded and ready to go down "the river St. Lawrence for Montréal, the Mohawk Indians were eager to follow them, which Col. Broadstreet absolutely forbade. We then went to work to plunder and demolish the fort."[9]

Bradstreet could not resist mentioning in his account that the French "embark'd under the greatest apparent affliction for the melancholy destruction they beheld . . . tears flow[ing] universally from their eyes." A provincial doctor who dined with Bradstreet several weeks after the raid claims that Bradstreet had a penchant for cruelty, forcing his French captives to personally "knock out y' Heads of 40 Hogsheads of Wine" before he would let them leave. And while this secondhand anecdote that Bradstreet made the French destroy their wine before leaving for Montreal rings true, it would not have been for the implied reason given by Dr. Rea: namely, that Bradstreet was trying to humiliate them. To his credit, it was probably a conscious public display, not only for the benefit of the French prisoners, but for his entire force, especially the Haudenosaunee, that alcohol was *not* part of the plunder and that drunkenness would not be tolerated.[10]

It was therefore in the French POWs' best interests to help destroy this one part of the captured stores as quickly as possible before departure. Bradstreet knew that the French prisoners, cognizant that their families' safety depended on it, were the best option to see this crucial task done quickly without any pilfering, and thus allowing him to keep his men focused on the many other more critical tasks at hand. The French "had been under the most dreadful apprehensions" that Bradstreet would not be able to control his "ravenous beasts" in the aftermath, much like Montcalm's allies the previous summer at Fort William Henry. The raid commander instead offered the Haudenosaunee free rein to plunder whatever goods they wanted (except alcohol) and "by that means were diverted from the thoughts of scalping."[11]

The British commander's preferential treatment for the Haudenosaunee contingent did not go unnoticed by the provincials. Some took umbrage that the Natives who had not done any heavy lifting at the portages, nor helped with the siege works, were given carte blanche to take whatever they wanted, most of which "were of the valuable kinds." Charles Clinton grumbled that only the Indians were exempt from unloading their plunder for equal distribution upon their return and that many "took among themselves all the fine Guns." Bradstreet acknowledged that some warriors had had extremely good fortune in their selections. He noted that "several of them on their return to the Mohocks country" sold their plunder "to the amount of three, four (and one) to the value of five hundred pounds in lace, paint, bever &c."[12]

Lt. Benjamin Bass, the normally taciturn New Englander of Williams's regiment, was moved to eloquence on the spoils of war found in abundance everywhere one looked: "The Stores of the fort were Exceeding many, Warlike Stores of all Sorts for the Endions and there was Sixtey Piecs of Cannon which was destroyed. The Chief [plunder] that we Brought off was Bailes of Cloath, Laist [lace] and Plain Coats and Shirts of all sizes a great number of Dear skins and fur of all sorts and Several other things."[13] Along with religious convictions and a desire for revenge, plunder had always been a prime motivating factor for most of the provincial soldiers who placed themselves in harm's way. New Englanders, despite their Puritanical leanings, had a strong predilection for looting, a behavioral trait that Bradstreet had picked up on while serving in the provincial army that had captured Louisbourg in 1745. He exploited it now. Not one account by a raid participant, nor any contemporary recording of the event secondhand, fails to mention, nor be impressed by, the magnitude of the stores and loot found at Fort Frontenac. (For a detailed breakdown of the plunder taken, see appendix K.)

Bradstreet, cognizant that some of his detractors might be critical of his motives concerning plunder, announced to his regimental agent back home in

Britain that he had deliberately excluded himself from any share in the prize money. "Instead of putting eight thousand pounds in my Pocket, which I might have done with justice," he wrote to Charles Gould on his return, "I have not taken one Shilling [in order] to encourage the people [and] given it all up to them."[14] The commander, who believed that he had many opponents, informed Gould that some had only agreed to him leading the expedition because they thought it doomed to failure. Now that he had achieved what he had set out to do and was returning victorious, those same false well-wishers—"the opposition . . . at headquarters"—would sharpen their knives and await his return. In his *Impartial Account*, published several months after the raid, a somewhat paranoid Bradstreet would claim that "a set of gentleman, envious of the rising character and fame of Col. Bradstreet," were attempting "to deprecate from the merits of [his] conquest; representing it as a 'mad injudicious scheme, the success of which was merely owing to chance and accident.'"[15]

Whether this was true or not is unclear. There are no extant letters or newspaper pieces that would indicate any cabal dedicated to holding Bradstreet back or besmirching his name in a concerted campaign. But themes of conspiracy and warring factions were the warp and woof of gossip in the London coffeehouses where individuals vying to influence public opinion, and more specifically, the London elite, plied their trade. But it may have been a complete fabrication on the part of Bradstreet, a strand of carefully calculated drama deliberately woven into the *Impartial Account*, complete with envious villains and humble heroes, all carefully designed to capture immediate attention and boost his reputation.

"A dupe of his own good faith and generosity of character"

By 1:00 a.m. on 26 August, the news that British forces were closing on Fort Frontenac had been delivered by courier to Vaudreuil in Montreal. The intelligence arriving from the fort, along with the captured documents (see appendix G) taken off the officers' servants killed above Oswego Falls at the outset of the raid, was the incontrovertible proof that finally got the governor to pay attention to what the Sieur de Noyan had been saying since the beginning of the month.

"The alarm was raised in Montréal and the *Generale* was beat!" recorded the colony gossip, the Sieur de Courville. "M. de Vaudreuil gave a dozen different orders which clearly stemmed from his irresolution [and] there was much manoeuvring and intrigue to see who would command the 1500 militia that he finally determined to send as help." It was quite clear that the Generalissimo had been unnerved by the raid and was, in fact, nonplussed that he had been outmaneuvered. To lead the counterexpedition, Vaudreuil chose the Sieur François Lefebvre-Duplessis Fabert, town major of Montreal, "a man of spirit and intelligence, who squandered it all away by his lacklustre performance and ignorance." It is worth noting that the sixty-nine-year-old colonial regular had—at his own request and because of ill health—been relieved of much more active commands in the pays d'en haut because of chronic illness.[16]

The perceptive adjutant of the Bearn regiment, who was in Montreal at the time, recorded the sluggish response and sequence of events that then followed:

> 27th—[Town] Major Duplessis, of Montréal, went to Lachine with all the Colonial and Militia officers, a great many Militia and Indians.
>
> 28th—Had word that M. Duplessis was not yet gone; the getting on board is slow work as they are delayed by the want of many things ...; forwarded thither some more Militia and Indians.
>
> 29th—Remainder of Militia set out for Lachine under M. de Contrecour's orders. A courier [Lt. d'Irnon La Plante] arrived from Frontenac with assurances that when he left, the English were crossing over towards the fort; he thinks, from the number of barges, that there are 1,500 or 2,000 men; that M. de Noyan dispatched him with the intelligence, after having made the best defensive arrangements; that the sloops are in the bay in the rear of the fort; that on the night of his departure [25 August], he had heard the report of cannon; this stupid courier [en route] had caused the return of 150 Indians or Canadians who were going to the relief of the fort.[17]

By the time word had arrived in Montreal, it was probably already too late.

By 30 August, everyone in Montreal had heard that Fort Frontenac had fallen three days earlier. On 1 September, they all learned firsthand the details of the forty-eight-hour siege from members of the Frontenac garrison who arrived after their three-day trip down the St. Lawrence. The same day, Vaudreuil ordered thirty bark canoes to be sent upriver to La Présentation, from whence they were to convey five hundred men, provisions, and ammunition with as many pro-French warriors that could be mustered to reinforce Niagara.[18]

Not surprisingly, the "blame for the loss of Cataraqui fell on the post commander, Sieur de Noyan. He, however, allowed himself to be persuaded by de Vaudreuil, in whom he trusted, to leave all explanations of the causes of the disaster to him," wrote the Sieur de Courville. The governor had allegedly reassured the fort commandant upon his return that there were "no grounds for self-reproach" and that "the cause of the failure lay with [Vaudreuil] alone. Accordingly [de Noyan] gave no official written account of the surrender, leaving de Vaudreuil to make his explanations." But then Vaudreuil did a complete volte-face and "threw the entire blame on de Noyan saying that age had weakened his judgement [and] at the same time asking for his retirement." A sympathetic Courville characterized the old soldier as "a dupe of his own good faith and generosity of character."[19] Surprisingly, the only contemporary document acknowledging that the doughty French commander and his tiny garrison had punched well above their weight was a letter written by one of his opponents. Veteran Lt. John McKane (McKeane), of the Independents, told his superior upon his return that throughout the siege "the French behaved very brave before they gave up the fort."[20]

"Set adrift on the lake"

The main problem for Bradstreet after dispatching the prisoners of war to Montreal was to figure out quickly what to take and what to destroy. Hours after the surrender, the British stripped the interior fort of anything of value, including gunpowder from the main magazine. Several of the fort's guns that were still operable (several had burst or had been dismounted) were loaded and used to batter down the walls at point-blank range. They were then spiked and their trunnions knocked off, and all wooden structures inside the fort were set alight. The evening of the surrender was marked with more conflagration as Major Wall of the Rhode Islanders and others watched as "two snows, two schooners and three sloops" were torched and sank to the bottom of the inner harbor.[21]

The next challenge on the day of surrender was what to do with the post's embarrassment of riches. Garret Albertson and his colleagues were overwhelmed by "the many hundreds of barrels of beef, pork, molasses, and hogs-fat which we could not possibly transport over the lake." "Outside of the fort were about ten or a dozen houses chiefly used as stores, but the principal warehouse was on the wharf which was about two hundred feet in length and about 25 in breadth," wrote Bradstreet. "A great variety of Indian goods and provisions [in] prodigious quantity was on the wharf piled up against the storehouse along the whole length [and] judged to be at least ten thousand barrels." Bradstreet and his staff officers were concerned that the returning bateaux would be "too deep laden with provisions, &c. and too much crowded to admit of any considerable addition to their cargoes, without greatly endangering them on Lake Ontario."[22]

The solution of how to destroy the contents of thousands of barrels of liquids or foodstuffs in the storehouses was simple but effective, albeit wasteful. "We beat in the heads of the barrels," Albertson recalled, then "tumbled them down a steep bank into the river St. Lawrence." They were actually dumping the barrels into the inner Cataraqui harbor, which was the delta of the Cataraqui River, not the St. Lawrence, another indication that the rank and file, as well as their leadership, had no clue as to the local topography. Bradstreet would admit somewhat wistfully that the total haul of plunder taken at Fort Frontenac, including the ships' cargoes, was not even "one-fourth part of what was burnt in the stores and onboard the vessels."[23]

On the 28th in the morning, the British set fire to what remained: "houses, the barracks, the breastwork, fences and everything that would burn." That the raiders did not achieve total destruction of the fort and its settlement in the twenty-four hours (27–28 August) allotted by Bradstreet was readily apparent to their opponents who showed up a few days later—palls of smoke still rising from the burned-out buildings and warehouses. The tardy relief force reported back that the fort's ovens were still intact and fully operational, that most of the walls and stone structures of the fort were still standing, and that artillery captured in 1756 at Oswego was still lying outside the fort. They also found six French twelve-pounders that had been overlooked by Bradstreet's men in their haste to leave, untouched and in perfect condition. These would later be used to arm the two new French sloops that Governor Vaudreuil ordered constructed over the 1758–59 winter at Pointe au Baril near Oswegatchie.

By noon, everything was ablaze and Bradstreet, concerned for security, ordered the men into their boats. They crossed over to Île aux Cochons to spend the night in a more defensible location. To carry some of the plunder as well as some members of the expedition, the *Marquise de Vaudreuil* and the *Montcalm* had been refloated on the morning of 28 August. Both were found to be still fully loaded with furs and trade goods.[24] The *Marquise de Vaudreuil* was laden with a year's worth of furs and skins *from* Niagara, while the brigantine *Montcalm* had been filled with provisions, arms, gunpowder, and Indian trade goods from the stores and magazines of Fort Frontenac and had been bound *for* Niagara (see appendix K for List of Plunder taken). Carpenters quickly plugged any shot holes near the waterlines, and Capt. Peter Jacquet with his battoemen took charge of repairing all sails and rigging that had been damaged in the warships' alleged last-ditch attempt to escape. To the cargoes above were added all the wounded, the train of siege artillery, four British brass six-pounders taken at Oswego, two brass wall guns, seventy-eight barrels of gunpowder, as well as extra barrels of provisions.

Bradstreet placed his second-in-command, Charles Clinton, in charge of the detachments returning in the two captured ships, which included the rangers, the artillery detachment with their guns, and the New York Independents, as well as experienced sailors and mariners drawn from the ranks of the several detachments to act as crew. Peter Jacquet took command of the eighteen-gun *Montcalm*, which was the former brigantine *London* he had helped construct two summers ago at Oswego. Bradstreet would stay with the bateaux and bring up the rear. Though Bradstreet had intended for the two ships with the majority of the plunder, the wounded, and his train of artillery to leave that day for Oswego, Thomas Butler recorded that the ships had to remain moored until the following morning, 29 August, as the wind was "pretty hard ahead."[25]

The return trip for Bradstreet's raiders over the lake to Oswego was uneventful, the ships and their cargoes making the trip in a single day, then dropping anchor at Oswego the evening of 29 August. For those returning with Bradstreet in the bateaux, it was a different story, as many were exhausted through lack of sleep and an excess of hard labor. A provincial doctor recounted, after having dined with Bradstreet upon his return, that the raid commander had to use a different motivational tool to jump-start his flagging men and keep them focused after their bout of adrenaline-fueled looting. According to Dr. Caleb Rea, Bradstreet now informed his men that he had "from good authority that some of y' Mohawk Tribes intended on his retreat, in case he did not Succede to waylay him and cutt off all his army. This he never let his men know 'til on their return."[26]

Clinton wrote a letter from Oswego on 30 August to his regimental colonel, Oliver Delancey, at Fort Stanwix reporting his arrival there with the ships the day before. But Bradstreet and the bateaux "had not come, nor can be expected till the weather is more moderate for a little breeze raises great swells on this lake." The first bateaux finally arrived at midnight on the 30th, and they continued to come in throughout the wee hours of the 31st. A last inspection of the two captured ships was made at first light by Bradstreet, after which he had them "set on fire . . . with the remains of their cargoes and set adrift on the lake." The bateaux were then loaded for their journey upriver, while Bradstreet had the gunners bury four captured brass six-pounders and note their locations for retrieval on next year's campaign. The remainder of the artillery train would return to the new fort and become part of its armament.

"A toylesome Slavish Expedition to the men"

At noon on 1 September, Bradstreet ordered eight men on board each bateau, while "the remainder march'd as a flank guard. Towards evening, we halted at the six-mile creek, our boats on account of the deep loading, and the great force of the stream against them, could not be carried farther." The next day, they arrived at Oswego Falls, where they had spent a day and a half on their outward journey getting over and down to Oswego. Going back against the current was infinitely more difficult, and it would take three days to get above the falls.

On 4 September, the men "Rose up very Early, Got over all our boats with vast slavery, the men being all the time they wrought with them up to their Breasts in the Rapid Current." It was here that some of the Yorkers jettisoned two brass swivel guns they had taken as trophies. Clinton confessed that "We Could not Carry Any further two Brass Patteraras we took from the French so we, therefore, threw them into the River just below the Falls near the west shore where they may be easily taken up at Some Convenient time if Swego be Built again Or any other Occation Require them." The boats were emptied, for the most part, their cargoes unloaded and carried on the backs of men acting as pack-mules. That said, the boats were still vulnerable to the many rocky shoals they were hauled over, so "that Some of Our Boats [were] Stove to Pieces on the rocks . . . and Some Racked to pieces Dragging them," wrote Clinton. The cargoes and boats were carried up the portage and then reloaded above the falls over a three-day period; on 4 September, they "set off about 9 of the clock and Got to an Island above the three rivers where we incamped." At first light on 5 September, Lieutenant Bass recorded that he found one of the men in his company had died during the night from his exertions at the falls, and he was quickly buried on the island before Bradstreet had them all on the move again just after sunrise.

The hardship did not end. "The Current Set Strong against us," Clinton wrote, "and Many Stoney places and Shoal Rifts in the River Oblidged the men in the Boats to go into the Stream and hale them Along, where they were often

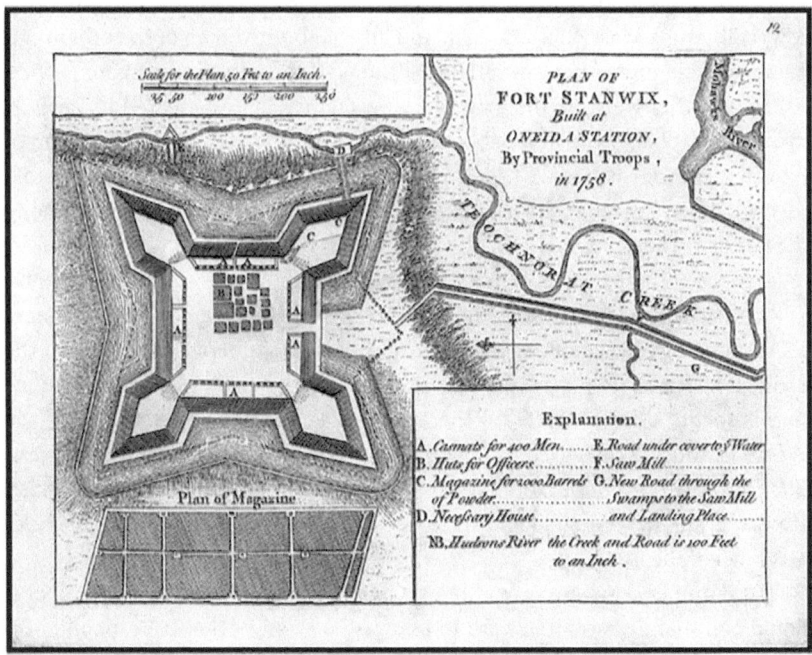

The new fort

Fort Stanwix was constructed in 1758 by provincial regiments to guard the key portage at the Oneida Carrying Place and protect the western settlements of the Mohawk Valley against French or Indian attacks. Its first garrison was a contingent of 400 men of the Fraser Highlanders and a detachment of Royal Artillery. Fort Stanwix National Monument, a reconstructed structure built by the National Park Service, now occupies the site. Courtesy of Toronto Public Library.

wet up to their armpits." Fatigue, by now, must have weighed heavily on everyone, for each night on the Oswego to Fort Stanwix leg of the journey, half the force remained on guard all night while the other half slept. For older officers like the sixty-eight-year-old Clinton, the strain must have been enormous, and witnessing Bradstreet driving the men along he finally became convinced that the glorious raid was no more than "a toylesome Slavish Expedition to the men, tho' in the End, a successful one to the Public."

"Joyfull Newse of our Armeys Sucksees at Caterouga"

While their compatriots at Cataraqui commenced an orgy of destruction on Sunday, 27 August, those provincials who had remained behind at the Great Carrying Place were engaged in more mundane pursuits. Since the departure of his company under Captain Parker on 16 August, Dorr had performed endless guard duties and supervised fatigue parties as well as construction of a smallpox hospital away from the camp. Now, for a second Sabbath day in a row, Williams's Massachusetts men and all able-bodied men of the other regiments worked on the new fort all day without the benefit of any divine service. At sunset, after work on the 27th, the Rev. Daniel Shute squeezed in "a short discourse [it] being the first Sabbath after ye Confirmation of ye reduction of Louisbourg" for his flock. Choosing his passage from Chronicles 16:31, he told them: "Let the heavens be glad, and let the earth rejoice: and let men say among the nations, The Lord reigneth."[27]

A more military form of rejoicing had already occurred days earlier on 23 August when General Stanwix received dispatches confirming the rumors of Amherst's great victory at Louisbourg in July. He ordered a parade and the firing of a "feu de joie" (fire of joy) in the camp. Ens. Moses Dorr, who was new to this sort of thing, reported: "There were 21 Peices of Cannon fired and the Whole Camp was Drawn round the Lines and whosaed [huzzaed] three times." Buried at the bottom of Dorr's diary was a more important milestone, added almost as an afterthought: "On the same day at 4 PM the first Stick of timber was Layd of the fort."

The commencement of Fort Stanwix was a decisive moment in the operational commander's desired plan to establish a strong defensive capability on this approach, as well as a physical and tangible proof for the Six Nations that British promises to protect them from the French were genuine. It was also an important operation to prepare for next year's campaign, by providing an important staging area and jumping-off point for reestablishing a fort and shipyard at Oswego and building an offensive marine capability on the lake.[28]

It was on the evening of 2 September, ten days later, that Ensign Dorr, at the Great Carrying Place, was able to report that "just at Sun Seat [sunset] there came an Endien on an Express from Colo Brodstret which brought the Joyfull Newse of our Armeys Suckses at Caterouga or fort Frontenac that they had taken the place with the Lose [loss] of But one man and Seventeen wounded." General Stanwix again ordered a celebration and "imediatly order'd twenty-one pieces of Artilery to Be Discharg'd and hove three shells and wen finished we hozzaed three times. And we rejoiced with Great Joy for the Scseas [success]." A few days later, on 8 September, the members of Dorr's company straggled in from Lake Oneida, having taken three days to make headway up the log-encumbered Wood Creek to the start of the western portage of the Great Carrying Place. Two days later, Dorr traveled to Fort Newport, where he "met Capt Parker and the most part of his Company in Prite goo health with Joy."[29]

Ensign Dorr along with other officers who had not been on the raid had been ordered to the fort to oversee the distribution of the plunder. These officers were instructed to act as a prize committee to see "Justice done in this Distribution . . . of Goods." Another member, Dorr's friend and senior Lt. Benjamin Bass, wrote:

> We marcht with some of the Weakist By Land to Bools fort and thear halted by order of Coll. Bradstreet and as our Battoas came up they were Strickly Serched and also the men's Packs and Colected ower Plonder together and after gathering it Divide it to each Regiment their proportion and then was brought to fort Newport and then Divided into Companeys and Leut Bass and Ensign Dorr and Ensign Fisk Devided ower Company's [share of] Plonder amongst the men.[30]

At Fort Bull Bradstreet had ordered that "Every thing taken from the French on this Enterprize be immediately Unladen and put on Shoar . . . and Any Person who shall not Comply with this order may Expect to be severely punished." He also detailed five hundred men "under the Command of Lieu^t Col Corsa Remain at [Fort Bull] for the protection of Goods and to see the last of the . . . Battoes up."[31]

That justice was done is debatable. The raid's second-in-command was not overly pleased with the distribution. Clinton complained that "these Gentleman who Remained 5 or 6 Days to Divide the plunder" did so "in such a manner that, all I got of it, I offer'd for thirty Shillings," concluding that "I never Saw any Account yet how they Managed it, or what the whole came to." Sgt. Garret Albertson of the Blues recorded that the lowest soldier "shared about 7 lbs 10 shillings per man, of the plunder we had taken," this estimate being lower than the £13 sterling per man roughly calculated by Fred Anderson for the Massachusetts men who participated.[32]

For the Massachusetts men and others, the agony of victory was just starting. Dorr's journal records the death of seven men from his regiment in the space of a week. By the end of the month, the casualty rate at the Great Carrying Place was even more staggering. On 29 September, Brigadier Stanwix reported to Abercromby that of the "5,600 men you ordered for these services only 2,750 remained fit for duty" with "near a thousand numbers of which are dead & dying daily, for by all accts the Enterprize was perform'd with so much expedition and fateague that few could well bear it, & I believe [Bradstreet's] great success was wholly owing to it."[33] During just one week in September 1758, the new General Hospital at Albany with its three hundred beds was stretched to breaking point with more than five hundred admitted patients recorded in one week. These numbers would have been higher but for strict orders to discharge from the hospital all "provincials as soon as they are able to crawl." It is problematic, however, to differentiate the raid casualties from the mounting casualties of the units working at the Fort Stanwix site, as smallpox had broken out in both the Stanwix and Lake George camps necessitating special smallpox hospitals to be set up separate from the main hospitals. The orderly books that have survived from Fort Stanwix's construction record bateaux convoys leaving every two or three days, carrying the sick down

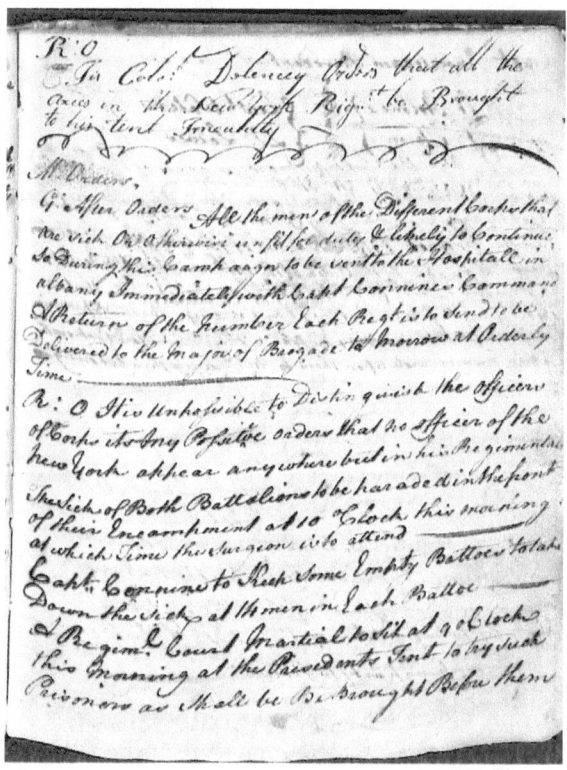

The butcher's bill

A page from the orderly book of Goose Van Schaik dated 23 September 1758 details the transportation arrangements of the sick and wounded from Fort Stanwix to Albany. It reads in part: "All the men of the Different Corps that are sick or otherwise unfit and likely to continue so during this Campaign to be sent to the Hospital in Albany with Capt. Canine's Command. A Return of the Number Each Regt. is to send to be delivered to the Major of Brigade tomorrow at orderly time." Courtesy of the Fort Ticonderoga Museum Collection.

to Schenectady, as well as several deaths per day, with burials noted but the causes of the deaths unspecified.[34]

The four companies of Williams's Massachusetts Regiment returned to find that their regimental doctor, who had remained behind at Fort Stanwix, had succumbed to smallpox along with their chaplain. Two of the returning company commanders, Timothy Parker and Richard Atkins, also took ill and were immediately sent down to Schenectady. At the end of the campaign when the debilitated Massachusetts troops finally marched home, the *Boston Evening Post* reported in November 1758: "We learn from the Westward, that as Capt. Richard Atkins was returning... he was seized with a violent Fever and died."[35]

Regiments that had been dysfunctional before the raid, such as the Rhode Islanders and Jerseymen, now started to disintegrate. With men dead and dying in the tent lines around the fort in large numbers every day since the return from the raid, senior officers departed, leaving their most junior officers and sergeants to clean up the mess. The first one to go down the line of communications was Bradstreet himself on 10 September, albeit summoned by Abercromby. The troops he had used for the mad dash across the lake, with the exception of his beloved battoemen, were no longer his responsibility, and he washed his hands of them.

Major Wall would later complain to the governor of Rhode Island that their regimental surgeon, Dr. Hunter, had never accompanied the regiment to the Great Carrying Place. Instead, he and the chaplain, Dr. John Bass, who also doubled as one of the two regimental surgeon's mates, chose to stay with their colonel in the comfort of Albany. Upon returning from the raid, the last remaining Rhode Island surgeon's mate, Leach, fell ill and was sent down to Schenectady, as were Lieutenant Colonel Potter and most of the other field officers. Colonel Babcock came up from Schenectady to help in November, still hobbling on his wounded leg, but the passed-over Daniel Wall had had enough of being the de facto lieutenant colonel of the Rhode Island Regiment and resigned his commission.[36]

By 22 October, just three weeks later, the death toll had risen yet again, with another 1,250 men dead, dying, or sent down to Albany. General Stanwix started to voice his concerns about completing the fort in time for the winter. Writing to his superior Abercromby from the Great Carrying Place, he calculated that "from the 5600 intended for the service this way that not 1500 [were now] left fit for duty & and these I'm sending down in Boat loads every day." He was also blunt in his assessment of the main causes. "I think all the Provincials, whilst with me, have behaved well, but they are really worn out, worked down & fairly jaded with Fatigue, to which the Bateaux Service and Cadaraqui has not a little contributed."[37]

One of those boatloads that Stanwix sent down is described in some detail by an invalid soldier of the Jersey Blues who remarkably survived his illness. Sergeant Albertson confessed that since they had first set off soaking wet on the expedition, he had been sick and "scarcely enjoyed one day's health." But it was upon his return to the New Jersey camp at the Fort Stanwix construction site that he felt himself weaken and rapidly grow "daily more feeble and unwell."

The sergeant's medical nightmare was just beginning, and by no means was it unique to just him. Hundreds of provincial soldiers like Albertson were left to fend for themselves upon their return, with many NCOs and officers foremost among the stricken, which only hastened unit disintegration. Albertson's story is their story writ large, and thus his raw narrative is quoted here at some length:

> Lieut. [Abraham] Bonnel asked me if I would rather go down to my captain [William] Douglass, at Schenectady. I answered, "Yes." He then took me to the doctor, who bid me put out my tongue. I did so; he then felt my pulse, and I immediately fainted away.
>
> When I came to my senses, the first thing I observed, was my sitting down; Bonnel and my corporal Thos. Hill were holding me up and bathing my face with spirits. I heard the doctor say, "It is not worthwhile to send him down to Schenectady, he will not live!" which hurt my feelings very much.
>
> Bonnel and my corporal went with me to my tent; Bonnel asked me if I had a desire to go to my captain at Schenectady. I answered "Yes!" He said he would send his waiter [servant], Josiah Bryan, to take care of me, until he came down, which he did.... Accordingly, the next day, he accompanied me down to bateaux, with one Stephen Barns, a sergeant from Philipsburg in Greenwich, and Jeremiah Foster, a second cousin of mine, both sick. We sat down on the bank of the river, while the bateau was making ready to start; Barns sat close by my side, fell back, and I believe in one minute was dead.
>
> Bonnel thought I appeared as low as Barns, which hurt my feeling very much; however, I and Foster embarked on board, went down the Mohawk river until we arrived in a few days at Schenectady, where Captain Douglass was, who was wounded in the battle of Ticonderoga.
>
> I desired a furlough to go home; he thought I was not able, and said he would give me one in the morning, which he did.... I embarked in a wagon for Albany, about 14 miles distant, with a number of sick and wounded, an unmerciful driver, through a pine swamp crossway. He drove on a trot, and the poor creatures with myself, begged, pleaded and screamed; I thought I must die in the wagon.
>
> At length we arrived at Albany, the town was so crowded with sick and wounded soldiers, that it was very difficult to get in a house to lodge; but at length got into a poor widow woman's chamber, which was crowded with soldiers, with my cousin Foster, lost my blanket and continued weak and feeble.
>
> Next morning we embarked on board a sloop for New York, with a doctor on board, who administered to me some medicine, and said, if I would call at

his house in New York, he would give me something to help me; I requested my friend Foster to take notice of the house as the doctor pointed it out.

Accordingly, we landed and walked up the street a small distance, when on a sudden I choked up and fell down; I thought I was dying, something appeared to rise up in my throat as big as my fist; the peopled gathered and asked Foster, "What is the matter with the man?" I retained my senses and reason and heard all that was said. I then told my friend we would return to the sloop, which we did.

On our return, we met William Rea, then a merchant in Quaker Town, New Jersey; he had been well acquainted with me and my father's family, but did not know me now. He asked Foster who I was? he told him; he then asked, if I wanted money. I told him "No." Did I want to send any word to my father? I said, "Yes!" to meet me in Brunswick such a day as the captain of the sloop said he would be there. Mr. Rea was faithful to his word. My father sent a man and horses and met me at the time appointed.[38]

Typhus, which most accounts refer to as camp fever, showed no respect for officer or enlisted man. On 15 September, Capt. Ebenezer Seely, the Ulster County company commander and James Clinton's superior for the raid, "requested by Letter to Resign his Commission," and Colonel Delancey "accepted it on his representing himself as Unfit for service in that station and want of Health."[39] A week later, James Clinton fell deathly ill on 23 September while dining with his father and Colonel Delancey. "My son James took sick that afternoon," wrote Clinton. "Was Bled [and] the next day he had a violent fever, a pain in his head and Back, [and] took a vomit.... The next day his fever Encreased." The senior Clinton, who had already lost his eldest son that year to smallpox, now faced the possibility that he would lose another son to a fatal disease. A younger son, also named James, had died years ago of measles on the passage over from Ireland.

A distraught Clinton "took a Resolution to go with him to Schenectady till he and I would Recover as Many Others did" and "went [to] Apply to Col Delancy And the General who freely Gave their Consent." The Clintons, however, were forced to stop at Fort Herkimer as James Clinton's fever worsened, rendering him unfit to travel further. Clinton "was Obliged to Stay there till [his son] was a little better which was 17 days." It was probably never far from his mind while at Fort Herkimer for two weeks that they were only twenty-five miles upriver (as the crow flies) from Frey House, the place where Charles Clinton had had the vivid and disturbing dream of his dead father lying in his coffin. The seventeen-day convalescence period must have been pure agony for the elder Clinton. One of the last lines in his journal reads: "I wish we had Never Stired one pennyworth out of the fort but Consumed the Whole [by fire] with the Provisions. We would not [have] had the trouble of Carrying it for Greedy R[oo]ks."[40]

AN IMPARTIAL

ACCOUNT

OF

Lieut. Col. BRADSTREET's

EXPEDITION

TOO

FORT FRONTENAC.

TO WHICH ARE ADDED,

A few Reflections on the Conduct of that Enterprize, and the Advantages refulting from its Succefs.

By a VOLUNTEER on the Expedition.

LONDON:

Printed for T. WILCOX, oppofite the *New Church* in the *Strand*; W. OWEN, *Temple-Bar*, M. COOPER, *Pater-Nofter-Row*; and Mr. COOKE, at the *Royal-Exchange*.

M.DCC.LIX.

Impartial account? Title page of a pamphlet entitled "An Impartial Account of Lieut. Col. Bradstreet's Expedition to Fort Frontenac... by a Volunteer on That Expedition." It is now certain that this "anonymous" pamphlet published a year after the raid was authored by John Bradstreet himself, Unfortunately, this less than "Impartial Account" has long been used by historians as the principal source document for the account of the raid, thus shrouding the contributions made by hardy provincials from New York, Massachusetts, Rhode Island, and New Jersey. Author's collection.

CHAPTER 6

Aftermath

It is not well done, mark you now,
take the tales out of my mouth, ere it is made and finished.

—Shakespeare, Henry V

The French were dismayed but not devastated by the news of the successful raid; one French logistician laconically admitted in his monthly report to Marshal de Belle Isle in France that they had certainly been "cramped in the direction of Lake Ontario by the unfortunate affair of Frontenac." André Doreil, the commissary of the regular troops, writing to the minister of war, was blunt on the massive intelligence failure and who was to blame: "M. de Vaudreuil has remained in too great security in regard to the important post of Frontenac, and he is the dupe of the overconfidence he has placed in the Indians, whose services he needs, but they must always be treated with caution and distrust."[1]

But his first concern as a logistician was the loss of the invaluable squadron of ships at Cataraqui and what that loss would entail. "I tremble with fear that we have not had the precaution nor time to burn the sloops and bateaux which we had at Frontenac and that the enemy will profit by them to cut us off, absolutely, from all access to Lake Ontario, whereby all our people beyond it will be made prisoners." Montcalm and other regulars took the opportunity to snipe and profit at the governor's discomfort of the moment for having accepted a little too much risk along his lightly defended lines of communication on the Lakes. The French general wrote to the minister of war: "You will find it difficult to understand, my Lord, why . . . our sloops were not kept armed and cruising. I can give no answer to your astonishment, except that I am, myself, as much surprised and astonished." He added that the small fleet "assured to us the superiority on Lake Ontario which we now lose. 'Twill be still worse should the enemy reduce Niagara, which is a strong post for this country."[2]

On 3 September, Doreil the commissary added a postscript to his lengthy letter to his minister that his worst fears were

> well-founded, my Lord; the enemy is master of the post of Frontenac or Cataracouy since the 27th of August. No precaution was taken with our navy. The English, more careful than we, have burnt it, with the exception of two 20-gun brigs, which they have preserved, the more effectually to exclude us from Lake Ontario. The provisions and merchandize destined for supplying all our posts in the Upper Countries, to which Frontenac, bad as it was, served as an entrepot, are lost, and what is still more vexatious, is the loss of considerable artillery.... Everything is now to be feared for Fort Niagara which, indeed, is ... but as bare as Frontenac.[3]

On confirmation of the surrender, Vaudreuil wrote to his superior minimizing the loss of the fort. The real loss, he argued, was not the locale but "that of our two biggest barks, which are in the possession of the English." It was this turn of events that gave him "real disquiet about Niagara which is destitute of men and supplies, [its commander] M. de Vassan having sent a party to the defence of M. de Ligneries at the Ohio." The normally vain and narcissistic governor humbly confessed that he had underestimated the British, strong in his belief that they "would not dare to enter the lake on which we had vessels," but only after he had listed all the other possible excuses and allocated blame elsewhere. The first person he threw to the wolves was his Haudenosaunee emissary. He claimed that "the assurances the 5 Iroquois Nations had given M. de Longueuil that they would come to me in 20 days ... were, for me, motives of tranquillity." Next was De Noyan, who he believed could have, at least, burned the vessels and that "this is the only reproach that I have to make to M. de Noyan."[4]

The late doyen of Canadian historians William Eccles and others believe that the "tranquillity" was a mere illusion, as many ulterior motives seethed below the surface. Food shortages had not only created famine among the civilian population of New France the previous year. Their allies the Seneca, who normally had surplus crops to sell to the French each year, suffered shortages from drought in 1757, as did the Delaware and Shawnee; Seneca leaders applied for assistance from the French at Fort Niagara and were turned away. It was then they finally realized that the French were on their last legs and could no longer be relied on. Eccles and others believe that despite the setback at Ticonderoga, the Six Nations had witnessed the combined might of the British-American troops there, acknowledging the army had "fine limbs" but still "had no head." That lack would be addressed the following year in the 1759 Niagara campaign.

Previously, the French factions within the Six Nations, many of whom had clan or family members living at Oswegatchie near Fort Frontenac, or at Kahnawake near Montreal, had always kept Vaudreuil well informed of British plans and preparations; however, on this occasion, they had been unusually mute. The Sieur de Longueuil, a longtime trusted friend and adopted brother of the Onondaga, had been prevented in July from going up the Oswego River because they alleged they could not guarantee his safety. Eccles posits that the western Haudenosaunee regarded it as "in their interests to have the British destroy Fort Frontenac, located as it was on lands they claimed as theirs." When the French had destroyed Oswego in 1756, they had "pointedly thanked Vaudreuil for having re-established the Five Nations in lands that belonged to them."[5]

By the end of October, Vaudreuil was in a much happier frame of mind vis-à-vis Fort Frontenac. Any fears he had of the British exploiting the potential advantages they had gained with the capture of his last two warships on Lake Ontario and, perhaps, seizing a weakly held Fort Niagara had dissipated on the news that Bradstreet's forces "had nothing more compelling [in mind] than to withdraw and even to burn the two large barks that they had captured. They fled with such haste," he crowed, "that most of them abandoned their clothes and even their muskets so that Colonel Bradstreet instead of striving to re-establish Choueguen [Oswego] withdrew to the old Fort Bull at the Carrying Place."[6]

After the fall of both Louisbourg and Frontenac, Montcalm was invited by a worried Vaudreuil to propose some new direction and guidance for the future defense of the colony. Montcalm was under no illusions that the key terrain and center of gravity for New France, given the motions of Britain's armies and fleets in 1758, were the key cities of Quebec and Montreal. With clear operational foresight, Montcalm did not hold back. He favored bringing in all detachments from all the isolated forts on the Great Lakes ("the branches of the tree") and concentrating them with all the regular forces defensively at the three main entry points to New France ("the trunk of the tree"): La Galette, on the St. Lawrence above Montreal in the west, where he recommended a fort be built; Île aux Noix, at the foot of Lake Champlain in the south; and Quebec, the capital, in the east. He firmly believed that

> it is no longer the time when a few scalps or the burning [of] a few houses is any advantage or even an object. Petty means, petty ideas, petty Councils about details are now dangerous, and waste material and time; circumstances exact determined and decisive measures. The war is entirely changed in this part of the world according to the manner the English are attacking us; nothing less is at stake than the utter and impending loss of the Colony or its salvation, that is to say, the postponement of its fall . . . 'tis the trunk of the tree that's attacked; whatever concerns the branches is of the greatest indifference.[7]

"Welcome once more to breathe thy native Air"

One group of people overjoyed at the news of Bradstreet's successful capture of Fort Frontenac and its 125 occupants were the beneficiaries of the terms of capitulation: long-held British prisoners of war throughout New France. Captives like Capt. William Martin of the Royal Regiment of Artillery, who had languished at Quebec City since his capture at Fort Beauséjour three years earlier, and Jost Johannes Petrie, a Palatine justice of the peace captured at German Flatts with his entire family in November 1757, were just two of many expectant prisoners awaiting exchange.

But perhaps the most famous and celebrated American prisoner of the entire French and Indian War was the loved and respected Col. Peter Schuyler, the paterfamilias of all hostages in New France.[8] The perennial commander of the New Jersey Regiment (also known as the "Jersey Blues") since the previous war, the forty-eight-year-old Jerseyman was captured with half his regiment at Oswego in 1756. While the majority of his soldiers were released on parole that same year, he and the regimental surgeon, Benjamin Stakes, continued to be held at Quebec.

Prisoner Robert Eastburn, a blacksmith captured at Fort Bull in 1756, fondly remembered arriving in Quebec City, where "the honourable Colonel Peter Schuyler, hearing of my coming there, kindly sent for me, and after inquiries about my Welfare, generously told me I should be supplied and need not trouble myself for Support! This public-spirited gentleman, who is indeed an honour to his country, did in like manner nobly relieve many other poor prisoners at Quebec!" Jean Lowry, who was taken on the Pennsylvania frontier with her children in 1756, described Colonel Schuyler as "singularly kind unto and careful of me and many others, for which I can never be sufficiently thankful. He provided me a Room in Quebec, and everything needful for me, and often sent me Victuals from his own Table, this I think still quite singular for a Gentleman of his distinction."[9]

Peter Schuyler went back to New Jersey on parole in October 1757 but was required to return to Quebec after six months, unless a cartel could be arranged before then. He arrived in New York City on 19 November 1757 to a hero's welcome, houses in the city illuminated, a large bonfire set ablaze on the common, and an "elegant entertainment" given him at the King's Arms Tavern. According to the *New York Post Boy*, "The General Public testified Great Joy on his safe Arrival." Schuyler's return prompted one of America's budding female poets, Annis Boudinot Stockton, to put pen to paper. The maudlin result was her first published poem, "To the Honorable Col. Peter Schuyler," which appeared in the *New York Mercury* newspaper and the *New American Magazine*.

Audiences were informed that the gushing ode to the returning officer "was wrote by a young Lady of the Province of New Jersey, during the few Minutes Col. Schuyler staid at Prince-Town, the last Week, on his way to Trenton, and presented him in the most agreeable Manner." The first two lines read: "Dear to each Muse, and to thy Country dear / Welcome once more to breathe thy native Air," and the paean ended, "Ev'n future Ages shall enroll thy Name / In sacred Annals of immortal Fame." Schuyler's hometown of Newark greeted him "with the discharge of thirteen pieces of cannon," an honor usually reserved for major generals and rear admirals.[10]

The *New York Mercury* also followed Schuyler's final release from captivity in November 1758 with great interest, reporting that "he brought with him to Fort Edward 114 Persons (including 25 Woman and Children, which he purchased from the French at a very high Price) among whom are Major Putnam, Captain Martin of the Train, Mr. Stone [Shorne] of the Inniskilling Regiment, Two of the Jersey officers and Doctor Stakes." All of the released prisoners, the paper claimed, were "continually praising their deliverer, BRADSTREET," and saying it was "an unlucky thing he did not go to Niagra as there were only 15 Men at that Place when he took Frontenac . . . and that [the French] were in the greatest confusion at Montreal, throwing up Trenches, expecting the whole English Army there."[11]

Schuyler and his redeemed colleagues returned to New York City via Schenectady, where the Palatine settlers and militiamen of his group, numbering some two dozen, bid adieu and returned to families and loved ones up the Mohawk Valley. Maj. Israel Putnam personally escorted Mrs. Jemima Howe and her three children eastward to Northampton, Massachusetts, along with a sickly Sylvanus Johnson, son of the colony's most famous captive of the war, Susannah Johnson, author of *A Narrative of the Captivity of Mrs. Johnson*.[12]

Schuyler would attend to personal business at home over the winter of 1758-59 and would rejoin his beloved Jersey Blues under General Amherst's command for the 1759 and 1760 campaigns. He and his Jerseymen would serve in Amherst's army that descended the St. Lawrence to capture Montreal, entering the city in September 1760. No doubt Schuyler saw many of his former French and Canadien acquaintances there from his three years in captivity. In November 1760, he retired to his beloved estate, Peterboro, on the banks of the Passaic River, but as one of his biographers put it, he "did not live long to enjoy the blessings of the peace which he had helped to secure." The "worthy old Colonel" died there on 7 March 1762. Perhaps his best epitaph is found in the *New York Mercury*, which characterized him as "a brave and loyal Subject, who despised his own Ease, and all the Delights of an affluent Fortune, for the Service of his Country."[13]

The impact these released captives from New France had on their families and respective communities was enormous. They were undeniable and overwhelming proof to all New Englanders that the hand of Providence had once more blessed God's chosen peoples. Sermons of thanksgiving were offered, and the ordeals of the various released prisoners at the hands of the Papists and heathen savages passed through the colonies like a brush fire. Most vexing of all, however, was the news that some captive children who had not been redeemed, like Susannah Johnson's and Jemima Howe's daughters, were being converted to Catholicism. Recruiting for the 1759 campaign would be brisk.

Schuyler was not the only "hero" to be immortalized in verse after the raid. Bradstreet and his victory garnered at least one fulsome ode dedicated to his "conqu'ring fame" in the press entitled "On Col. Bradstreet's Success," which first appeared in the *New London Summary* on 29 September 1758. It was quickly picked up by other papers, the *Boston News-Letter* publishing it on 12 October 1758, and the *New Hampshire Gazette* following suit on 20 October 1758. The anonymous author, who signed himself "Americanus," waxed lyrical about the raid commander with nary a mention of the provincial soldiers who had made it all happen:

> Envy, detraction, seek your dark retreat;
> There gnaw your chains, there curse the brave and great;
> But know, heroic Bradstreet's name shall shine,
> Through all the annals of succeeding time.
> May heav'n some great illustrious bard inspire,
> With genius equal, and with equal fire;
> O chief! to sound abroad your conqu'ring fame,
> And in his works immortalize his name.
> Till then, permit a bard but young in song,
> To aid your triumphs as they roll along.[14]

And while all this celebration of the moment may have been music to Bradstreet's ears, he would wait in vain for any mark of particular distinction or reward from Pitt or His Majesty the king in the coming twelve months. A year later, he was bitterly writing to his agent in England that "I nether hear nor see the least of any other preferment for Cadaraqui." Bradstreet became disenchanted with his quartermaster duties and yearned for a more active and high-profile role, claiming his principal employment as a logistician for the next year's campaign to be "a mortification as I cannot describe."[15]

Bradstreet died the same year as Sir William Johnson, 1774; both were spared the spectacle of neighbors going to war on each other. They were predeceased by several notable raid alumni. Thomas Butler, forty-three, the chief of scouts, would die almost a year to the day of the raid in 1759 of a prolonged illness, no doubt brought on by the grueling pace he had to set from the outset of the raid, trying to keep ahead of the hard-charging Bradstreet with the main body. Capt. William Ogilvie, forty-two, of the Independents would die of yellow fever aboard a ship off Havana in 1762. Ononwarogo, or Red Head, the Onondaga sachem, would die of alcohol poisoning at Fort Ontario in 1764 while waiting for the expedition against Pontiac and the relief of Detroit. Thomas Sowers, the engineer, would be wounded in the head a year after the raid while supervising the construction of Fort Ontario at Oswego. He would recover, however, to become Britain's chief engineer in North America but then succumbed to an epileptic seizure in the spring of 1774, brought on by the head trauma he sustained some fifteen years earlier.

Charles Clinton would never return to military service, but his son James Clinton would recover over the winter and command a company the following year at the 1759 siege of Niagara, joined by his younger brother, George. James would finish the Seven Years' War as a colonel commanding one of the three New York provincial regiments along with two other distinguished raid alumni, Nathaniel Woodhull and Isaac Corsa. The latter would go back to being a merchant in New York and would choose to remain loyal when the War of Independence finally arrived. His former colleagues must have looked out for their former brother-in-arms, for after a short confinement, Corsa was released on parole for the duration of the war. He died on his estate in his eightieth year in 1807, "respected and beloved." The steadfast Woodhull would become one of the early martyrs of the war, captured and sabered by British cavalry near Jamaica, Long Island, allegedly after he had surrendered. Despite his rank of brigadier general, he would die unattended in a British prison, which provoked outrage throughout the former colonies.

James Clinton would rise to the rank of brigadier general in the Continental Army, serving most of the Revolutionary War in the Northern Department under the command of his old colleague Maj. Gen. Phillip John Schuyler, one of Bradstreet's protégés. During the Saratoga campaign, Clinton commanded Fort Montgomery in the Hudson Highlands but was able to escape from the fort when it fell to British forces. In 1779, his brigade, in tandem with the troops of Maj. Gen. John Sullivan, would carry out a scorched-earth campaign against the Haudenosaunee, methodically destroying at least forty Iroquois villages throughout western New York. In October 1781, he took his brigade southward to join Washington's army at Yorktown and was present for the British surrender. He retired from military service at the end of the war. George Clinton would also do well, becoming the first governor of the State of New York in 1777, an office he held for twenty-one years and through which he exerted a larger influence than any other man in the early development of the fledgling Empire State. Charles Clinton's youngest son would close an eventful life while filling the chair of vice president of the United States under two different presidents.

Fellow officers of the New York Regiment such as Goose Van Schaick, Marinus Willett, and Christopher Yates all became senior officers in their own right. John Cochran, the surgeon's mate of the Independents, became a doctor after the French and Indian War and married the only sister of Philip Schuyler. In 1781, Cochran was promoted to director general of the military hospitals of the Continental Army and was notable also for his contributions regarding smallpox inoculations of the soldiers at Valley Forge.

Last but not least, Sgt. Garret Albertson of the Jersey Blues went home, married, and took up a trade as a wagon maker "until the American Revolution; when I was again called upon to go forward in the service of my country, which I readily complied with, and served on the frontiers along the sea coast several months, in different capacities as sergeant, lieutenant, adjutant, second major of the second regiment of Hunterdon county militia." He died in 1813, at the age of seventy-eight, one year after writing his memoirs, which he signed off with these words:

> I've had a tedious journey,
> And tiresome it is true;
> But see how many dangers,
> The Lord has brought me through.[16]

"No settled Plan for profitting by the Success we had"

General Abercromby was perceived by some of his subordinates as having acted rashly when approving the raid after his major setback at Ticonderoga. In their minds, his dispatching of such a large force with artillery and equipment to the south and west from his main line of operations in order to allow his chief logistician to lead an operation against Fort Frontenac was highly questionable. Just two weeks after Bradstreet's departure, two of Abercromby's principal brigadier generals at the Lake George camp drafted a letter pressing for him to resume the offensive and to launch a second attack northward against Ticonderoga. In it, Brigadiers Thomas Gage and James (Jacques) Prevost hinted darkly that he might face censure at home; for try as they might, they could not

> see how you are going to justify to the Nation why you left our army without an Adjutant-General as well as severe understaffing in the rations, transport and hospital departments: an economy that will ruin the conduct of the King's business and gain you the blame of all people of good sense. . . . We know Sir that you will provide a quantity of specious pretexts to justify the non-efficiency of

the army and its unfortunate success: the lack of experience of regular troops in "woodland warfare"; the Provincials that we cannot trust and the lack of cooperation from the officers of the public departments.[17]

Perhaps the most contentious issue in the aftermath of the raid was the burning of the last two captured ships at Oswego on 31 August 1758. When reaction from home was finally received back in North America the following spring, the anxious Bradstreet, who was expecting some recognition for his small victory, heard instead that Pitt was "displeas'd at my not bringing *all* the Vessells and provisions to Oswego which I took last year at Frontenac."[18] Pitt had seen what should have been apparent to the most untrained of military observers in the theater: that by destroying the last two serviceable warships on Lake Ontario, Bradstreet had not only deprived the French of their mastery of the lake but had denied it to the British as well. Other observers, such as Lord Loudoun's personal physician, Dr. Richard Huck, who had remained behind in North America after Abercromby's predecessor had been recalled, observed in a letter to his patron that Abercromby had had "no settled Plan for profitting by the Success we had at Cadarqui.—We might with the Like Facility have taken Niagara. . . . Or we might have preserved the Shipping and taken Post at Oswego. But except the Distruction of the Place, the shipping, the Provisions and Indian Presents, we reaped no other Advantage from it."[19]

Abercromby himself only belatedly realized, upon receipt of Bradstreet's first communiqué reporting his success at Cataraqui, that the possession of the only two remaining warships on the lake would give him a distinct and immediate advantage over the French. On 18 September 1758, when Bradstreet's forces were already at the Oneida Carrying Place dividing up their spoils, and the charred hulks of the two captured ships were resting at the bottom of Lake Ontario fifty miles to the west, Abercromby instructed Brigadier General Stanwix to tell Bradstreet "that if the two Vessels he brought to Oswego, be still afloat, . . . I desire they may not be burnt or destroy'd; on the Contrary, I shou'd have them well mann'd and keep the Lake as long as possible, constantly Cruizing and keeping the Enemy in continual Alarm, which may be productive of drawing off some of their Force from this Quarter and facilitate any Enterprize we may resolve on here."

This belated decision is yet another example of how Bradstreet's standalone raid and assigned objectives were not integrated or synthesized with the original larger operational design of Abercromby's campaign. Bradstreet's reaction upon receipt of this directive to maintain the ships on the lake in order to disrupt French lines of communication is unrecorded, but when his actions were questioned at the operational-strategic level of command the following year, he was unwilling to be Abercromby's scapegoat or to share any blame for the fumbling and blundering of his commander.

Instead of utilizing an "I was just following orders" defense, he went on the offensive in his letters home, imputing "the fault was in Genl. Abercromby," who was "in opposition to my best endeavours to get his leave to bring everything I should take there [at Frontenac] to Oswego and establish myself." In his *Impartial Account*, he was even more critical of his former commander, stating that *if* Abercromby had only listened to him "our advantages might have been multiplied almost beyond imagination." He was quick, with the benefit of hindsight, to portray himself as the more foresighted and astute officer, observing that

> *if* only two thousand Provincial troops, which were kept unemploy'd at Lake George, had been order'd to follow us, and take post at Oswego, we might have thrown up some defensible works, and brought over and preserved all the shipping, artillery, ammunition and provisions fort Frontenac would have amply supplied us with. We might then have had it in our power to have taken Niagara and secured that important pass, long the object of the nation's desire.[20]

But that was a big *if*. Bradstreet conveniently ignored that Abercromby's army of provincials and regulars were "employ'd" at the time entrenching and blocking Montcalm's army from moving southward (though the latter had no intention of doing so), as well as making preparations for mounting a second attempt to move north on Pitt's assigned, but not forgotten objectives. Bradstreet also ignored the stark fact that Fort Niagara was in Seneca territory and that no diplomatic negotiations had been conducted for passage of a large armed British force through their country for such a contingency.

Upon his return, this may have been the motivation behind his claims that the loyalty of all the Six Nations was in doubt; indeed, this caution may have given Abercromby serious pause to think that perhaps he should order a strike against Niagara. But Bradstreet's naive allegations of complete disloyalty on the part of the Haudenosaunee Confederacy mostly had the effect of enraging the superintendent of Indians, who quickly dispelled Bradstreet's flimsy evidence and managed to reassure his commander that the DQMG was completely overexaggerating the extent of the Six Nations' disaffection. Sir William told his superior in remarkably restrained prose that "from Every Circumstance by which I am able to form a Judgement," Bradstreet's so-called "Intelligence" was "groundless and without reason."[21]

In effect, Johnson told Abercromby to leave the Indian diplomacy to him and to let him get on with his job. Ironically, it would be Sir William Johnson who garnered the laurels the following year at the 1759 siege and capture of Fort

Cartouche scene

A line drawing showing Sir William Johnson presenting medallions of George III to loyal sachems of the Haudenosaunee Confederacy at the end of the French and Indian War. Johnson died two years before the outbreak of the Revolutionary War and thus was saved the spectacle of the burning of the valleys and disintegration of the Confederacy. Courtesy of Library of Congress.

Niagara, aided and abetted by the largest contingent of the Haudenosaunee Confederacy to take part in the war to date.

"Total destruction and devastation"

In 1778, George Washington received a package from his good friend Maj. Gen. Philip Schuyler, lately retired from the Northern Department and completely exonerated of any negligence in the loss of Ticonderoga in a recent court-martial of October 1778. Schuyler had been proposing an expedition to destroy British shipping on Lake Ontario since January 1778, no doubt inspired by the adventures twenty years earlier of Col. John Bradstreet, the bold "Battoe-Master General" and hero of Frontenac. Bradstreet had died two years before the Revolutionary War started, and Schuyler, his longtime friend, confidant, and protégé, had been the executor of the will and had inherited all of Bradstreet's military belongings. Schuyler had sent one of his most treasured keepsakes to Washington for his perusal: Bradstreet's personal journal of the 1758 expedition to take Fort Frontenac.[22]

Washington had first heard of "the brave and active Bradstreet" in 1756 through tales of his derring-do at Oswego against the French and Indians, which was reported widely in the newspapers of the day and letters from friends like George Chew and Beverly Robinson. But then Bradstreet's star had dimmed, damped by the dismal tragedy of Oswego a few weeks later and the apparent graft of Governor Shirley and his cronies. But Bradstreet had emerged from that cloud of scandal like a bright penny.

At the time of Bradstreet's Raid, Washington was in command of the 1st Virginia Regiment on General Forbes's 1758 campaign to capture Fort Duquesne; he affectionately remembered getting a letter on 11 September 1758 from his hungover friend George Chew. An old friend from Washington's early days in Virginia who had left the Old Dominion to establish himself as a merchant and port surveyor in New London, Connecticut, Chew hailed the raid as "a most Glorious stroak" but begged off providing details and, instead, sent newspaper clippings of the affair, claiming his "head something out of order having Sat up late last night and finished several Bottles to the health of Col° Broadstreet and his army."

Bradstreet's journal looked to be still wrapped in its original oilskin pouch, its flap secured with a blue ribbon. Inside Washington found a calfskin quarto-size journal, and after he had read the first few paragraphs, he felt compelled to take up his pen and copy down large extracts of valuable information relating to the terrain and distances encountered while traveling from Fort Stanwix to Lake Ontario. Remarkably, most segments read word-for-word with the *Impartial Account* published by Bradstreet in 1759, incontrovertible proof of the Irish-Acadian's authorship.

On 27 April 1779, Washington wrote back to Schuyler telling him he was

> done with the Papers you were so obliging as to lend me and only wait for a safe conveyance to return them—In the journal of Col° Bradstreet's Expedition to Fort Frontenac—the author when he gets to the head of the Oneida lake makes this observation "about half a Mile from the lake a creek called the Fish-kill empties itself into Wood creek; It is by the rout[e] of this Creek the Indians from Oswegatchie come to Oneida & from thence make incursions & commit ravages on the Inhabitants of the Mohawks Country; . . . their journey to the Mouth of this Creek is usually performed in three days, and its distance from Oswegatchie about 100 Miles" . . . if the distance is no greater than is mentioned above & a way can be had fit for the transportation of Artillery & stores it presents itself to me as the most certain plan for reducing the upper Posts of the Enemy, & their force on the lake as their communication with Canada may be cut . . . I shall esteem it as a particular favour to have this Country & rout[e] well explored.[23]

And while he never did order another invasion of Canada, General Washington would, early the following year, order the largest-ever campaign mounted against North American Indians to date. Relentless raids by the Haudenosaunee (with the principal exception of the Oneida, who supported the American rebels) and Col. John Butler and his rangers, had been conducted with impunity on the northern frontier for the first two years of the war. Washington and Congress decided to strike back decisively. Washington authorized General Sullivan, accompanied by Brig. Gen. James Clinton, to rain down "total destruction and devastation" upon their settlements across upstate New York so their "country may not merely be overrun, but destroyed."[24] The Haudenosaunee were too distracted by their own internal divisions to see the crisis looming for the Confederacy. By August, the Sullivan expedition was moving through Iroquois country meeting little resistance; Clinton's brigade, adept at riverine warfare after years of chasing Butler's raiding parties up and down the valley for the early years of the war, now went to work. In keeping with explicit orders from Washington, American regiments set ablaze every village in their path. This was genocide on a grand and unapologetic scale.

"I am well persuaded," claimed General Sullivan to Congress afterward, "that, except one town situated near the Allegana, about 50 miles from the Chinessee [Genesee], there is not a single town left in the country of the Five Nations." The campaign saw the conflagration of forty Iroquois villages, left hundreds homeless, and caused mass migration to Niagara, where many of the Haudenosaunee perished from exposure and starvation during a harsh, frigid winter.[25]

The Haudenosaunee Confederacy, arguably the strongest and most respected Indian government during the colonial period, would never recover. And while individual war parties in tandem with Butler's Rangers and Sir John Johnson's Royal Yorkers would continue to launch raids sporadically over the next few years, it was clear the expedition had caused widespread famine and the dispersion of many Haudenosaunee families and bands from their traditional territories. It also severely impacted the Confederacy's traditional political order, though some embers were carried north to Canada by substantial numbers of the Loyalist Haudenosaunee. They established a new and enduring Council Fire in a small community on the Grand River that would grow into modern-day Brantford, Ontario.[26]

Fort Niagara

The former French fort, which had dominated the Seneca lands at the head of Lake Ontario for over thirty years, fell in 1759 to British forces led by Sir William Johnson and Gen. John Prideaux, allied with the largest numbers of Haudenosaunee warriors to participate in the war to date. Courtesy of the artist, Robert Griffing, Paramount Press.

CHAPTER 7

Assessment

Forbear to judge, for we are sinners all.
Close up his eyes and draw the curtain close;
And let us all to meditation.

—Shakespeare, Henry VI

During the recounting of this 1758 raid, it has become apparent that several myths are still in play surrounding it. While it achieved more in terms of captured and destroyed matériel on the physical plane than Robert Rogers's St. Francis raid conducted the following year, it quickly faded from everyone's mind. The latter raid, covered extensively by the New England press, saw Rogers's command sustain even heavier casualties proportionally than Bradstreet's (two-thirds to one-third), but it accomplished a coup on the psychological plane. While, in reality, it was a vicious and ruthless attack on a defenseless Indian village—about thirty women, children, and old men were killed, and every building except the church was burned to the ground—it served as a stark warning of what would happen to tribes who continued to support or assist the French in any way. Most tribes chose to take a neutral knee in 1760. The St. Francis raid became the toast of New England because it was satisfying retribution doled out on a biblical scale, and its colorful leader, Robert Rogers, a New Hampshire man, was hailed as a savior of the New England frontier.[1]

At the beginning of the twentieth century, New York's state historian fumed that a cabal of New England historians led by Francis Parkman and George Bancroft had deliberately ignored or downplayed the destruction of Fort Frontenac in 1758. Bradstreet and New York's feat of arms at Frontenac, he claimed, rankled the Brahmins of the Bay Colony so much that "the importance of the aid rendered by New York in the attack and capture of Fort Frontenac was minimized as much as possible." The Hon. James Austin Holden, perhaps inspired by the outbreak of the First World War, was ready to die on the barricades for New York history.

"For a hundred years, the history of New York, its mighty deeds, its magnificent achievements, and the works and lives of its founders and leaders, have been written principally from a New England standpoint," Holden noted in an address to the New York Historical Association, but he went on to promise that would all change on his watch. "If, during the time I am in office, by the help of such organizations as this, I shall succeed in restoring to New York its rightful prestige and the honour and renown which belong to it properly," then he would be satisfied that his "time and strength and life have not been given for naught."[2]

Conspiracies aside, the first myth examined—and now, hopefully, dispelled—was that Bradstreet's raid achieved total surprise. This claim has been shown to be patently untrue: the French knew, or deduced, from troop and artillery movements up the Mohawk in July and from various warnings by the Seneca and Onondaga in July, that a force was going against Cataraqui. Intelligence collated from interrogated deserters and the capture of actual documents detailing the composition of the raiding force a full week before it struck at Fort Frontenac have been consistently ignored by respectable historians content to believe Bradstreet at face value.

The myth of little or no casualties has also been laid to rest, and as to the myth of French supply routes being irrevocably severed, French Canadian scholars scoff and beg to differ. Guy Frégault disagrees with any portrayal of the colony being cut in two as a result of the raid. In his opinion, New France was certainly "weakened by the loss of Frontenac, but there still was Niagara."[3] Historian René Chartrand has also disputed the rather fatuous contemporary British claims that the lifeline of the traditional French Great Lakes empire had been severed with the fall of a single static fort. Chartrand points out that the Ottawa River–Lake Huron route was the main trade "highway" to the French posts on Lakes Huron, Michigan, and Superior, and, to a certain extent, Detroit and Lake Erie. "For the French, the loss of Frontenac was a disagreeable surprise," he writes, "but it merely was a temporary break in the Lake Ontario–upper St Lawrence route. It was not seen as a strategic or tactical disaster as long as the link was maintained. This was confirmed by the fact they did not even bother to restore or reoccupy Fort Frontenac as a military post."[4]

Shrugging off the loss of Fort Frontenac, though, is part of the old French Canadian nationalist narrative that Canada could have survived but for the lack of supplies and reinforcements from France, the corruption of the Frenchman Bigot, and the defeatism of Montcalm that led to disaster at Quebec. This is a politically focused and thus flawed approach to assessing the operational or strategic impact of the loss of Fort Frontenac. The plain, unvarnished truth was that a famous fort that proudly bore the name of a doughty governor of days gone by was now wiped off the map. Destruction of the oldest fort in the Great Lakes area, a key depot and a diplomatic center, was bound to make an impression on indigenous communities. By 1758, the flow of supplies from Canada to communities in the west was already drying up, a cause for wary consideration by all allies of the French.

Closer to home, it came as a profound shock to Canadien colonists. A legendary base had fallen in a day! It did not help that all the released French prisoners arrived in Montreal just three days after the surrender of the fort and passed on their personal accounts of the debacle. There was no way for Vaudreuil to hide the truth or sugarcoat what the defeat meant except in his letters sent back to France. The raid also affected the morale of the French high command despite claims to the contrary. Montcalm, a French regular, had a brilliant victory at Carillon, but the Canadian-born governor presided over a humiliating defeat. The destruction of Fort Frontenac drove the existing divisions between the two men even deeper, making the journals of Montcalm and Bougainville and the letters of Vaudreuil, all rife with scathing criticisms and counteraccusations, sometimes almost painful to read. As Canadian historian George F. Stanley summarized, both men "had their blind spots and neither really understood the point of view of the other."[5]

It has been shown that John Bradstreet's raid as executed did not fit into the British operational plan designed for 1758. It was an add-on, never integrated or synchronized within the original Ticonderoga campaign plan executed by Maj. Gen. James Abercromby. Fort Frontenac was not considered a relevant operational objective by Pitt, nor relative to the overwhelming forces being applied on the central land approach or the main sea approach leading to the strategic objective of New France. By contrast, John Bradstreet's original raid in Lord Loudoun's 1758 campaign plan was a daring opening gambit, designed as a diversion to be conducted in the spring as soon as the ice broke up. Simultaneously, a major thrust to the north against Ticonderoga and Crown Point would be made at the end of May using British regulars only, long before French troops could reinforce the small winter garrisons. Instead, the midsummer raid was authorized by a desperate commander on the defensive, late in the campaign, the operation never fully thought through as to what actual effects were desired or how the raid could best support or achieve Abercromby's assigned operational objectives.

At the operational level of war, it could be charitably argued that Abercromby used Bradstreet to fix his enemy in place with a tactical "left hook," much like Bougainville had mused in his journal in mid-July when speculating on likely destinations for mass troop movements with artillery up the Mohawk Valley. But this would constitute a defensive maneuver vice an offensive one, and one that would not contribute any immediate effects toward the successful achievement of Abercromby's assigned "offensive" operational objectives on the Lake Champlain axis. Whether he liked it or not, for Bradstreet's raid to fit into his campaign design, Abercromby would have had to have been seriously intending to renew the offensive. Instead, we can now conclude that he was just going through the motions or, more likely, just incompetent.

For Bradstreet, there was never any doubt as to what his assigned objective was, or what his tasks were, once on site. As the tactical commander, he was to reduce the fort and, in essence, destroy everything he found there—stores, weapons, trade goods, shipping—then return. It was a simple spoiling attack, and therefore his orders did not state, nor indeed imply, that he was required to achieve operational effects such as neutralizing Indian tribes or establishing naval control of the lake. These potential second-order effects that might accrue from the raid, while part and parcel of the arguments he had personally deployed over the past three years to justify the attempt being made, were not part of Pitt's strategic design assigned to Abercromby.

In 1759, when Bradstreet's raid was not receiving the appropriate attention he thought it deserved from the home authorities in Britain, and he, with it, being neglected for preferment or promotion, he started to claim, in hindsight, that the raid was more than just a tactical victory. Indeed, he announced, with some creative and unsubstantiated assertions, that his raid had achieved very important "advantages" or effects that were "undoubtedly . . . of the highest importance to the general interest of the colonies." Today, with the benefit of additional hindsight (in addition to that of Bradstreet's), it is worthwhile to examine some of his claims to assess whether they are indeed true, and, if so, whether they had any impact on the operational or strategic end states of the 1758 campaign year. Bradstreet alleged that

> the taking of Cadaraqui . . . has depriv'd the enemy of Lake Ontario; has frustrated their scheme of making an incursion into this province; has kept the Five Nations in a state of neutrality; has influenced the Indians on the frontiers of Pensilvania, Jersey and Virginia to a peace; has facilitated the expedition against Fort Duquesne; has broken the chain of attachment and interest, which subsisted between the French and the Indians on the Ohio, the lakes and the surrounding country.[6]

Some of the above claims are wishful thinking, such as depriving of the enemy of Lake Ontario; in fact, the French still had possession of the only three standing forts/trading posts on the Lake Ontario–St. Lawrence system (Fort Niagara, Fort Rouillé [Toronto], and La Présentation). Furthermore, by the time of the publication of his *Impartial Account*, the French were again "masters" of the lake. Vaudreuil ordered the immediate construction of two new warships in November 1758 at Point au Baril near La Présentation, and by April the following year, the French had launched the schooner *Iroquoise* and the brig *Outaouoise*, each about eighty feet in length and armed with swivels and ten twelve-pounder guns apiece.[7]

While the raid certainly "cramped" the capability of the French to smoothly resupply their posts further west, and temporarily neutralized their ability to maintain naval mastery of the lake by destroying their two principal warships/transports, Fort Frontenac was not, as Anderson has styled it, "the indispensable link." Fort Niagara, which has a much better claim to this title, remained in French hands at the southern end of Lake Ontario astride the line of communications between it and Lake Erie further south. Control of Lake Ontario or "dominion of the lake" depended on which side was serious about maintaining warships on it. The failure of the British to retain the two captured ships, combined with their postponement of the reoccupation of Oswego until the following year, handed back to their opponent any operational initiative or advantage that had been gained by Bradstreet's raid.

Thus the raid did not stop, or even neutralize, French use or control of the lake as Bradstreet claimed. There is no physical evidence that his spoiling attack gainfully contributed to the successful achievement of any operational or strategic objectives. It is interesting to note that Bradstreet himself perhaps realized this as other, larger events unfolded around him and dwarfed the significance of his raid. His 1759 *Impartial Account* went so far as to claim the raid had caused intangible and unmeasurable effects in the psychological plane, such as the "influencing" of Indian tribes and the aiding of diplomatic efforts.[8] And while certainly news of his capture of the French fort and destruction of the French lake fleet was fresh in the minds of those tribal representatives and colonial administrators who met at Easton, Delaware, in October 1758 to sign a new accord, the raid was not the driving force behind the accord process. Negotiations had been two years in the making, and the treaty's signing was due mainly to the untiring efforts of Sir William Johnson, Frederick Post, Conrad Weiser, the Pennsylvanian government, and many other players.[9]

In reviewing the detailed planning that led to the destruction of Fort Frontenac in 1758 and the effects that Bradstreet's raid achieved relative to Pitt's overall design, and Abercromby's assigned theater objective, the tactical raid can be styled as a "nice-to-have" versus a "must-have" in the overall scheme of things. Abercromby was ultimately outmaneuvered by his own subordinate, who, for purely personal reasons of glory and preferment, led him off his "critical path" and, in so doing, siphoned off essential resources (including Bradstreet's skills as DQMG) from the principal campaign at hand. Abercromby never should

Brahmin of the Bay Colony
Francis Parkman was the first serious American historian to write of the Seven Years' War in North America. His scholarship, however, is now considered faulty, racially biased, and overly dependent on the accounts of one or two journals. Author's collection.

have been sidetracked from his assigned operational objective, and his failure to mount a second attempt on Ticonderoga and Crown Point, then exploiting onward to Montreal, can be laid, in large part, at Bradstreet's door. That Abercromby's stalled campaign had had a major strategic effect on the entire tempo of the theater plan for North America was obvious to the most casual of observers. Dr. Richard Huck observed to his former commander and patron the Earl of Loudoun:

> Your Lordship will be disappointed, as will the whole Nation, by the Inactivity of our Fleets and Armies after the Reduction of Louisbourg. . . . The bad Behaviour of the French rendered Louisbourg an easy Conquest, tho it is thought much more Time was spent upon it than was necessary. The Admiral is blamed, I do not know how justly, for not sending the two Ships of the Line, and five or six Frigates up the River S Lawrence. This might have prevented that large Supply of Provisions which the French have received this Summer. I do not know what Ships of War the Enemy had at Quebec, but exclusive of that, the Reduction of that Place would have been as easy a Conquest as Cadaraqui. They had no Troops there.[10]

British regulars were not the only ones critical of the year's stuttering missteps. Perhaps the last word on aftermath perceptions should go to the lowly ensign Moses Dorr, the Massachusetts provincial who witnessed the formation and launching of Bradstreet's forces at the Oneida Carrying Place, including their pitiful return. Dorr ended his private 1758 journal with the telling words: "this Day the Last of the Year & the End of this Year's Campaign and Not Canada Taken Yet."[11]

"Naked truths" and a "strategic coup"

Well has it been said that "on the actual day of battle naked truths may be picked up for the asking, [but] by the following morning they have already begun to get into their uniforms."[12] There are always two sides to every story, and every interested party involved or affected by the raid at the time, winner or loser, had something to say. And while a review of the contemporary "spins" or observations after the event is useful in trying sort out some of the "naked truths" and arriving at some conclusions, there is a third category of interpreters or "after-the-event" observers to be considered as well, albeit nonparticipatory—the historians. The various interpretations of Bradstreet's raid by a sampling of various leading nineteenth-, twentieth-, and twenty-first-century historians of American, British, and Canadian extraction are instructive. The one applicable metric to measure whether they addressed the event objectively is to ask the question: "Did they slavishly adopt Bradstreet's depiction of the event as a "strategic coup" or perhaps, just perhaps, have they independently deduced and discovered that the tactically executed raid may have transcended the operational level of war and achieved strategic effects?

Francis Parkman (1823–93), the first serious historian to write of the Seven Years' War in North America, had mixed feelings about John Bradstreet, especially his role during Pontiac's Uprising in the Ohio country and on the upper Great Lakes in 1764. However, his assessment and treatment of Bradstreet's raid on Fort Frontenac as a "brilliant masterstroke" have become gospel for historians who came after. Parkman was first to claim the fort was of "strategic importance," which thus imbued Bradstreet's successful raid with having achieved "strategic" effects. But any balanced examination of contemporary French accounts or modern analysis of the raid within the actual strategic imperatives of the day reveals such an assessment to be unpersuasive. A recent analysis of Parkman's style of writing and researching history has shown him to have been overly dependent on one or two journals of an event, repeating them verbatim or paraphrasing the statements and opinions made in them with little or no analysis as to their validity or relevance to other contemporaneous events.[13]

In his opus, *France and England in North America*, first published in 1884, Parkman claims that "the important post of Fort Frontenac... controlled Lake Ontario," an assertion readily disclaimed by French military officers and civilian administrators of the day. For the most part, Parkman's account of the raid is a thinly disguised paraphrase of Bradstreet's various versions of the event with some supporting excerpts drawn from Bradstreet's directed letter-writing campaign to American and British newspapers. For example, compare Parkman's "analysis" to Bradstreet's hindsight:

> *Bradstreet:* If only two thousand Provincial troops, which were kept unemploy'd at Lake George, had been order'd to follow us, and take post at Oswego, we might have thrown up some defensible works, and brought over and preserved all the shipping, artillery, ammunition and provisions.
>
> *Parkman:* If Bradstreet had been followed by another body of men to reoccupy and rebuild Oswego, thus recovering a harbour on Lake Ontario, all the captured French vessels could have been brought thither, and the command of this inland sea assured at once.

Parkman's summary of the raid's effects is classic Bradstreet: "Command of Lake Ontario was gone. New France was cut in two; and unless the severed parts could speedily reunite, all the posts of the interior would be in imminent jeopardy." In the early twentieth century, British historian John Fortescue, in his ten-volume *History of the British Army*, leaned heavily on the works of Francis Parkman for details of the North American events in which the king's troops participated, and thus, unsurprisingly, his take on Bradstreet's raid closely echoes Parkman: "The command of Lake Ontario was lost to the French [and] their communications north and south were severed."

Pulitzer prize–winning historian L. H. Gipson followed on the heels of Fortescue with his fifteen-volume *The British Empire before the American Revolution*, in which he styled the Seven Years' War as *The Great War for Empire*. In his opinion, "the French Empire in the New World had been shaken to its very foundations... by the destruction of Cadaraqui, the key to the entrance [egress] of [the St. Lawrence] river as well as to the Great Lakes region."[14]

Gipson too would simply paraphrase Parkman and speculate on "what if" Bradstreet had "known that Fort Niagara had only a garrison of forty men"? Surely "he would doubtless have moved upon it and thereby added immeasurably to the laurels he and his troops had already won." But unfortunately, Gipson opines, Bradstreet had not, and therefore had to be content in the knowledge that "the objective that he had had in mind had been attained without the loss of a single man." Again, one is left with unsupported assertions with no analysis as to whether the raid was relevant, sanctioned by indigenous people in the area of operations, an effective use of resources, or even necessary for the successful attainment of Abercromby's assigned objectives.[15]

French-Canadian historian and nationalist Guy Frégault, never slow to disparage the regular forces of both mother nations in the conflict, believes that the destruction of Fort Frontenac was not a "masterstroke" as James Wolfe styled it, but more of "a hit-and-run raid [for] Bradstreet beat a hasty retreat after burning the fort and the French ships in the port." Highlighting the positive actions taken by the Canadian-born governor to ameliorate the situation at Niagara (sending immediate reinforcements and new supplies), Frégault believed that Fort Niagara, at the juncture of Lake Ontario and Lake Erie, was the true indispensable link with Detroit and the western forts of the colony.[16]

A twenty-first-century assessment by Fred Anderson in *Crucible of War* imbues the bold Bradstreet with "strategic insight," as do Parkman and Fortescue, but rightly identifies the destruction of the fort as of little consequence. Instead, it is the destruction of "the whole of French shipping and naval strength on Lake Ontario" that he claims "would have a catastrophic impact on the Indian trade of the *pays d'en haut* as well as on the installations of the Ohio country to defend themselves," and this is certainly true. However, if one admits that these installations were little more than glorified fur trading posts and not strategic sites (mere "branches of the tree" in Montcalm's words), then again, Bradstreet's raid can be viewed in the proper perspective.[17]

A contemporary of Anderson, Ian K. Steele, perhaps the most preeminent Canadian historian of the period living today, agrees that the objective was not strategic but astutely adds that "Abercromby violated Pitt's instructions and authorized a raid into untenable country . . . that did not offset the Fort Carillon [Ticonderoga] disaster." Despite these recalibrated assessments of the perceived importance of Bradstreet's raid by two of the leading contemporary authorities, recent popular histories are content to regurgitate Parkman and Gipson and continue the myth of Bradstreet's raid as a brilliant strategic masterstroke.[18]

Part of my remit with this study has been to scrape away the superficial varnish that has accumulated over the years obscuring the faces of the true heroes of John Bradstreet's raid—the provincial soldiers of the colonies. By letting many of the participants of the raid give voice to their own experiences, as well as consulting French sources, I have been able to retell the story of the raid with a more balanced narrative of what transpired at the French fort in 1758. Any history that places an undue emphasis on the commander in an operation tends to create an incomplete picture that negates any comprehensive understanding of the inner workings of a campaign and their effects on the participants.

If an old soldier might be permitted a last word. Good commanders never turn their backs on their men, or as the urbane Charles Clinton, Bradstreet's provincial second-in-command, put it, treat them with "vast slavery." John Bradstreet was indeed the consummate hard-charging logistician who created a much needed riverine capability for the British army, an operational capability put to good use transporting armies in the years that followed at the siege and capture of Fort Niagara in 1759 and in the final descent of Amherst's army down the St. Lawrence River in 1760. But Bradstreet's claim to fame must be as a military innovator, not as a leader or a commander, and the legacy of the raid must no longer be his exclusive purview.

Benjamin Franklin's use of the 1758 raid as a shining example of provincial pluck and fortitude in a letter to a London newspaper a few months after the fact was the unvarnished "naked truth." He noted it was "the Provincials who made that long and admirable march into the enemies country, took and destroyed Fort Frontenac, with the whole French fleet on the lakes and struck terror into the heart of Canada."[19]

Simply put, it was the blood and sweat of provincials from Rhode Island, Massachusetts, New Jersey, and New York that caused a legendary French fort to fall in the wilderness and a new British fort to rise up at the strategic Oneida Carrying Place—Fort Stanwix. Moreover, the development of command capabilities in the provincial officer corps that participated in the hit-and-run raid cannot be underestimated. The valuable expertise gained by an outstanding cadre of junior American-born officers on the raid would give them a solid foundation and an invaluable corpus of operational knowledge with regard to riverine operations and their complex logistics, which proved vital for the next war. At the commencement of the Revolutionary War, the alumni of the 1758 raid were perhaps some of the best combat-trained, semiprofessional soldiers extant in the Thirteen Colonies They stood ready to assume their mantles of command with an old familiarity, albeit some with sorrow, as they faced off against old comrades-in-arms. But not once in Bradstreet's *Impartial Account* were the provincial soldiers or their officers on the 1758 raid praised or acknowledged by their American-born commander for their backbreaking work and achievements. Yet, the "anonymous" author of the *Impartial Account* had no problem praising the British regulars who took part on the expedition—the gunners, his engineer, and his commissary. Perhaps most astonishing of all, Bradstreet praised himself as a "daring and bold" officer who led his force from the front "with bravery and prudence."[20]

Is that a bullfrog I hear?

Appendix A

Parade State of Fort Frontenac Garrison, 27 August 1758[1]

Note: An asterisk following a name indicates that the individual was killed during the siege.

Companies

Sergeants (2)

Rene Troussienne *called* Vadeboncouer	of St-Luc
Pierre de Cor *called* la Joye & wife	of No. 8 Company

Corporals (3)

Claude Quentin *called* St. Quentin	of Herbin
J. B^te Dolet *called* Damien	of La Roche
Jacques Miles *called* Besançon	of Denny

Soldiers (43)

Sans Soucy, Gunner	
Biard, Gunner*	
Jean Richter *called* Paris	of la Valtoi
Jean Massey *called* LaPlante	[ditto]
Pierre Verdoir *called* Vive l'ete	of la Bouvais
Jean Petitier *called* Beaupre	of Cabanac
Jacques Berbe *called* La Forge	of Virier
Francois Ouvre *called* La Bonte	[ditto]
Pierre Figinerre *called* Sisteron	of La Corne, Senior
Antoine Hemer *called* Hemer	[ditto]
Pierre Cordier *called* Cordier	of Chevalier La Corne

Pierre La Roche *called* Brindamour   [ditto]
Etienne Roumlord *called* Idem   [ditto]
Alexandre Cacton *called* St. Esprit   of Vassan
Jean Fidel *called* Quercy   of Bonne
Jean Crudel *called* Crudel   [ditto]
Jean Gentil *called* Jolicoeur*   [ditto]
Michel Fraye *called* La Rose   [ditto]
Baltazard Conteler *called* Baltazard   of Contrecour
Thibeault Dictye *called* Dictye   [ditto]
Simon Nicolas Gruger *called* Jolicoeur   of St-Arn
Andre Charle Vallet *called* Carillon   of Boucherville
Yves Bouillet *called* La Violette   [ditto]
Jean Pulade *called* Songay   of Lorimier
Laurent Husimond *called* St. Laurent   [ditto]
Bazille Rachin *called* de Langedoc   of St. Vincent
Thomat Gaudon *called* La Rose   of Vergon
Tibeault Teydre *called* Teydre   of de Lignerie
Jean Yster *called* Yster   of la Collombierre
Joseph Mules *called* Harbee   [ditto]
François Pary *called* Pary   [ditto]
Jean Fraitge *called* Fraize   of Villier
Matthieux Chichot *called* St. Pierre   of La Roche
François Matier *called* St. François   [ditto]
Aristophile Erlingra *called* Erlingra   [ditto]
Christian Jacob *called* Jacob   [ditto]
Jean Godefride *called* St. Jean   of la Perriere
Jean Seguin *called* St. Jean   [ditto]
Phillippe Tellier *called* La Rose   of Courtemanche
Jean Vaguener *called* Vaguener   of Boisbert
Hardy Mal *called* Vorm   of de Gaspe
Jean Delais *called* Sans Chagrin   of No. 1 Company
Pierre Gagoua *called* St. Pierre   of Denny

Officers (5)[2]

Capitaine [Payen] de Noyan
Lieutenant de Viviers, his wife & son
Lieutenant de la Plante & his two sons
Ensign [Pierre-Charles Daneau] de Muy[3]
Cadet La Couture

Total Military Personnel: 53 all ranks

"I promise to effect the return of a number of persons equal to those who have been handed back to me by Colonel Bradstreet after the capitulation made at Fort Frontenac on 27 August 1758."

Appendix B

List of the King's Employees at Fort Frontenac, 27 August 1758[1]

Joseph Papin, King's Storekeeper
Jean Louis Tanasson, Assistant Storekeeper
Francois Papin, Clerk in said Stores
Le Vitre, Ship's Carpenter
La Douceur, Ship's Carpenter
Martin, Cooper
Maurul, Carter & wife
Perrot, House Carpenter
Dumat, Carter, his wife & three children
Goudau, Surgeon
Girard, Currier
Dejardins, Currier
La Malice, Cowherd
Malboeuf, Mower
Guivin, Mower
Billet, Mower
Guimant, Mower
La Combe, Blacksmith & wife
Amiot, Armourer & wife
La Mercier & two children
The Storekeeper's Maid

Commissary Employees

Du Vernay, Chief Clerk, & wife
Tonnoir, Assistant Clerk
La Neau, Baker, & his wife and child
Grigoire, Cooper

Appendix B

Canadian Voyageurs

Rene Lanaurais	Bte Labelle
Joseph La Combe	Provencal
Jan Aubin	des Longchamp
Louis Roy	Pinard
Jh. leVelle	Jean Le Vert
LaPage, wife & four children	Seize Ville
Daunais	Jean Avarre
Va de bon Coeur	Pierre Coutenaux
Bouchet	Pierre Beaulieu
Amable Beaulieu	Louis Maureaux
Francois Raymonde	Des Jardin
Toussin Labelle	four Settlers, names unknown

Total Civilian Personnel: 75 men, women, and children

"I promise to effect the return of a number of persons equal to those who have been handed back to me by Colonel Bradstreet after the capitulation made at Fort Frontenac on 27 August 1758."

Appendix C

Ships Captured or Destroyed by Bradstreet's Forces, 27–31 August 1758

Name	Guns	Built	Rig	Remarks
Hurault	12	ca. 1753, Frontenac	schooner	Destroyed 28 August 1758, Cataraqui harbor
Victor	6	ca. 1753, Frontenac	sloop	Destroyed 28 August 1758, Cataraqui harbor
Louise	6	ca. 1753, Frontenac	schooner	Destroyed 28 August 1758, Cataraqui harbor
Marquise de Vaudreuil	16	1755, Frontenac	schooner	Captain: René-Hippolyte Pepin, Sieur de LaForce. Used as floating battery at siege of fort 25–26 August; burned at Oswego, 31 August 1758
London	18	1756, Oswego	brigantine	Prize taken by French at Oswego, 1756; under command of Sieur de la Broquerie, and used as floating battery at siege of fort 25–26 August; burned at Oswego, 31 August 1758
Mohawk	12	1756, Oswego	sloop	Prize taken by French in 1756 at Oswego; destroyed 28 August 1758, Cataraqui harbor
Ontario	6	1755, Oswego	sloop	Prize taken by French in 1756 at Oswego; destroyed 28 August 1758, Cataraqui harbor

Name	Guns	Built	Rig	Remarks
Vigilant	?	1755, Oswego	schooner	Prize taken by French in 1756 at Oswego; destroyed 28 August 1758, Cataraqui harbor
George	?	1755, Oswego	schooner	Prize taken by French in 1756 at Oswego; destroyed 28 August 1758, Cataraqui harbor

Source: Excerpted and adapted from Tables 4 and 5 in Malcolmson, *Warships of the Great Lakes*, 17–19.

Appendix D

Order of Battle and Strengths of British and American Forces at Siege of Fort Frontenac, 1758[1]

Note: An asterisk following a name denotes the individual was wounded.

Staff (9)

Raid Commander	Lt. Col. John Bradstreet, DQMG
Second-in-Command	Lt. Col. Charles Clinton, NYR
Adjutant	Lt. Archibald Montague Brown, NYIC*
Commissary	Lt. George Coventry, 55th Foot
Engineer	Lt. Thomas Sowers, RE
Commander, Royal Artillery	Capt.-Lt. James Stephens, RA
Captain of Scouts	Capt. Thomas Butler, Indian Service
Captain of Battoes	Capt. Peter Jacquet, Battoemen
Senior Surgeon	Dr. Richard Shuckburgh, New York Independent Company (NYIC)

British Regulars (179)

Composite NY Independent Coy (153)	Capt. William Ogilvie, NYIC[2]
Det., 24th Coy, 2nd Bn, Royal Artillery (26)	Capt.-Lt. James Stephens, RA
	Lt. John Wilson, RA

Provincial Detachments (2,474)

Col. Oliver Delancey's NY Regt. (1,090)	
1st Detachment (529)	Lt. Col. Charles Clinton
2nd Detachment (561)	Lt. Col. Isaac Corsa*
Col. Joseph Williams's Mass. Regt.	
Detachment (423)	Maj. William Arbuthnot

Col. Thomas Doty's Mass. Regt.
  Detachment (241)
Col. Henry Babcock's Rhode Island Regt.
  Detachment (318)
Col. John Johnson's Jersey Blues
  Detachment (402)

Provincial Auxiliaries (379)

Bradstreet's Battoemen (276)
Wendell's Coy, Rogers Rangers (61)

Indigenous Warriors (42)

Maj. Richard Godfrey

Lt. Col. John Potter Jr.

Capt. Joseph Ellis

Capt. Peter Jacquet
Lt. William Hair (Hare)

Red Head (Ononwarogo)
Capt. John Butler, IS
Capt. John Lotteridge, IS

Ordnance

4 x Brass 12-pdrs
2 x Iron 8-pdr howitzers
2 x 12-pdr Royal Brass howitzers

Recapitulation

Staff Officers	9
Infantry, Regulars	153
Infantry, Provincials	2,474
Artillery	26
Rangers	61
Battoemen	276
Native Warriors	42
Total	**3,041** All ranks (with eight pieces of artillery).

Appendix E

Composite Detachment of Col. Joseph Williams's Massachusetts Regiment, 13 August 1758

Detachment Commander: Maj. William Arbuthnot
Detachment Adjutant: Lt. Job Cushman Barker

Composite Companies

Capt. Timothy Parker	Capt. Richard Atkins	Capt. Joseph Billings	Capt. Samuel Glover
Lt. Benjamin Bass Lt. Benjamin Davis (White's) Ens. George Fisk (White's)	Lt. Samuel Wetherhead Lt. Samuel Berry (Slocum's) Ens. Thom. Colson (Slocum's)	Lt. — Lt. (Butterfield's) Ens. Michael Martin	Lt. George Hannon (Angier's) Lt. Giles Harris (Angier's) Ens. Edward Emerson
1 sgt. 2 sgts. (White's)	2 sgts. 2 sgts. (Slocum's)	2 sgts. 2 sgts. (Ward's)	2 sgts. 2 sgts. (Angier's)
2 cpls. 2 cpls. (White's)	2 cpls. 2 cpls. (Slocum's)	2 cpls. 2 cpls. (Ward's)	2 cpls. 1 cpl. (Angier's)
52 pvts. 42 pvts. (White's)	44 pvts. 46 pvts. (Slocum's) 6 pvts. (Butterfield's)	46 pvts. 46 pvts. (Ward's) 4 pvts. (Butterfield's)	50 pvts. 29 pvts. (Angier's) 19 pvts. (Butterfield's)
Coy. Total— 108 all ranks	Coy. Total— 108 all ranks	Coy. Total— 108 all ranks	Coy. Total— 108 all ranks

Detachment Total—432 All Ranks

Source: Excerpted and adapted from [Capt. Richard Atkins], Atkin's Orderly Book, 1758, in "The Expedition to Fort Craven, Oneida Great Carrying Place and Frontenac in 1758,"*Colonial Wars: A Quarterly Magazine* (Boston, 1913), 180–81, 202–3.

Appendix F

Return Taken of the Detachment of the New York Regiment at Camp on Oneida Lake, 18 August 1758

Detachment Commander: Lt. Col. Charles Clinton (2nd Bn)
Second-in-Command: Lt. Col. Isaac Corsa (1st Bn)
Detachment Major: Maj. Nathaniel Woodhull (2nd Bn)

Company	Captain	Subs	Sgts	Privates
Capt. Daniel Wright (2nd Bn)	1	3	6	103
Capt. Goose Van Schaik (3rd Bn)	1	3	5	82
Capt. Ebenezer Seely (2nd Bn)	1	1	3	50
Capt. Peter Stuyvesant (2nd Bn)	1	1	5	75
Capt. Christopher Yates (3rd Bn)	1	2	3	73
Capt. Elias Hand (2nd Bn)	1	2	4	72
Capt. Richard Hewlett (2nd Bn)	1	2	5	56
Capt. Samuel Badgely (3rd Bn)	1	3	3	96
Capt. Thom. Arrowsmith (2nd Bn)	1	3	5	82
Capt. William Humphreys (3rd Bn)	1	2	3	85
Capt. Peter Dubois (1st Bn)	1	3	7	99
Capt. Jonathan Ogden (1st Bn)	1	2	3	92
Subtotals	12	27	54	995
TOTAL				1,091
				All ranks

Source: Excerpted and adapted from "A Return Taken of the Detachment of the New York Regimt on ye Expedition, Camp at Lake Onida [sic] 18 August 1758," in Clinton's *Journal*, 305. The New York Regiment's contribution to the expedition was initially announced as 1,112 all ranks in General Stanwix's General Orders dated 11 August 1758 at the Oneida Carrying Place. This total was adjusted down to 1,091 all ranks the following week at Lake Oneida, 18 August, due to disease, desertions, and injuries en route, a wastage of 21 men.

Appendix G

Col. Bradstreet's Instructions to the Commander of a Scouting Party

Note: These instructions were *not* for Capt. Thomas Wells of Bradstreet's Battoemen, as most historians have assumed, but for an unnamed company commander and his men, most likely the rangers and indigenous warriors under Captain of Scouts Thomas Butler. Note that all movement of bateaux above Oswego Falls was to be done in darkness to avoid detection. Author's emphasis.

Sir, I have given orders to Captain [Thomas] Wells, who is in the Bateaux department, to join you to-night with eleven men in one barge, and *you will take your company* and the barges you have, so as to advance in the manner following, viz: You will to-morrow (14 August) descend Wood creek, pass *in the night* Lake Oneida as far as the mouth of the Onondaga river, and *the following night* proceed as far as the Island, one mile and a half above and on this side of the Choueguen rapids [Oswego Falls], which Captain Wells will indicate to you; and from that place you will scout continually as far as Choueguen, to see what can possibly be discovered, until I join you, observing not to allow yourself to be seen by friends or others, and your scouts will not follow the ordinary route as far as the Choueguen rapids, nor in going to Choueguen either.

13 August [1758].

Appendix H

Meteorological Data (Lake Ontario Leg), 22–31 August 1758

Date	Location	First/Last Light	Moonrise Brightness %	Remarks/Observations
Tuesday, 22 August	Ruins at Oswego/ in transit	5:10 a.m. 6:54 p.m.	9:10 p.m. 75%	BRADSTREET: At 11 [a.m.] embarked... The weather being calm and favorable, the opportunity of advancing as far as possible was not to be neglected; for on the least rise of wind, the swell is very great: this obliged us to keep along shore, that we might land, and draw up our boats, whenever the wind heighten'd. CLINTON: "the whole fleet set sail about 11 [a.m.] the Clock on Lake Ontario, and made Good Way. BRADSTREET: We continued rowing till about two oclock in the morning, and then came to in a fine bay.

162 APPENDIX H

Date	Location	First/Last Light	Moonrise Brightness %	Remarks/Observations
Wednesday, 23 August	in transit / Lake Ontario	5:12 a.m. 6:52 p.m.	9:52 p.m. 66%	BRADSTREET: At eight in the morning, embarked, but the wind and sea rising, we were obliged very soon to put ashore again. At three in the afternoon embark'd again and at ten oclock [p.m.] halted. CLINTON: sailed till about 2 of the Clock at Night then Came to at the NE shore in a Cove. Stayed there 'til about 7 in the Morning then set sail and proceeded on our voyage till about 9 of the Clock in the forenoon, at which time we were Pretty far advanced into the Lake and the Pilots observing the wind likely to Blow Which upon this Lake Raises a very Great Sea, it was thought best to make into Shore and stay and See what the weather would do. This Lake is very Large the Sun Rises and Setts in it often in the year.
Thursday, 24 August	in transit / Lake Ontario	5:13 a.m. 6:50 p.m.	10:25 p.m. 55%	BRADSTREET: At two in the morning, the report of four discharges of cannon at Cadaraqui were distinctly heard, our distance from thence being about 15 miles. ... the wind continued very high all this day till about four in the afternoon when we embark'd, and in the evening landed on the south side of an island which lies in the mouth of St Lawrence fronting Cadaraqui, about six miles distant.

APPENDIX H 163

Date	Location	First/Last Light	Moonrise Brightness %	Remarks/Observations
Friday, 25 August	Garden Island/ Fort Frontenac (44° 14' N, 76° 29' W)	5:14 a.m. 6:48 p.m.	11:01 p.m. 44%	MONTCALM: Firstly, the two brigs could have been saved instead of having them waiting around a place that could not be saved, and that *on Friday, a north east wind blew strongly* that could have taken them away to safety [author's emphasis]. BRADSTREET: At daylight, embark'd again and at about eight oclock [a.m.] came in sight of Fort Frontenac, and landed on a small island [Garden Island], about three miles distant from it. The water in the bay being very rough, prevented our crossing of it at this time.... at five oclock it was thought practible to land ... the whole immediately embark'd and at six in the evening landed without the least opposition. SOWERS: An attempt was made at Nine at Night to Board the vessels in the Harbour but without success. [OLSON: (Moon in 3rd quarter) Moon would not be in the sky (approx) from sunset to midnight, but from midnight to sunrise.]

Date	Location	First/Last Light	Moonrise Brightness %	Remarks/Observations
Saturday, 26 August	Fort Frontenac	5:15 a.m. 6:46 p.m.	11:42 p.m. 34%	BRADSTREET: At an hour before day [first light] the whole stood to their arms: at daylight all the boats were moved to a bay nearer the fort.
				BASS: This morning at Daybrake Landed our Cannon.
				WALL: As soon as it was dusk, we approached up to the breastwork of the enemy.
				ALBERTSON: under cover of a dark night, about half the army marched under the bank of the lake and got into the French settlement near the fort in profound silence, went to work, repaired and fortified the entrenchment planted the cannon and mortar pieces long before daylight and opened fire upon the fort.
				BRADSTREET: On our approach towards the west bastion, the noise and rustling, which the fascines made among the bushes, discovered [betrayed] our advancing party on that quarter: as the night was very dark they only fired on the sound.

APPENDIX H 165

Date	Location	First/Last Light	Moonrise Brightness %	Remarks/Observations
Sunday, 27 August	Fort Frontenac	5:17 a.m. 6:45 p.m.	—	BRADSTREET: The enemy after discovering our situation to the west by assistance of the moon which rose about four oclock [a.m.] kept an incessant fire upon us . . . after day light, Mr Wilson began to cannonade the fort. BASS: This morning at Daybrake we began our Fire. WALL: At daybreak, began to throw shells which continued very hot until seven oclock [a.m.]. BRADSTREET: the vessels [attempted] to run off . . . which they found impracticable, *the wind being unfavourable* [author's emphasis]. ALBERTSON: a brig and schooner, which they took from us the year before at Old Oswego, loaded with fire-arms, clothing and furs, endeavored to make out into the lake, but *the wind being calm*, could not [author's emphasis].
Monday, 28 August	Fort Frontenac	5:18 a.m. 6:43 p.m.	—	BUTLER: We are making ready to set off this day but the wind is pretty hard ahead." [viz. prevailing winds from the southwest thus preventing ships from sailing out of harbor]. SHUTE: [at Oneida Carrying Place] Very Hot. At sunset a very smart shower, and heavy Thunder, high wind and hard rain in the night.

Date	Location	First/Last Light	Moonrise Brightness %	Remarks/Observations
Tuesday, 29 August	in transit	5:20 a.m. 6:41 p.m.	—	BRADSTREET: On the 29th at daybreak we embark'd but the wind coming ahead [blowing from the southwest] and the sea growing too rough to continue on it, we halted at 10 oclock [a.m.] about twenty miles distant. At 3 oclock sailed again, and in the evening came to at an island on which we continued.
				DORR: [at Oneida Carrying Place] Last night it rained and stormed as hard as I ever have seen it in all my Life.
				SHUTE: [at Oneida Carrying Place] Cool after ye thunder.
Wednesday, 30 August	in transit	5:21 a.m. 6:39 p.m.	—	SHUTE: [at Oneida Carrying Place] Very cold last night.
Thursday, 31 August	Oswego	5:22 a.m. 6:37 p.m.	—	SHUTE: [at Oneida Carrying Place] Pleasant.

I am indebted to Dr. Don Olson, a noted astrophysicist at Texas State University, and his colleague Roger Sinnott, of *Sky & Telescope* magazine, for their precision and patience in calculating the 1758 moon and first/last light data for Bradstreet's expedition. Dr. Olson has provided computer-generated data for many other historical events that have hinged upon meteorological events, such as the tides and moonlight on the St. Lawrence for General Wolfe's 1759 descent (see Donald W. Olson et al., "Perfect Tide, Ideal Moon: An Unappreciated Aspect of Wolfe's Generalship at Québec, 1759," *Sky & Telescope*, October 2002, 957–74) and the extant moon and tidal conditions for Paul Revere's "Row & Ride" (see Donald W. Olson and Russell B. Doescher, "Astronomical Computing: Paul Revere's Ride," *Sky & Telescope*, April 1992, 437–40.)

Appendix I

Bradstreet's "Orders for Landing," Cataraqui, 25 August 1758

Note: These orders are an amalgam of the three copies of the same order given verbally dated 25 August 1758 in "Camp At an Island in Lake Ontario Near Fort Frontinack," in Atkins' Orderly Book, 206–7; Clinton *Journal*, 307; and VSOB, 91–93, respectively.

Lieut Col° Curso [Corsa] & Major Ondle [Woodhull] with all the whale boats in the front, Capt Ogilvie with the Regulars. Next Lieut Col° Clinton with the Yorkers next to the Regulars. The Train next to the Yorkers. Major Arbuthnot with Col° Williams next to the Train. Capt. Ellis with the Jersey men next to Col° Williams. Lieut Col° Potter with the Road Island Troops to bring up the Rear—

The whole to Range the Shore in one Line within Six feet of each other if possible, and when the Signal is given for Landing, the whole to turn the heads of their Boats to the Shore & push to it with the Greatest Resolution & Dispatch, taking care not to fire a single shot till Landed & formed two deep in the front of their Boats & then push forward on the Enemy, except the Regulars & those in the Train Battoes who are to Remain a Guard to the Boats & provisions.—

The Rangers & Indians to Land in the Rear of the whole, & take to the woods immediately to flank the Enemy.—

The Signal for marching will be firing a Howitzer—

And all the Troops are to take notice that our Indians have Red Gimp in their hair & be Extremely Careful not to fire upon them.—

If no Enemy Appear on the Landing, the whole to stand fast in the front of their Boats Except the Indians & Rangers; who are to scout some Distance Round to see what they Can Discover.—

One man to be Left in Each Battoe & Whale Boat & to be now appointed for that purpose to prevent Confusion.—

In Landing, the whole spaces of half the Length of the Boat & the six feet between each must be Kept to prevent Confusion & to have Room to form.—

The Commanding Officers of Corps to receive provisions for today & tomorrow & give orders that it be Cooked Immediately—

No man to fire his piece on any account whatsoever. If any officer sees his men fire his piece he is to confine him & will be punished Immediately—

this part of the orders to be read to the men.—

Col° Bradstreet Recommends to every Commanding Officer of a Corps to see that each officer in their Respective Corps be careful in observing the above orders—

Appendix J

Conditions of Surrender, Fort Frontenac, 27 August 1758

Conditions upon which M' de Noyan, Knight of the Royal and Military Order of Saint Louis, King's Lieutenant at the town of Three Rivers, King's Commandant at Fort Frontenac, proposes to surrender it to his Britannic Majesty, 27 August 1758:

I.

The Sieur de Noyan promises to surrender Fort Frontenac complete with all its dependencies, to Colonel Bradstreet, commandant of the English troops.

II.

That the officers and soldiers of the garrison and others at this post, will remain prisoners of war, until an agreement be concluded by the Marquis de Montcalm and the English General for their exchange.

III.

That the sick and wounded shall be attended to at the expense of the King of Great Britain.

IV.

That he will guarantee the officers, soldiers and all other persons whatsoever now actually in the fort against all insults on the part of the English soldiers and Indians.

V.

The Colonel will permit the vestments and sacred vessels of the chapel to be removed in the baggage of the Chaplain, and he, Sieur de Noyan, promises to give up faithfully all the munitions of war and provisions, and all the goods & tools which are now in the storehouses of the said fort.

VI.

The said Sieur de Noyan asks that there be furnished to him, his soldiers and the rest of the persons with him in the fort, transport to carry their baggage and necessaries for the voyage.

Frontenac, 27 August 1758.

Colonel Bradstreet, in consideration of the infirmities of M. de Noyan, Commandant of this fort, permits him to return to Mont Real and to take four men; also Mdme. Duvivier, Mdme. Barollon and the other women belonging to this fort who are without men.

[Signed] Bradstreet and De Noyan

M. de Noyan engages to procure Colonel Schuyler in exchange for himself, or for some other person if it is found that M. Schuyler has been already exchanged. After the capitulation, Colonel Bradstreet permits all the French in Fort Frontenac to depart for Mont Real in Canada, under the promise made by M. de Noyan to return an equal number of people and of the same quality as soon as it can be done, and to send them to Fort George.

Fort Frontenac, the 27 August 1758

[Signed] De Noyan and M. Bradstreet

Appendix K

List of Plunder "divided at Bulls fort," 8 September 1758

178 Gold and silver laced Hatts
33 Pieces of gold lace
16 Pieces of silver lace
400 Pieces of ribband
445 Pieces of gartering
45 Pieces of ferriting
238 Pieces of napp'd frieze
3690 Mens shirts
828 Pair of full'd woolen stockings
1978 Woolen caps
1674 Plain coats
375 Callimancoe gowns
689 Childrens gown and frocks
1110 Blankets
120 Ruggs
313 Laced coats
85 Pieces of white linnen
16 Pieces of striped ditto
56 Pieces of cross barr'd stuff
662 Childrens shirts
270 Bags of vermillion
55 Fox skins
53 Otter skins
4950 Racoon skins
360 Bever skins
4007 Deer & Elk skins

732 Bear skins
152 Pieces of Ticklenburgh
383 Skains of tent cord
147 Fine fuzees
400 Muskets
46 Pair of Pistols
205 Brass kettles
78 Barrels of Gunpowder (never divided, but sent to the magazine at fort Stanwix on the Oneida Carrying Place)

Extracted from Bradstreet's *Impartial Account*, 25–26. To the barrels of gunpowder "not divided," one might add four British brass six-pounders. Captured at Oswego in 1756, then recovered at Cataraqui in 1758 and taken back to Oswego, these guns were buried and recovered again the following summer during the building of Fort Ontario.

Glossary of Eighteenth-Century and Modern Military Terms

Terms and definitions are taken and, in some cases, adapted from the four following publications: Donald E. Graves. *French Military Terminology, 1670–1815, A Technical Glossary* (St. John, New Brunswick, 1979); B. L. Dunnigan. *Siege, 1759: The Campaign against Niagara* (Youngstown, OH, 1996), 139–40; Canada, Department of National Defence, B-GJ-005-500/FP-000, *CF Operational Planning Process* (Ottawa, 2008); Canada, Department of National Defence, B-GJ-005-300/FP-000, *Canadian Forces Operations* (Ottawa, 2005).

abatis.   Expedient anti-personnel obstacle constructed from felled trees with branches trimmed and sharpened. Put in front of defenses to slow down enemy infantry.

aide-de-camp.   An officer appointed to assist a general in preparing and executing orders.

approaches.   Trenches dug by besieging forces toward a fortress, allowing troops to approach their objective under cover.

area of operations.   That portion of an area of war necessary for military operations and for the administration of such operations.

bastion.   A projecting part of a fortification, consisting of four sides (two faces and two flanks) and allowing defenders to fire enfilade along the main walls.

bateau(x).   A sturdy, clinker-built, flat-bottomed boat used by both the French and the English, usually made with an oak bottom and pine sides, capable of carrying a cargo of one to two tons upstream against the current and as much as five tons on the return trip.

battery.   A protected emplacement for besiegers' or defenders' artillery.

branch plan.   A type of contingency plan built into the basic plan for adjusting the ongoing operation, if necessary, to ensure the maintenance of the overall operational design.

broadside.   An aimed salvo of guns from a battery.

campaign.   A series of military operations in one theater of operations designed to achieve a specific strategic objective.

campaign plan. A plan for a series of related military operations aimed to accomplish a specific strategic objective, normally within a given time and space.

capability. The state of having sufficient power, skills and ability to carry out a military activity or operation.

compagnies franches de la marine. Independent companies of French infantry raised by the Ministry of Marine to garrison overseas colonies.

curtain. A section of a stone rampart or wall that connects two bastions.

decisive Points. Desired effects to be produced in time and space, decisive points must be identified in the operational planning process so they can be successfully integrated and logically applied. The progressive achievement of decisive points results in the successful achievement of the objective.

embrasure. An opening made in a parapet of a wall or an earthen embankment of a battery, allowing cannon to fire through it while the gunners remain under cover.

enfilade. Fire directed from a flank against a fortification or a body of troops.

fascine. A tightly bound bundle of sticks or branches used to build up and reinforce earthen walls.

flank. That part of a bastion joining the face to the curtain; also the side or end of a line of fortifications or a line of troops.

gabion. A large basket, woven of twigs, without top or bottom, designed to be filled with earth to rapidly build up a parapet.

grapeshot. Anti-personnel ammunition consisting of small balls tightly bagged and corded around a spindle and fired from a cannon.

invest. To surround and cut off a fortified place from outside aid.

lines of operations. Critical paths of effort in time and space, designed to sequentially and logically achieve desired effects or battle capabilities leading to a designated end state; they help a commander in the planning phase to ensure that all the critical activities required to achieve objectives are fully synchronized and integrated.

maneuver. To seek to attain a position of advantage in respect to the opposition from which force can be threatened or applied. At the operational level of war the term refers to areas where an adversary cannot focus appropriate combat power or attention. It also speaks to the agility of a commander's mental faculties and how he applies his knowledge to leverage the operating environment to his best advantage.

objective. A clearly defined and obtainable goal for a military operation, such as seizing a terrain feature, neutralizing an enemy's force or capability, or achieving some other desired outcome essential to the commander's plan and toward which the operation is directed.

operational art. The skill of employing military forces to attain strategic objectives in a theater of war or theater of operations through the design, organization, and conduct of campaigns and major operations.

operational command. The authority granted to a commander to assign missions or tasks to subordinate commanders, deploy units, reassign forces, or retain or delegate operational and/or tactical control as deemed necessary. It does not of itself include responsibility for administration or logistics.

operational level of war. The level of war at which campaigns and major operations are planned, conducted, and sustained to accomplish strategic objectives within theaters or areas of operations.

parapet. A wall giving protection to troops and guns.

rampart. The main wall of a fortress.
sally. A sudden attack by the defenders against the trenches and works of the besiegers.
sortie. A party of defenders who sally out against the besiegers.
strategic level of war. The level of war at which a nation or group of nations determines national or alliance security objectives and develops and uses national resources to accomplish those objectives.
tactical command. The authority delegated to a commander to assign tasks to forces under his command for the accomplishment of the mission assigned by higher authority.
tactical control. The detailed local direction and control of movements or maneuver necessary to accomplish missions or tasks assigned.
tactical level of war. The level of war at which battles and engagements are planned and executed to accomplish military objectives assigned to tactical units or task forces.
theater of operations. Area within a theater of war within which operations are directed toward a common strategic objective.
theater of war. The continental territory, including adjoining sea areas, in which a war is conducted. Operations in a theater of war are invariably joint and usually combined. A theater of war normally comprises *several* theaters of operations.
troupes de la marine. Regular soldiers of the French navy.
troupes de terre. Regular soldiers of the French army.

Abbreviations

AB	Abercromby Papers, Huntington Library, San Marino, CA
Albertson *Memoirs*	Albertson, *A Short Account of the Life, Travels and Adventures of Garret Albertson, Sr.*
Bass *Journal*	Bass, "Account of the Capture of Fort Frontenac by the Detachment under the Command of Col. Bradstreet"
BFTM	*Bulletin of the Fort Ticonderoga Museum*
BL	British Library
Bougainville *Journals*	Bougainville, *Adventure in the Wilderness: The American Journals of Louis Antoine de Bougainville, 1756–1760*
Cleaveland *Journal*	Cleaveland, "Journal of the Rev. John Cleaveland, June 14, 1758–October 25, 1758"
Clinton *Journal*	Clinton, "Colonel Charles Clinton's Journal of His Campaigns in New York July to October, 1758, during the French War"
CO	Colonial Office Papers, The National Archives, UK (formerly PRO)
Courville *Mémoires*	Aumasson de Courville, *Mémoires sur le Canada, depuis 1749 jusqu'à 1760*
CWP	*Correspondence of William Pitt*
DCB	*Dictionary of Canadian Biography*
"Détail"	"Détail de la prise de frontenac," in Montcalm, *Journal des campagnes du marquis de Montcalm*, vol. 11, pt. 6 [du 13 août 1758 au 27 mars 1759
Dorr *Journal*	Dorr, "A Journal of an Expedition against Canaday by Moses Dorr Ensin of Capt. Parkers Company Roxbury May 25 1758"
Impartial Account	[Bradstreet], *Impartial Account of Lieut. Col. Bradstreet's Expedition to Fort Frontenac....*
JJA	Amherst, *Journals of Jeffery Amherst*
LO	Loudoun Papers, Huntington Library, San Marino, CA
MA	Pargellis, *Military Affairs in North America 1758–1763*
NYCD	*Documents Relative to the Colonial History of the State of New York*

Pouchot *Memoirs*	Pouchot, *Memoirs on the Late War in North America between France and England*
PPP	Godfrey, *Pursuit of Profit and Preferment in Colonial North America*
Shute *Journal*	Shute, "A Journal of the Reverend Daniel Shute, D.D., Chaplain in the Expedition to Canada in 1758"
Rea *Journal*	Rea, *The Journal of Dr. Caleb Rea, Written during the Expedition against Ticonderoga in 1758*
RFF	Preston and Lamontagne, *Royal Fort Frontenac*
SWJP	*Papers of Sir William Johnson*
VSOB	Van Schaick's Orderly Book
Wall's Account	Major Daniel Wall to Governor Hopkins, 17 September 1758, Oneida Station, in *Records of the Colony of Rhode Island and Providence Plantations in New England*, vol. 11

Notes

Preface

1. For the only biography of Jean-Baptiste Bradstreet, see William G. Godfrey, *Pursuit of Profit and Preferment in Colonial North America: John Bradstreet's Quest:* (Waterloo, ON, 1982). Unfortunately, as its subtitle suggests, it is weighted toward the pursuit of profit and preferment without any real attempt at assessing Bradstreet as a military commander, focusing instead on the Anglo-Acadian officer's ambitions, schemes, and patronage links based primarily on correspondence with his regimental agents, the Gould family.
2. For this study, I will use bateau (sing.) and bateaux (pl.), unless the word is found within a quotation. Bradstreet's paramilitary unit of boat specialists will be referred to as Bradstreet's *battoemen* as is done in contemporary accounts and news stories. For complete details on the construction of bateaux and the various types used, see Robert E. Hager's excellent monograph *Mohawk River Boats and Navigation before 1820* (Syracuse, NY, 1987).
3. For Abercromby's blatant attempts to control the flow of information back to England after the Ticonderoga debacle, see Ian McCulloch, "'Believe Us, Sir, This Will Impress Few People': Spin-Doctoring—18th-Century Style," *BFTM* 16, no. 1 (1998): 92–107. See also *Impartial Account*. It is now certain that this "anonymous" pamphlet was authored by John Bradstreet, as several large extracts of his private 1758 journal of the raid were transcribed by George Washington in 1778 and match its text almost verbatim. See George Washington Papers, Series 4, General Correspondence: *John Bradstreet's Journal of 1759* [sic] *Expedition to Fort Frontenac, December 1778, Extracts by George Washington*, 1 January 1778, accessed 17 October 2020, https://picryl.com/media/george-washington-papers-series-4-general-correspondence-john-bradstreets-journal-a87ee0.
4. John Keegan, *The Face of Battle* (London, 1976), 33.
5. Quoted in *MA*, 188n. Unconventional spellings, errors in spelling, and variant spellings have been carefully transcribed from the original sources and thus are reproduced as written.
6. "Extract of a Letter from an Officer in Albany," 13 September 1758, *London Chronicle*, 25–27 January 1759. The anonymous author of this letter identifies himself as an officer in the same regiment as Bradstreet, the 60th Foot (Royal Americans). His display of detailed insider knowledge of the planning, preparations, and future

operations of the army point to him being a staff officer at General Abercromby's HQ. Of the three principal aides-de-camp—James Cunningham (45th Foot), James Abercrombie (42nd), and James Delancey (60th)—only the latter, the oldest son of Col. Oliver Delancey, who commanded the New York provincial regiment, fits the bill.

7. Donald Stoker, "There Was No Offensive-Defensive Confederate Strategy," *Journal of Military History* 73 (April 2009): 571–72.

Chapter 1

1. "Excerpt of a Letter from a Gentleman . . . ," 24 August 1758, Lake George Camp, reprinted in the *London Chronicle; or, Universal Evening Post*, 21–23 December 1758. After describing the situation of Ticonderoga and Crown Point, the unidentified author discussed at length the chief characteristics of New England and New York as he observed them.
2. *London Chronicle; or, Universal Evening Post*, 10–12 May 1759. Paul Leicester Ford first identified Franklin as the author of this letter in 1889, and Verner W. Crane established the matter definitively in 1950 by pointing out the similarities of thought and treatment in certain passages with other of Franklin's writings. Paul L. Ford, *Franklin Bibliography: A List of Books Written by, or Relating to, Benjamin Franklin* (Brooklyn, NY, 1889), 283; Verner W. Crane, ed., *Benjamin Franklin's Letters to the Press, 1758–1775* (Chapel Hill, NC [1950]), 9.
3. *The Annual Register; or, a View of the History, Politicks, and Literature for the Year 1763*, 7th ed. (London, 1796), 28–29.
4. See Fred Anderson's excellent *A People's Army: Massachusetts Soldiers and Society in the Seven Years' War* (Chapel Hill, NC, 1984), 26–62; and Kevin Sweeney, "The Very Model of a Modern Major General," *Amherst Magazine* 61, no. 1 (Fall 2008): 26.
5. A modern definition of riverine warfare is: "Operations conducted by forces organized to cope with and exploit the unique characteristics of a riverine area, to locate and destroy hostile forces, and/or to achieve or maintain control of the riverine area." US Department of Defense, JP 1–02, *DOD Dictionary of Military and Associated Terms* (12 April 2001, as amended through 31 October 2009), 121.
6. For excellent articles on eighteenth-century riverine warfare, see D. Peter MacLeod, "The French Siege of Oswego in 1756: Inland Naval Warfare in North America," *American Neptune* 49, no. 4 (1989): 262–71; W. A. B. Douglas, "Le Saint Laurent: Une Voie d'Acces Strategique," *Cap-aux-Diamants*, no. 43 (1995): 19–23; Ian Glenn MacDonald, "Whaleboats, Row-Galleys and Floating Batteries: British Gunboats in the 1760 Canada Campaign" (MA thesis, Queen's University, Kingston, 1999); and Joseph F. Meany Jr., "Batteaux and 'Battoe Men': An American Colonial Response to the Problem of Logistics in Mountain Warfare," New York State Museum [1998].
7. For a concise discussion of New France's capability to be self-supporting, as well as the impact of food shortages and rationing on military capability, as well as on civilian and Indian populations, see G. F. Stanley, *New France: The Last Phase, 1744–1760* (Toronto, 1968), 191–96.
8. Ian K. Steele, *Guerillas and Grenadiers: The Struggle for Canada, 1689—1760* (Toronto, 1974), 70–71; on the reluctance of Indian tribes to go on the warpath,

unless the French supplied foodstuffs and other necessities for their communities, see D. Peter MacLeod, *The Canadian Iroquois and the Seven Years' War* (Toronto, 1996), 114; on the combat effectiveness of the *compagnies franches de la marine* over the seventy-year period, see two articles by W. J. Eccles: "The French Forces in North America during the Seven Years' War," in *DCB*, 3:xv–xxiii; and "The Social, the Economic and the Political Significance of the Military Establishment in New France," *Canadian Historical Review* 52, no. 1 (1971): 1–22; see also Jay Cassel, "The Troupes de la Marine in Canada, 1683–1760: Men and Material" (PhD diss., University of Toronto, 1987). Cassel discusses the origins of the marines, or colonial regulars, their organization and command, patterns of military life, recruitment, the nonmilitary economic activities of the soldiers, transportation, clothing, weapons, artillery, rations and nutrition, shelter, medical care, and remuneration.

9. Steele, *Guerillas and Grenadiers*, 70–71; Eccles, "French Forces in North America," xvii.
10. Eccles, "French Forces in North America," xxvi; see also Jay Cassel's excellent article "The Militia Legend: Canadians at War, 1665–1760," in *Canadian Military History since the 17th Century: Proceedings of the Canadian Military History Conference, Ottawa, 5–9 May 2000*, ed. Yves Landry (Ottawa, 2000), 59–67; and Martin Nicolai, "A Different Kind of Courage: The French Military and the Canadian Irregular Soldier during the Seven Years' War," *Canadian Historical Review* 70, no. 1 (1989): 53–75.
11. MacLeod, *Canadian Iroquois*, 19–36; Pouchot *Memoirs*; Bougainville *Journals*, 59–60.
12. MacLeod, *Canadian Iroquois*, 19–36.
13. See Ian K. Steele, *Warpaths: Invasions of North America* (Oxford, 1991), 110–207.
14. For example, see the account of Gaspard-Joseph Chaussegros de Léry's 1756 raid on Fort Bull at the Oneida Carry, in MacLeod, *Canadian Iroquois*, 29–33, detailing how indigenous allies melted away when told their objective was a fort.
15. Food from France had to arrive via a famous bottleneck called the St. Lawrence River, which froze several months of the year. See James Pritchard, *Louis XV's Navy, 1748–1762: A Study of Organization and Administration* (Kingston, ON, 1987), which recounts how the French navy tried to cope with this operational constraint and, ultimately, why it failed. See also Stanley, *New France*, 191–96.
16. Marquis de Montcalm, "Reflections on the Measures to Be Adopted for the Defence of the Colony" [n.d.], in *NYCD*, 10:874.
17. For the best account of how the Six Nations diplomatically and sometimes adroitly played both the French and English off against one another during the Seven Years' War, see chapter 2, "Parallel Warfare," in MacLeod, *Canadian Iroquois*, 19–36; see also Jon Parmenter and Mark Power Robison's excellent "The Perils and Possibilities of Wartime Neutrality on the Edges of Empire: Iroquois and Acadians between the French and British in North America, 1744—1760," *Diplomatic History* 31, no. 2 (2007): 167–206; and Greg Rogers, "Petite Politique: The British, French, Iroquois, and Everyday Power in the Lake Ontario Borderlands, 1724–1760" (PhD diss., University of Maine, 2016), Electronic Theses and Dissertations, 2506, accessed 20 September 2020, http://digitalcommons.library.umaine.edu/etd/2506.
18. George Washington to Dinwiddie, 18 July 1755; and George Washington to Warner Lewis, 14 August 1755—both in *Papers of Washington*, 1:339.

19. Benjamin Franklin, *Autobiography*, ed. John Bigelow (New York, 1927), 271.
20. For the best contemporary account of the siege, see Patrick Mackellar, "A Journal of the Transactions at Oswego from the 16th of May to the 14th of August 1756," in *MA*, 187–89, 200. See also Peter Way, "Soldiers of Misfortune: New England Regulars and the Fall of Oswego, 1755-1756," *Massachusetts Historical Review* 3 (2001): 49–88.
21. Pargellis believes that Lord Loudoun's removal was unfair and unjustified; he claims the Scottish peer was the first commander to clearly see "American conditions demanded experts not numbers. [Loudoun] did what his predecessors should have done, and when he was superseded, England lost the ablest administrator in matters of detail that the war produced." *MA*, xviii.
22. Lord Loudoun to Holderness, 16 August–17 October 1757, quoted in M. John Cardwell, "Mismanagement: The 1758 British Expedition against Carillon," in *BFTM* 15, no. 4 (1992): 241–42.
23. S. M. Pargellis, *Lord Loudoun in North America* (New Haven, CT, 1933 [reprint, 1968]), 231.
24. See Lord Loudoun to Pitt, 14 February 1758, in *CWP*, 1:192–93; see also Pargellis, *Lord Loudoun*, 356–57.
25. Pitt to General Abercromby, 30 December 1757, Whitehall, *CWP*, 1:143–51. See also James Robertson to the Earl of Morton, 18 December 1758, *MA*, 429.
26. W. J. Eccles, "French Imperial Policy for the Great Lakes Basin," in David Curtis Skaggs and Larry L. Nelson, eds., *The Sixty Years' War for the Great Lakes, 1754-1814* (East Lansing, MI, 2001), 37–38. For the best and most scholarly accounts of the Siege of Louisbourg, see the late Hugh Boscawen's *The Capture of Louisbourg, 1758* (Norman, OK, 2011); and A. J. B. Johnston's *Endgame 1758: The Promise, the Glory, and the Despair of Louisbourg's Last Decade* (Lincoln, NE, 2007).
27. John Bradstreet to Gould, 13 March 1758, quoted in *PPP*, 116. Unless otherwise noted, all emphases in quotations are the author's.
28. For detailed accounts of the 1758 Ticonderoga campaign, see Ian McCulloch, "'Like Roaring Lions Breaking from Their Chains': The Battle of Ticonderoga, 8 July 1758," in *Fighting for Canada: Seven Battles, 1758-1945*, ed. Donald E. Graves (Toronto, 2000), 24–80; John Shy, "James Abercromby and the Campaign of 1758" (MA thesis, University of Vermont, 1957); and William R. Nester, *The Epic Battles for Ticonderoga, 1758* (Albany, 2008).
29. *RFF*, 3, 85–101, 186–87. For the events leading up to and including the construction of the first fort, see various French documents from 22–25.
30. Capitaine Anne-Joseph-Hippolyte Maures, Comte de Malartic, to Count d'Argenson, Camp at Cataracoui, 6 October 1755, *RFF*, 248.
31. Memorandum, Capitaine Charles de Plantavit, Chevalier de la Pause, "Observation and Notes on Fort Frontenac" [1756], *RFF*, 250–53.
32. Capitaine Francois le Mercier, "Memorandum on the Artillery of Canada," 30 October 1756, Montreal, *RFF*, 254; M. Doreil to Marshal de Belle Isle, 31 August 1758, Quebec, in *NYCD*, 10:834.
33. David Lee, "Payen de Noyan, Pierre," in *DCB*, vol. 2 (Toronto, 2003–), accessed 19 May 2020, http://www.biographi.ca/en/bio/payen_de_noyan_pierre_2E.html.
34. "On lui avoit donné ce commandement, qui étoît au-dessous de son grade, pour améliorer ses affaires qui étoient extrêmement dérangées." Courville *Mémoires*, 113–14. For an excellent discussion of Courville the man and his memoirs, see

Marc-André D'Amours, "Entre deux régimes: Louis-Léonard Aumasson de Courville et ses Mémoires" (PhD diss., History Department, University of Montreal, 2016).
35. This breakdown of the garrison's complement is taken from the parade state given by the French commandant on surrender (see appendixes A and B) and does not include the indigenous allies, nor the boat crews and their officers who abandoned their ships and escaped. *RFF*, 258–59.
36. *Impartial Account*, 8–9. Bradstreet's "most accurate intelligence relative to the state of Fort Frontenac and the condition of the shipping" did not come from Sir William Johnson but from an Onondaga sachem and warrior named Ononwarogo, or Red Head, who came to Oswego in 1755 and "being courteously received and caresses'd by Mr. Bradstreet... made a tender of his services." See John Bradstreet to William Shirley, 29 May 1755, in *SWJP*, 2:547–50. The ambitious, unbridled Bradstreet slid into his new role immediately, sniffing out and identifying the operating environment he was confronted with, and then, like quicksilver, spreading and filling all the nooks and crannies where he perceived leadership was lacking. In a sense, he was also a spymaster gathering intelligence for his mentor and boss, William Shirley. In this rather astonishing letter, the junior officer informs the commander in chief that he has "engag'd the principal Chief of the Miscisaga [Mississauga] Indians who came here to trade, to go to Colonel Johnson's & at [the Chief's] Request have sent a Belt of Wampum to his Nation who live on the North Side of the Lake; they are a numerous Nation, and live in Friendship with the Six Nations, and certain I am, if I had Authority with proper presents and provisions, I could engage many Indians to go to the Westward with us." This probably was written about the time when Bradstreet started to incur the lasting enmity of SWJ by what others perceived to be an attempt, on the Irish-Acadian's part, to secure Johnson's job with the Six Nations. See Goldsbrow Banyar's analysis of Bradstreet's ambitions in Banyar to Johnson, 18 November 1755, *SWJP*, 2:39, where he claims that Bradstreet "now aims at the Superintendancy of Indian affairs, at least as to the foreign and uppermost of the five Nations." Sir Charles Hardy, the governor of New York, and no fan of his Massachusetts counterpart, would write a scathing indictment of Bradstreet's bona fides as an Indian expert to Lord Germain: "I must observe to your Lordship that [Shirley's] principal Indian Ambassador is Mr. Broadstreet who never saw one of the Castles till his going this year to Oswego and now takes upon him to know more than any-body in this Country." Hardy to Halifax, 27 November 1755, *MA*, 152.
37. *PPP*, 105.
38. John Bradstreet to Sir Richard Lyttleton, 5 September 1757, quoted in *PPP*, 101.
39. William Shirley to Robinson, 19 December 1755, New York, in William Shirley, *Correspondence of William Shirley, Governor of Massachusetts and Military Commander in America, 1731–1760*, ed. Charles Henry Lincoln (New York, 1912), 2:345–46.
40. Oswegatchie, La Présentation, and La Galette were all synonymous to the British but were technically different spots in the same locale. Fort de La Présentation was a palisaded mission fort built in 1749 at the confluence of the Oswegatchie River and the St. Lawrence River and so named by the French Sulpician priest Abbé Picquet. It was also sometimes known as Fort La Galette because of an older

French fort on the northern side of the river that appeared on British maps. As to Shirley's prescience, it was just three years later that the French built their own fort (Fort Lévis) on one of the islands near La Galette, the same year Oswego and Fort Ontario were being rebuilt by the British as a new forward operating base. Shirley to Robinson, 19 December 1755, 2:346.
41. Shirley to Robinson, 19 December 1755, 2:346.
42. Shirley to Robinson, 19 December 1755, 2:346.
43. John Bradstreet to Sir Richard Lyttleton, 5 September 1757, quoted in Lawrence Henry Gipson, *The Great War for the Empire: The Victorious Years, 1758-1760*, vol. 7 of *The British Empire before the American Revolution* (New York, 1949), 237n.
44. See "Memorial" of Bradstreet to Loudoun, 4 January 1758, LO, 6895. See also the draft "Plan of Instructions to Capt. John Bradstreet," 25 January 1758, drawn up by then adjutant general, Col. John Forbes, in *The Writings of General John Forbes Relating to His North American Service*, ed. Alfred Proctor James (Wenasha, WI, 1938), 31-32.
45. Lord Loudoun to William Pitt, 14 February 1758, *CWP*, 1:194.
46. Godfrey's sole source for a March 1758 council cites a very dubious and ambiguous passage in Benson J. Lossing's colorful *Life and Times of Philip Schuyler* (New York, 1872), 1:146. See also Harold E. Mahan, *Benson J. Lossing and Historical Writing in the United States* (Westport, CT, 1996), 128-31.
47. James Abercromby to William Pitt, 16 March 1758, New York, *CWP*, 1:208.
48. *Impartial Account*, 5.
49. *Impartial Account*, 6. George Augustus, Lord Viscount Howe, eldest son of Sir Edward Scrope, second Lord Viscount Howe, in the peerage of Ireland, was born in 1725 and succeeded to the title on the death of his father in 1735. In early 1757, he was ordered to America, being then colonel-commandant of the 3rd Battalion, 60th Foot (Royal Americans), and arrived at Halifax in July 1757. On 28 September 1757, he was appointed colonel of the 55th foot, and on 29 December 1757, brigadier general in America. After Howe was killed in an ambush on 6 July prior to the Battle of Ticonderoga, his corpse was escorted to Albany for interment by Philip Schuyler, a protégé of John Bradstreet and captain in Delancey's Yorkers. Howe was buried in St. Peter's Church in Albany. Massachusetts erected a monument to his memory in Westminster Abbey at an expense of £250. Lord Howe was a Member of Parliament for Nottingham at the time of his death. *NYCD*, 10:735.
50. *NYCD*, 10:735.
51. See Stephen Brumwell, "Band of Brothers," *History Today* 58, no. 6 (June 2008): 25-31; and Ian McCulloch," Stream of Consciousness: Searching for Lord Howe...," *Adirondack Life* 33, no. 3 (May-June 2002): 20-25.
52. Rufus Putnam, *The Memoirs of General Rufus Putnam and Certain Official Papers and Correspondence,1738-1824*, ed. Rowena Buell (Boston, 1903), 23.
53. Albertson *Memoirs.*

Chapter 2

1. The reference to "Deo-Wahne-Sta" as the indigenous term for the Oneida Carrying Place is found in scores of published materials that discuss the history of the area, but it seems that the indigenous roots of the name might be questionable as there is no record of the term's use in documents earlier than 1845. Daniel K.

Richter, *Ordeal of the Longhouse: The Peoples of the Iroquois League in the Era of European Colonization* (Chapel Hill, NC, 1992), 262. An Oneida historian posits that *Tiowestah* may be a corruption of *Latihuwaha:wí* ("They carry their canoes"). See Kandice Watson, "The Oneida Carry: An Important Link in Haudenosaunee Travels," *Oneida* website, accessed 29 July 2021, https://www.oneidaindiannation.com/the-oneida-carry-an-important-link-in-haudenosaunee-travels/.
2. For those interested, there has been a substantial body of research into Iroquois/Haudenosaunee politics and diplomacy: Gille Havard, *Empire et métissages* (2003) and *The Great Peace of Montreal of 1701* (2001); Francis Jennings, *The Ambiguous Iroquois Empire* (1984) and (ed.) *The History and Culture of Iroquois Diplomacy* (1985); Daniel K. Richter and James H. Merrell, eds., *Beyond the Covenant Chain* (1987); Timothy J. Shannon, *Iroquois Diplomacy on the Early American Frontier* (2009); Richard White, *The Middle Ground* (1991); and Yves F. Zoltvany, *Philippe de Rigaud de Vaudreuil, Governor of New France, 1703–1725* (1974).
3. For an excellent analysis of how the Oneida and other members of the Haudenosaunee Confederacy plugged into the labor markets of the Mohawk Valley in times of war and peace, see Gail D. MacLeitch, *Imperial Entanglements: Iroquois Change and Persistence on the Frontiers of Empire* (Philadelphia, 2011), 85–122.
4. For detailed discussion of all aspects of bateau design and development, see Hager, *Mohawk River Boats and Navigation*. For the latest archaeological revelations and discoveries relating to Seven Years' War bateaux and their role, see J. W. Zarzynski, *Ghost Fleet Awakened: Lake George's Sunken Bateaux of 1758* (Albany, 2019). For the French equivalent of the bateaux, see C. Dagneau, "The 'Batteaux Plats' of New France," *International Journal of Nautical Archaeology* 33 (2004): 281–96.
5. Fragment from Unknown Person to Johnson, 30 April 1758, Herkemers [sic], *SWJP*, 3:987.
6. General Abercromby to Sir William Johnson, 20 May 1758, Albany, *SWJP*, 9:906.
7. Johnson to Abercromby, 1 June 1758, Fort Johnson, *SWJP*, 9:920. For bios of these ranger officers see Ian McCulloch and Earl Chapman, eds., *Orderly Books of the 78th Regiment of Foot, Fort Stanwix, New York, November 1758–April 1759* (Montreal, 2011), 13, 34, 42–43.
8. For an interesting discussion of the woes of the New York Independents, see Pargellis, *Lord Loudoun,*, 329–30. See also S. M. Pargellis, "The Four Independent Companies of New York," in *Essays in Colonial History Presented to Charles McLean Andrews by His Students* (New Haven, CT, 1931), 96–123.
9. George Croghan to Sir William Johnson, 31 May 1758, Fort Hendrick, *SWJP*, 11:915.
10. *NYCD*, 10:719; although each of the regular regiments, the *troupes de terre*, were tasked to provide a sixty-four-man picket (with the two battalions of the Berri regiment providing one between them), La Reine had departed already for Carillon before Levis's detachment was organized at Montreal. Thus the regular component of the French raid comprised six pickets of light infantry drawn from the Royal Roussillon, Berri, Bearn, Guyenne, La Sarre, and Languedoc regiments for a total of 402 all ranks. Bougainville *Journals*, 211–14.
11. James Robertson to the Earl of Morton, 19 December 1758, New York, *MA*, 429–32.
12. Dr. Richard Shuckburgh (1708–16 August 1773) was born in London, son of Richard and Anne Shuckburgh. After his medical training, he immigrated to America, where he was commissioned as one of the two surgeons to the four New York

Independent Companies on 25 June 1737; he also served as surgeon to the Mohawks. He resigned his surgeon's commission in 1760 in order to take advantage of new employment with Sir William Johnson. Force reductions after the war, however, found him looking for a new job, and General Amherst's personal involvement helped him purchase a commission as surgeon to the 17th Foot on 29 December 1762. He was forced to sell land he had acquired in the Mohawk Valley in order to pay for the commission. Shuckburgh accompanied his regiment to Detroit in 1764, remaining there for one year. When Johnson's secretary died in 1765, he was offered the job of secretary of Indian affairs and took it, resigning from the army on 9 May 1768. He died of an apoplectic fit on 16 August 1773 in Albany, New York. "Richard Shuckburgh," in *JJA*, 2:309.

13. For a detailed scholarly discussion of the true origins of the song "Yankee Doodle," see Oscar George Theodore Sonneck, "Report on 'The Star-Spangled Banner,' 'Hail Columbia,' 'America,' 'Yankee Doodle' . . ." (Washington, 1909), 79–126; also, for a lively, but lighter-weight discussion, see David Hackett Fisher, *Liberty and Freedom: A Visual History of America's Founding Ideas* (New York, 2005), 215–20.
14. Peter Kalm, *Travels in North America*, trans. and ed. Adolph B. Benson (New York, 1937; reprint, 1964), 1:343–45.
15. VSOB, 1 June–3 November 1758. Many thanks to Matt Keagle and Rich Strum on the Fort Ticonderoga Museum staff for making scans of the original orderly book available for this study.
16. *New American Magazine*, 5 June 1758, in "Newspaper Extracts," *Documents Relating to the Colonial History of the State of New Jersey* (Paterson, 1898), 20:219.
17. Shute *Journal*, 5.
18. The two colonels specifically mentioned were "the two Col° W[illia]^{m}'s, Billy and Jose, but what end they had in it I won't pretend to guess but only observe that they have a great interest that way." Rea *Journal*, 14–15; the two individuals concerned were Cols. William Williams and Joseph Williams, distant cousins, and not brothers as stated in the original transcript annotated by a grandson. Fred Anderson has perpetuated the case of mistaken identity by anointing Joseph Williams, a native of Roxbury, just outside Boston, as one of the "powerful Connecticut Valley gentleman known as 'River Gods.'" Anderson, *People's Army*, 69. Dr. Kevin Sweeney, an authority on Connecticut colonial history and author of "River Gods and Related Minor Deities: The Williams Family and the Connecticut River Valley, 1637–1790," 2 vols. (PhD diss., Yale University, 1986), states that the said Col. Joseph Williams (1708–98) of Roxbury "was a member of a family branch that never left the old hometown of Roxbury and had little or nothing to do with the 'River Gods' of western Massachusetts. The Williamses in western Massachusetts and Connecticut did maintain contact with another branch of the family that remained in Roxbury as well, but not with the one of which Joseph was a member. And I'm not aware of their paths crossing during the 1750s. Colonel Joseph was a member of the Massachusetts House of Representatives in 1750, 1752–1754, 1757, 1760, 1762–1765, and 1767–1769. He was appointed a Justice of the Peace by the royal governor; hence his use of Esquire. The appointment as a JP and as a provincial colonel indicates that he was someone being courted by the colony's royal government, but he was nowhere near as important as the folks in western Mass. In the end the courtship was unsuccessful: he was a patriot and, at

67 years of age turned out for the Lexington alarm and helped direct militiamen on April 19th [1775]." Email to author, 1 March 2020.
19. Shute *Journal*, 5.
20. Shute *Journal*, 5.
21. See "Return of the Provincial Forces That Have Arrived in Albany from the 7th to the 20th of June, 1758, Both Inclusive," CO/5/50, f. 509. The other tardy Massachusetts regiments were those of Cols. Jonathan Bagley and Thomas Doty.
22. John Appy to Robert Wood, 2 July 1758, CO/5/50, ff. 188–97.
23. Entry, 19 June 1758, Rea *Journal*, 19; Entry, 23 June 1758, Cleaveland *Journal*, 99; Entry, 1 July 1758, Shute *Journal*, 5.
24. John Stanwix [formerly Roos] (1693–1766), army officer and politician, was baptized on 19 March 1693, the son of the Rev. John Roos, rector of Widmerpool, Nottinghamshire, and Matilda, the daughter of Thomas Stanwix of Carlisle. At the age of thirteen (in 1706), he was commissioned in the British army as an ensign and a lieutenant. He became a captain in the 28th Foot and served as its adjutant. He changed his family name from Roos to Stanwix on the death of his uncle, Thomas Stanwix. In 1741, he served as a major in the 10th Regiment of Marines, and in that year he stood for Parliament in the riding town of Carlisle, but was unseated on petition due to election irregularities. He was, however, returned in a by-election in 1746 and in the subsequent general elections of 1747 and 1754. He served as the lieutenant colonel to the Duke of Rutland's regiment raised to combat the Jacobite Uprising in 1745. In 1749, he became a royal equerry to Frederick, Prince of Wales, when his regiment was disbanded and he was put on half-pay. After the prince's death in 1753, he was made governor of Carlisle Castle for his loyal services. Two years later, he was made deputy quartermaster general of the forces. In 1756, on the outbreak of the Seven Years' War, he volunteered for service in America and was appointed colonel-commandant of the 1st Battalion of the 60th Foot, Royal American Regiment. Upon his arrival in America, he was appointed to the local rank of brigadier general and given the command of all forces to the south of the area of operations. Ironically, during 1757 his headquarters were located at Carlisle, Pennsylvania, the namesake of the castle and riding for which he had been previously responsible. After his relief by Gen. John Forbes in 1758, General Stanwix proceeded to Albany, whence he was ordered west into the Mohawk River Valley to build a new frontier fort at the Oneida Carrying Place. The fort was built by provincials and the Fraser Highlanders to secure that important position and reestablish communications with Lake Ontario. In 1759, he was ordered back to Pennsylvania to replace Forbes, who died after the capture of Fort Duquesne in December 1758, and thus was responsible for overseeing the construction of Fort Pitt (Pittsburgh). On 19 June 1759, Stanwix was appointed major general and relieved by Gen. Robert Monckton on 4 May 1760. Promoted to lieutenant general on 19 January 1761, he returned to England and was appointed lieutenant governor of the Isle of Wight. He was given the colonelcy of the 8th Foot and became a Member of Parliament for Appleby in Westmoreland. He drowned with his wife and daughter at sea while crossing from Ireland to Wales in *The Eagle* packet. *The History of Parliament: British Political, Social & Local History*, accessed 1 May 2020, https://www.historyofparliamentonline.org/volume/1754-1790/member/stanwix-john-1693-1766; "John Stanwix," in

Appleton's *Cyclopaedia of American Biography*, ed. J. G. Wilson and John Fiske (New York, 1900), 5:651.
25. Shute *Journal*, 5–6.
26. Capt. Elias Hand to Johnson, 14 June 1758, Stone Arabia, *SWJP*, 2:837. Details of the dispute are lost as the original letter was destroyed by fire and only an abstract description survives: "asking directions in view of a conflict of authority with Captain Bagely."
27. Clinton *Journal*, 298.
28. For a man touted as an enlightened liberal espousing the ideals of democracy (long before the break with the mother country, according to the many enthusiastic biographers of his famous Revolutionary War veteran sons), an apparent contradiction hovers on the periphery of Clinton's almost saintly persona: the fact he was a slave owner. While slavery would not be abolished by the British until 1833 and the Americans until 1865, Clinton senior (nor his sons for that matter) had no qualms about the institution of slavery in the mid-eighteenth century. On his death, he bequeathed eight of his nine slaves to his sons, giving only one her freedom as a promise to his dead daughter: "I give and bequeath to my Eldest son Charles, my Negro boys Robin and Dublin. . . . I give to my son [James] my Negro boys David and Isaac. . . . I give my son George, my Negro boys William and Samuel. My Negro Wench, Lettice, I intended to give to my Daughter Catherine but She being then very Sickly and having no Children she Desired if she died before me, I should Leave [Lettice] free which I promised to do . . . and give and bequeath to my said three sons. . . . my negro Peter and wench Pegg." Extract from "The Will of Charles Clinton," *Proceedings of the New York State Historical Association* 6 (1906): 166–68.

Cadwallader Colden, writing to friend in England in July 1758 before the raid, claimed how pleased he was that his fellow surveyor and friend Charles Clinton, the lieutenant colonel of the 2nd Battalion, Ulster County militia, was "pitched on to be second in command" for the raid and boasted Clinton had "received his commission on my recommendation." Cadwallader Colden to Peter Collinson, 29 July 1758, Flushing, Long Island, in Cadwallader Colden, *Letters and Papers of Cadwallader Colden*, vol. 5, *1755–1760* (New York, 1921), 254.
29. John Bradstreet to Charles Gould, 21 September 1758, Bradstreet Papers, Library and Archives Canada.
30. Abercromby to Pitt, 12 July 1758, *NYCD*, 10:727; Montcalm to Belle Isle, 12 July 1758, *NYCD*, 10:733; James Abercromby, "Return of the Officers Killed or Wounded, 8 July 1758," AB, 425.
31. William Hervey, *Journals of the Hon. William Hervey, in North America and Europe from 1755 to 1814; with Order Books at Montreal, 1760–1763* (Bury St. Edmunds, UK, 1906), 50; Captain Peter Dubois to friend, 10 July 1758, reprinted in *Gentleman's Magazine* (1758), 446.
32. *Impartial Account*, 6.
33. "At a Council of War, Held in Camp on the Banks of Lake George on Thursday, the 13th of July, 1758," LO, 438.
34. Abercromby to Bradstreet, 13 July 1758, Lake George, LO, 439.
35. Col. Melancthon Taylor Woolsey to brother, 26 July 1758, Schenectady, in Melancthon Taylor Woolsey, *Letters of Melancthon Taylor Woolsey: Colonel, New York Provincial Troops in the French and Indian War* (Champlain, QC, 1927), 18.

NOTES TO CHAPTER 2   189

36. "wanton Sacrefise"—Putnam, *Memoirs*, 75; "army is unhinged"—Colonel William Williams to his uncle Israel Williams, "Lake George (sorrowful situation) July ye 11th," in Israel Williams Papers, Massachusetts Historical Society; "confused rabble"—Colonel Henry Babcock to Governor Stephen Hopkins, 4 July 1758, Lake George Camp, in *Records of the Colony of Rhode Island and Providence Plantations in New England* (Providence, 1863), 6:163–64.
37. Pvt. Abner Barrow, "Fragment of the Diary of Abner Barrow," *Colonial Wars: A Quarterly Magazine* (Boston, 1913), 215. Sgt. Seth Tinkman also witnessed the same event and provides more detail, including the names of the ringleaders: "July 22 we were Ordered to Load up our Tents and Packs. Tents we loaded, but they would not Load their packs, and when we were ordered to march Capt [Abel] Keen's men Clubbed their Fire Locks and followed Sergt Rogers and several from other Companys, we were ordered to Surround them and Then took away their Fire Locks and carried them back to the Barracks and Confined them. The Two Sergts viz. Rogers and Cushing was pinioned and 4 more sent down to Albany that Night, the Rest were kept until further orders." Seth Tinkman, "Seth Tinkman's Diary, 1758," in *Contributions Biographical, Genealogical and Historical*, ed. Ebenezer Weaver Peirce (Boston, 1874), 126.
38. Stanwix to Abercromby, 6 August 1758, AB, 948.
39. *Impartial Account*, 27.
40. The "myth of total surprise" on the part of the French garrison manning Frontenac in August 1758 was introduced as early as Francis Parkman's and Lawrence Gipson's histories of the event, and it has been perpetuated ever since by a slew of respectable Canadian and American historians, including Guy Frégault ("The defenders had been taken completely by surprise"), in *Canada: The War of Conquest*, trans. Margaret Cameron (Toronto, 1969), 222; William Fowler ("The surprise was so complete that the French vessels were trapped at their moorings"), in *Empires at War: The French and Indian War and the Struggle for North America, 1754–1763* (New York, 2005), 154; Fred Anderson ("undetected they beached their boats on the Cataraqui promontory within a mile of Fort Frontenac"), in *The War That Made America* (New York, 2005), 150; and Guy Chet ("Bradstreet's attack surprised the garrison"), in *Conquering the American Wilderness: The Triumph of European Warfare in the Colonial Northeast* (Amherst, MA, 2003), 117. See chapter 7 for a detailed historiographical discussion of how historians slavishly copied one another, beginning with Parkman and ending with present-day pundits.
41. Dorr *Journal*, 456.
42. See the draft "Plan of Instructions to Capt. John Bradstreet," 25 January 1758, in Forbes, *Writings*, 31–32.
43. Colden to Peter Collinson, 29 July 1758, Flushing, Long Island, Colden, *Letters and Papers*, 5:254. Cadwallader Colden Sr. (1688–1776), born in Dunse, Scotland, was one of the most learned men in the colonies during the Seven Years' War, a true figure of the American Enlightenment. Originally he studied for the ministry at the University of Edinburgh, then removed to London upon graduation to study medicine. He immigrated to America in 1710 and set up a medical practice and a mercantile business in Philadelphia; he moved to New York Colony in 1720 to become the first surveyor general of the colony on the invitation the governor, Robert Hunter. He wrote about many aspects of science, astronomy, and mathematics and counted Benjamin Franklin among his scientific colleagues. He

wrote a critique of Sir Isaac Newton's *Principles of Action in Matter* in 1751 and also became a botanist of the new Linnaean system of classifying flora, making significant contributions to medical literature. In 1743, when an outbreak of yellow fever killed numerous people in New York City, Dr. Colden went house-to-house to treat the ailing people in order to identify the chief areas of infection firsthand. By examining the environs in which the stricken were most numerous, he correctly pinpointed filthy drinking water as the cause of the epidemic, and then he fought for stricter measures to protect the public water supplies.

44. Bougainville *Journals*, 246.
45. Charles Lee to Miss Sydney Lee, 18 June 1756, Schenectady, and 16 September 1758, Schenectady, in Charles Lee, *The Lee Papers* (New York, 1871), 1:4–8. Charles Lee was an adopted warrior of the Mohawk. A native of Wales and son of a colonel in the British service, Lee entered the army early in life; was commissioned a captain in the 44th Foot, 11 June 1756; a major of the 103rd, or Volunteer Hunters, 28 October 1761, and in 1762 served, with the local rank of colonel, in the auxiliary British force sent to Portugal, where he distinguished himself. Lee went on half-pay at the peace and entered the Polish service; became a brevet lieutenant colonel in May 1772, and after rambling all over Europe, came to America in 1773 and settled in Virginia. He resigned his British army commission in 1775, when he was appointed by Congress major general in the Continental Army. He served through the Revolutionary War until 1780 when, in consequence of disobeying General Washington's orders, he resigned his commission to avoid a court-martial, returned to his plantation in Virginia, sold his farm, and then removed to Philadelphia, where he died on 2 October 1782.
46. "An Indian Council," Sir William Johnson to the Six Nations, 22 July 1758, Fort Johnson, *SWJP* (1939) 9:952–53.
47. "An Indian Council."
48. Sir William Johnson to Captain Thomas Butler, 6 August 1758, Camp near Herkemer, *SWJP*, 9:966–67.
49. Bougainville *Journals*, 263–65.
50. Sieur de Courville, extract from Courville *Mémoires*, 114.
51. Clinton *Journal*, 305.
52. Stanwix to Abercromby, 20 August 1758, CO/5/50, pt. 3, 559. The new directive was intended to rectify a long-standing problem that had bedeviled relations between provincial and regular officers from the outset of the war. Officers holding the king's commission outranked provincial officers who held their commissions from colonial governors, and in a move to smooth over this irritant for the colonials, Pitt's administration tried to ameliorate the problem for the 1758 campaign by declaring all provincial officers forthwith would be equal in rank to their regular counterparts. The king's commission, however, would still trump a provincial commission of equal rank, but now a provincial lieutenant colonel would technically out rank a regular major, and since all provincial regiments were almost always commanded by a full colonel, regular lieutenant colonels would now also rank *below* a provincial colonel. In order to accommodate this disparity, and to ensure that regular officers were kept senior in rank to the provincials, a simple semantic solution was devised whereby all lieutenant colonel commanding officers serving in North America in 1758 were promoted to "Colonels in America"

(sometimes referred to as a brevet rank). Unfortunately for Lieutenant Colonel Bradstreet, the DQMG, this protective "topcover" had not been extended to him in the annual 1758 list of promotions from Whitehall, and the several provincial colonels at the Oneida Carrying Place knew of this oversight. For further details see *JJA*, 1:xx–xxiii.
53. Shute *Journal*, 12.
54. All parade state figures were taken from "Return of His Majesty's Troops Detached from the Oneida Station—15th August 1758 under the Command of Lieut. Colonel Bradstreet," AB; and "A Return Taken of the Detachment of the New York Regimt on ye Expedition, Camp at Lake Onida 18 August 1758," Clinton *Journal*, 305. Numbers initially announced and allocated to provincial regiments on 11 August at Oneida Station in General Stanwix's General Orders were adjusted downward daily as injuries, disease, and desertion took their toll.
55. "Plagy rogues"—2 October 1758, Lake George Camp, Cleaveland *Journal*, 228.
56. For an interesting discussion of career progression and class backgrounds, see E. H. Knoublach, "Mobilizing Provincials for War: The Social Composition of New York Forces in 1760," *New York History* 78, no. 2 (1997): 147–72, accessed 20 March 2020, www.jstor.org/stable/23181843. Interestingly, members of the upper-class gentry of the colonies were not interested in serving in the provincial regiments raised for the hostilities, preferring instead to serve with their local militias.
57. Entry, 8 August 1758, Camp at Fort Harkman, VSOB, 82.
58. See Brian Dunnigan, *Siege, 1759: The Campaign against Niagara* (Youngstown, OH, 1996), 54, 70–71; William B. Weeden, *Early Rhode Island: A Social History of the People* (New York, 1920), 298.
59. Thomas Cushing and Charles E. Sheppard, *History of the Counties of Gloucester, Salem, and Cumberland, New Jersey* (Philadelphia, 1883), 34, 39, 41, 116, 121.
60. Shute *Journal*, 12.
61. See Kevin M. Sweeney, "Firearms, Militias, and the Second Amendment," in *The Second Amendment on Trial: Critical Essays on District of Columbia v. Heller*, ed. Saul Cornell and Nathan Kozuskanich (Amherst, MA, 2013), Table 6, 332–33.
62. Joseph J. Smith, *Civil and Military List of Rhode Island* (Providence, RI, 1901), 1:176, 198, 203, 210.
63. Smith, 6:163–64.
64. Smith, 6:163–64.
65. For the best detailed study of the 1756 French raid, see Gilbert Hagerty, *Massacre at Fort Bull: The de Lery Expedition against Oneida Carry, 1756* (Providence, RI, 1971).
66. Albertson *Memoirs*.
67. A later entry in Sir William Johnson's "Journal of Indian Affairs" for 1758 specifically mentions that SWJ personally thanked the ten Seneca warriors for going on "Col. Bradstreet's Enterprize." See 31 October 1758, Fort Johnson, *SWJP*, 10:51.
68. John Butler to Sir William Johnson, 28 April and 7 and 25 May 1757, *SWJP*, 9:702–3, 777. On the serious impact war had on the Haudenosaunee nations' abilities to hunt and farm, see MacLeitch, *Imperial Entanglements*, 69–70, 100–104; for subsistence and economic impacts on the Seven Nations allied to the French, see MacLeod, *Canadian Iroquois*, 7–8, 11–18.
69. *Impartial Account*, 8.

70. Sir William Johnson addressed the leadership of all Six Nations a month after the raid's conclusion saying:

> Brethren of the Six Nations:— I am very glad to find some out of each of your Castles joined Col. Bradstreet & the Troops under his Command in the late Enterprize against Cadaraqui, and I congratulate you on the Extraordinary Success it was attended with; for as that Fort is now demolished your Country is so far freed from the Fetters of the French & they cannot now from thence alarm you by any hostile Preparations. I hope you will prevent them from encroaching again upon you, by never suffering them to rebuild this fort where a number of your Ancestors were treacherously & cruely Massacred.

(*Journal of Indian Affairs*, 23 September 1758, Fort Johnson, *SWJP*, 10:12)

71. A rough calculation of the breakdown of Haudenosaunee participation in the raid based on Sir William Johnson's correspondence and other sources indicate that, with ten Seneca, and a like number of Onondaga warriors deducted from the total of forty-two going, the remaining unidentified twenty-two Six Nations warriors that went on the raid were from the Mohawk, Oneida, Tuscarora, and Cayuga nations. In addition, another unexamined aspect of the 1758 raid is the number of indigenous warriors that actually went on the raid "under contract" to the British, not as Native warriors per se, but as battoemen, rangers, or foot soldiers clad in the provincial green or blue of such colonies as New York, Massachusetts, and New Jersey, all of which actively recruited Blacks and indigenous soldiers. See Brian D. Carroll, "From Warrior to Soldier: New England Indians in the Colonial Military, 1676–1763" (PhD diss., University of Connecticut, 2009); and Scott A. Padeni, "Forgotten Soldiers: The Role of Blacks in New York's Campaigns of the Seven Years' War," *BFTM* 16, no. 2 (1999): 152–69.
72. *Impartial Account*, 8–9.
73. For tables with computed times for the speed of land and water communications in North America based on dated correspondence and recorded reception of the same sent by both French and British in the Seven Years' War in North America, see Malcolm MacLeod's helpful appendix "Speed of Communications," in "French and British Strategy in the Lake Ontario Theatre of Operations, 1754–1760" (PhD. diss., University of Ottawa, 1974), 567–71.
74. Bradstreet to Abercromby, 15 August 1758, Oneida Carrying Place, AB, 452 (author's emphasis).

Chapter 3

1. Shute *Journal*, 13.
2. George Davis, *A Historical Sketch of Sturbridge and Southbridge* (West Brookfield, MA, 1856), 100–101.
3. Dorr *Journal*, 457.
4. Dorr *Journal*, 457.
5. *Impartial Account*, 11.
6. *Impartial Account*, 11.
7. Clinton *Journal*, 305.
8. Albertson *Memoirs*.

9. Rea *Journal*, 62.
10. Clinton *Journal*, 305.
11. *Impartial Account*, 13.
12. Albertson *Memoirs*.
13. Courville *Mémoires*, 114. The Sieur de Courville claims that Payen de Noyan became so incensed by Vaudreuil's complete indifference to his warnings that he demanded the governor recall him to Montreal: "le S. de Noyan voyant que ses avertissements n'opéroient rien, demanda à descendre, aimant mieux qu'un autre que lui fût la victime du Général; il lui écrivit en conséquence en lui réitérant que le secours pour la place pressoit. M. de Vaudreuil ayant reçu sa lettre, dit, en haussant les épaules, 'qu'il falloit que cette Officier eût peur?'" (The Sieur de Noyan saw that his warnings were having no effect, so he demanded that he be allowed to return down the river if he were to be the sacrificial lamb of the Governor; however Noyan consequently wrote again to Vaudreuil reiterating the urgent need for help. The Governor, on reading this letter, shrugged his shoulders and said: "What is it that makes this man so afraid?")
14. *Impartial Account*, 14.
15. *Impartial Account*, 14; Albertson *Memoirs*.
16. Stephen Cross, "Up to Ontario: Journal of Stephen Cross of Newbury Port . . . : The Activities of Newburyport Shipbuilders in Canada in 1756," *Essex Institute Historical Collections* 74 (1939): 343.
17. Cross, 343.
18. Albertson *Memoirs*.
19. *Impartial Account*, 14.
20. *Impartial Account*, 14.
21. *Impartial Account*, 15.
22. Bougainville *Journals*, 330; Bougainville to brother, 28 August 1756, "I forgot to tell you I have become an epigraph writer. On the ashes of Oswego, we planted a cross and a post with the [coat of] arms of France. On the cross I gave for a motto: '*In hoc signo Vicunt*'; on the post: '*Manibus date lilia plenis*.'" The latter is a Latin verse from Virgil's *Aeneid*, which reads: "Let fly lilies with hands full."
23. "Détail," 448–50. For all weather data, see Annex I.
24. Pouchot *Memoirs*, 388.
25. Robert Malcomson, *Warships of the Great Lakes, 1754–1834* (Annapolis, MD, 2001), 10–15; Ernest Green, "Corvettes of New France," *Ontario History* 35 (1943): 29–38.
26. The name of the lake could derive either from *Kanadario*, a Huron-Wendat word meaning "sparkling," "shining," or "beautiful" water, or from *Oni-tario*, a Haudonosaunee word meaning "beautiful lake." William Martin Beauchamp, *Indian Names of Places of New York* (New York, 1893), 89.
27. See Laforce's and the Sieur de la Broquerie's captured 1757 maps of Lake Ontario with insets of the harbors at Cataraqui, Oswego, and Niagara in the George III Collection of the British Library. See esp. "Carte Du Lac ontario nouvellement Rellevé avec ces port a grand pois a bitté Lescadre Engloisse & francoisse Leur gremant Leur Cantité de Canon" by the Sieur de la Broquerie, accessed 2 June 2021, https://collections.leventhalmap.org/search/commonwealth:hx11z323c; and "CARTE, ou plan Nouveau du Lac Ontario, avec touttes les isles et bayes qui y Sont rénfermées: Et les forts qui Sont Scitués Sur les bords du dit Lac" by the Sieur

de Laforce, accessed 2 June 2021, https://collections.leventhalmap.org/search/commonwealth:hx11z088k.
28. Pouchot *Memoirs*, 513–18; Yvon Desloges, "Laforce, René-Hippolyte," in *DCB*, vol. 5 (Toronto, 2003–), accessed 4 June 2020, http://www.biographi.ca/en/bio/laforce_rene_hippolyte_5E.html.
29. For best accounts of Canada's first freshwater naval battle see Malcomson, *Warships of the Great Lakes*, 10–15; W. L. Grant, "The Capture of Oswego by Montcalm in 1756, a Study in Naval Power; with an Appendix of Letters from Captain Houseman Broadley, Commander of the British Forces on Lake Ontario," *Mémoires et comptes rendus de la Société Royale du Canada/Proceedings and Transactions of the Royal Society of Canada*, 3rd ser., vol. 8 (1964): 193–214; and D. P. MacLeod, "The Canadians against the French: The Struggle for Control of the Expedition to Oswego in 1756," *Ontario History* 80, no. 2 (June 1988): 143–58.
30. *La Friponne* ("The Cheat") was the nickname of the vast system of corruption at play in New France at all levels. Entry, 1 September 1758, Fort Carillon, Bougainville *Journals*, 266; see also Pouchot *Memoirs*, 136.
31. For the rise and fall of the La Présentation Mission at Oswegatchie, see the biography of Abbe Picquet in Robert Lahaise, "Picquet, François," in *DCB*, vol. 4 (Toronto, 2003–), accessed 3 June 2021, http://www.biographi.ca/en/bio/picquet_francois_4E.html.
32. Bass *Journal*, 450.
33. Nathaniel Woodhull was born on 30 December 1722 in Smithtown, Long Island, to Nathaniel Woodhull Sr. and Sarah Smith. His family had been prominent in New York affairs since the mid-seventeenth century. In 1758, the thirty-six-year-old Woodhull was known as a competent militia officer and a muster master for Suffolk County. He transferred from the militia to the New York provincial regiment in the rank of major in April 1758. In 1760, Woodhull was made colonel of the Third New York Regiment and participated in the 1760 expedition against Montreal via Lake Ontario and the St. Lawrence. Woodhull kept a journal throughout the campaign and provides a provincial's view of the invasion of Canada under General Amherst. After the end of hostilities, he returned to farming and community affairs. In 1761, he married Ruth Floyd (1732–1822), the sister of William Floyd, a signer of the Declaration of Independence. Sentiment against British taxation of the colonies led to Suffolk County electing Woodhull to the Province of New York assembly, where he served from 1769 to 1775. As such, he spoke against the Crown's colonial policies and represented Suffolk in the convention that chose delegates to the First Continental Congress. In May 1775, the New York Provincial Congress assumed control of the colony and reorganized the militia. In August, Woodhull was elected president of the congress, and in October he was made brigadier general of the Suffolk and Queen's County militia. In August 1776, on the eve of the Battle of Long Island, Woodhull's militia was detailed to drive livestock east to prevent their falling into British hands. Woodhull's troops drove 1,400 cattle out onto the Hempstead Plains, but their commander was captured near Jamaica by a British cavalry detachment and was struck with a sword multiple times, suffering severe arm and head injuries. He was taken to a cattle transport serving as a prison ship in Gravesend Bay. A sympathetic British officer had him released to a hospital where his gangrenous arm was amputated

in an effort to save his life. Nathaniel Woodhull died on 20 September 1776, at age fifty-four, with his wife, Ruth, by his side. The general was buried at his family home in Mastic, Long Island. See "Nathaniel Woodhull," *Dictionary of American Biography* (New York, 1939), 20:492–93; and *NYCD*, 8:295–96.

34. Isaac Corsa was a wealthy merchant ("Corsa and Bull") of Huguenot extraction from New York City. He served as a captain of a Westchester company in Col. William Cockcroft's Regiment of the New York forces assembled in 1755. Two years later, he was captain of a New York company that served at Fort William Henry. In spring 1758, the experienced Corsa was promoted to major of the 1st Battalion, New York Regiment, and after the Battle of Ticonderoga, in July, to lieutenant colonel in the field to replace its fallen commander, Bartholomew Roux. One of two officers wounded during the Frontenac raid, he earned high praise from Bradstreet for leading his men from the front. Corsa would go on to command the 1st New York Regiment the following summer, but he and his Yorkers would be left at Oswego as part of the garrison and to help build a new Fort Ontario. In 1760, Corsa was promoted to full colonel of the 2nd New York Regiment and accompanied Amherst's expedition to capture Montreal. On the outbreak of the American Revolution, "he clung to the Crown" and on 12 August 1776 was arrested by order of General Washington and sent as prisoner to Norwich and Middleton. He was released upon giving his parole not to take up arms. He was married to Sarah Franklin, sister of Walter Franklin of Maspeth, and acquired the latter's estate upon his death. Colonel Corsa died at Flushing on 3 May 1803; his estate was later absorbed by Fordham University. See "Biographical Sketches," *Colonial Records of the New York Chamber of Commerce, 1768–1784* (New York, 1867), 129; and *JJA*, 1:79.

35. Clinton *Journal*, 306.
36. Bougainville *Journals*, 22.
37. *Impartial Account*, 16–17.
38. Lake seiches can occur quickly: on 13 July 1995, a large seiche on Lake Superior caused the water level to fall and then rise again by three feet (1 m) within fifteen minutes, leaving some boats hanging from the docks on their mooring lines when the water retreated. The same storm system that caused the 1995 seiche on Lake Superior produced a similar effect in Lake Huron, in which the water level at Port Huron changed by six feet (1.8 m) over two hours. On Lake Michigan, it cost eight fishermen their lives when a ten-foot (3 m) seiche hit the Chicago waterfront on 26 June 1954. See Alexander B. Rabinovich, "Seiches and Harbor Oscillations," in *Handbook of Coastal and Ocean Engineering*, ed. Young C. Kim (Los Angeles, 2012), 243–86; Ulrich Lemmin, "Surface Seiches," in *Encyclopedia of Lakes and Reservoirs*, ed. Lars Bengtsson et al. (Berlin, 2012), 751–53.
39. *Impartial Account*, 16; Albertson *Memoirs*.
40. Beauchamp, *Indian Names of Places*, 92.
41. Clinton *Journal*, 306.
42. Clinton *Journal*, 306; *Impartial Account*, 17–18.
43. *Impartial Account*, 17.
44. Pouchot *Memoirs*, 379. The Thousand Islands (French: Mille-Îles) are an archipelago of 1,864 islands that straddle the Canada–US border where Lake Ontario drains into the beginning of the St. Lawrence River in its northeast corner. Stretching for about fifty miles (80 km) downriver from Kingston, Ontario, the

Canadian islands are in the province of Ontario, and the US islands are in the New York state. The islands range in size from over forty square miles (100 sq. km) to smaller islands occupied by a single residence, or uninhabited outcroppings of rocks. To count as one of the Thousand Islands, emergent land within the river channel must have at least one square foot (0.093 sq. m) of land above water level year-round, and support at least two living trees.

45. See "Sketch of the River St Lawrence from Lake Ontario to Montreal by an Onondaga Indian," 1759, British Library Collection, Norman B. Leventhal Map and Education Center, accessed 29 July 2021, https://collections.leventhalmap.org/search/commonwealth:hx11z0861.
46. Clinton *Journal*, 307.
47. Albertson *Memoirs*.
48. In Woodland Indian rituals, ceremonies, and religious observances, tobacco was seen as a means of direct communication between humans and the spiritual powers. It was said that the *manidog* (spirits) were extremely fond of tobacco and that the only way they could get it was from humans, either by smoke from a pipe or by offerings of dry tobacco. In almost all facets of their lives, the Haudenosaunee people and other Great Lakes tribes solicited the spirits for acts of kindness and protection or to give thanks for past favors. Before setting out in a canoe, a safe return was assured by offering tobacco on the water. On journeys or hunts, warriors left a pinch of tobacco as an offering when they encountered certain features of the landscape, including waterfalls, misshapen trees, oddly shaped rocks, and lakes or islands believed to harbor spirits. Dry tobacco was placed at the base of a tree or shrub from which medicine was gathered, and a pinch was thrown in the water before each day of wild rice gathering to assure calm weather and a bountiful harvest. When storms approached, families protected themselves by placing a small amount of tobacco on a nearby rock or stump. Tobacco was placed at graves as an offering to the departed spirit. Requests to elders to relate oral traditions or other special knowledge were accompanied by a gift of tobacco. "Ceremonial Use of Tobacco," in Alanson Skinner, *The Mascoutens or Prairie Potawatomi Indians*, pt. 3: *Mythology and Folklore, Bulletin of the Public Museum of the City of Milwaukee* 6, no. 3 (1927): 327–411.
49. Albertson *Memoirs*.
50. Albertson *Memoirs*.

Chapter 4

1. "La nuit du vendredi au samedi, les deux barques furent tâtées par une trentaine de berges angloises qui furent repoussées avec perte d'une vingtaine d'hommes de leur part." (Our two ships were attacked by about 30 whaleboats of English but these were repulsed with the loss of about 20 men on their part.) "Détail," 448; Wall's Account, 166–67; Capt. Thomas Sowers to the Commissioners of the Ordnance, 1 October 1758, Schenectady on the Mohawk River, *RFF*, 267–68.
2. Lt. Archibald Macaulay to Capt. Horatio Gates, 30 August 1758, Oswego, CO/5/50, pt. 3, 661–62.
3. Cleaveland *Journal*, 227–28; *Impartial Account*, 20 (author's emphases).
4. Albertson *Memoirs*; Wall's Account, 167; Charles Clinton to Col. Oliver Delancey, 30 August 1758, Oswego, reprinted in *London Chronicle*, 28–31 October 1758; "Copy

of letter from Capt. Peter Jacquet to Capt. Daniel de Normandie, dated 3 August 1758, Oswego," *London Chronicle*, 28–31 October 1758; Capt. de Normandie to Cadwallader Colden, September 1758, Albany, Bundle 96, f. 78, Chatham MSS, BL.
5. *Impartial Account*, 18.
6. Seven British brass eighteen-pounders, sixteen-pounders, and fourteen-pounders captured two years previously at Oswego could also easily throw shot a mile, but there is no record of them being found in the captured fort by Bradstreet's men, which probably indicates they were too valuable for retention at a frontier post and were redeployed to a more important post such as Quebec or Louisbourg. For a list of British ordnance, ammunition, and powder captured by the French at Oswego and taken to Frontenac in 1756, see *NYCD*, Paris Docs, 12:444; most of the iron guns of Fort Frontenac were spiked by the French themselves before their 1758 surrender, making the task of neutralizing them for further use much easier for the British. Some trunnions were knocked off by the British, and such guns numbering some sixty pieces along with twenty mortars were found lying outside Fort Frontenac by Maj. John Ross in 1783 when he came to Cataraqui. Most of these cannons were later recovered from the bottom of Deadman's Bay below old Fort Henry, where two War of 1812 warships were deliberately sunk, the 1758 ordnance found by Ross having been repurposed as ships' ballast half a century later; see "List and Description of Iron Ordnance at Caderaque 16th of June 1783," in Richard Preston, ed., *Kingston before the War of 1812: A Collection of Documents* (Toronto, 1959), 20.
7. Albertson *Memoirs*.
8. Clinton to Delancey, 30 August 1758.
9. Albertson *Memoirs*; *Impartial Account*, 20.
10. See George Smith, *Universal Military Dictionary* (London, 1779; reprint, Ottawa, 1979), 87–88.
11. *Impartial Account*, 18 (author's emphasis).
12. *Impartial Account*, 19.
13. Rea *Journal*, 61.
14. *Impartial Account*, 19.
15. Clinton to Delancey, 30 August 1758; Interestingly, Bradstreet's field-expedient technique of using preexisting French breastworks to his advantage was the same move used by General Amherst the following year in his quick and dirty 1759 siege of Fort Ticonderoga. He too would occupy preexisting French earthworks, pierce and repurpose them for siege guns, then cow a weak and outnumbered garrison into vacating the objective.
16. *Impartial Account*, 20.
17. Louis-Auguste-Joseph-Victor d'Espinassy (1730–1806) was the son of Pierre-Francois d'Espinassy and Louise-Francoise Belhomme de Neuville. He was commissioned *ensigne en pied* in the 2ème compagnie du canonniers-bombariers du Canada on 19 March 1757 and, a year later, was repairing the defenses at Fort Niagara. In August 1758, he took a work party to Fort Frontenac to get quarried stone and was caught up in its defense. He and his men received high praise for his working of the guns during the raid. and upon the fort's capitulation he escaped and made his way back to Oswegatchie on foot with his men and the boat crews. A year later, he would marry the daughter of Capt. Guilliame de Lorimier, the French

officer who had commanded the small garrison at Oswegatchie, and in 1760, he resigned his commission and took his wife back to France. He later rejoined the army, for in 1777, while stationed at Île-de-France, he was made a chevalier of the Order of Saint-Louis and colonel-commandant of the companies at Île-de-France. He died at Pamplemousse, Île-de-France, in 1806. Marcel Fournier, *Les officers des troupes de la Marine au Canada, 1683–1760* (Quebec, 2017), 353–54; Aegidius Fauteux, *Les Chevaliers de St Louis en Canada* (Montreal, 1940), 218–19; François-Alexandre Aubert de La Chesnaye Des Bois, *Dictionnaire de la noblesse* . . . (Paris, 1873), 6:111.

18. "Détail," 448–49.
19. Jean-Guillaume Plantavit de la Pause, "Observations and Notes on Fort Frontenac," *RFF*, 251.
20. See Mitsuyoshi Yabe et al., "Chronological Restoration of Fort Frontenac in 3D for Heritage Visualization," *Journal of Civil Engineering and Architecture* 9 (2015): 1463–73.
21. La Pause, "Observations and Notes," *RFF*, 251.
22. La Pause, 251.
23. Dr. Alexander Coventry, *Memoirs of an Emigrant: The Journal of Alexander Coventry, M.D., in Scotland, the United States and Canada 1783–1831* (Albany, 1973), 173.
24. *Impartial Account*, 20n.
25. Albertson *Memoirs*; *Impartial Account*, 20.
26. Clinton *Journal*, 311.
27. "Détail," 448–49.
28. Wall's Account, 166–67.
29. "Détail," 448–49.
30. Bass *Journal*, 450.
31. *Impartial Account*, 22.
32. *Impartial Account*, 22.

Chapter 5

1. Albertson *Memoirs*.
2. Capt. Thomas Butler to Sir William Johnson, 28 August 1758, Cadaracqui, *RFF*, 262.
3. *Impartial Account*, 21.
4. Translation of letter by General Abercromby to Colonel Schuyler, 1 October 1758, Camp Lake George, enclosed in M. de Vaudreuil to M. de Massiac, 3 November 1758, Montreal, *NYCD*, 10:877–80.
5. Vaudreuil to Abercromby, 1 October 1758, Montreal, *NYCD*, 10:878–80. In this letter, Vaudreuil claims that the victim was "beheaded"; Albertson, who was there, asserts in his *Memoirs* that the victim had his head bashed in with a rock; Thomas Butler, who also was there, simply reported that the French sailor was scalped (Butler to Johnson, *RFF*, 262)—the latter occurrence the only point on which all three seemed to agree.
6. See General Abercromby to Pitt, 28 April 1758, New York; Col. Peter Schuyler to Pitt [n.d.; received 1 June 1758]; and Pitt to Abercromby, 10 June 1758, Whitehall—all in *CWP*, 225–34, 268–69.

7. Clinton *Journal*, 311.
8. *Boston News-Letter*, 21 September 1758; *Boston Evening Post*, 18 September 1758; *Boston Weekly Advertiser*, 18 September 1758.
9. Albertson *Memoirs*.
10. Rea *Journal*, 61; *Impartial Account*, 21.
11. *Impartial Account*, 21–22.
12. Clinton *Journal*, 315; *Impartial Account*, 25.
13. Bass *Journal*, 450. At least one historian has argued that a New Englander's masculinity was also another underlying motivational factor, militarism being a symbol of manhood. Going to war was not just a political necessity or financially rewarding activity, but also a societal one. Ann Little posits that New England soldiers needed to show their masculine superiority over the Catholics, especially as they typically depicted Catholics as being effeminate. Ann M. Little, *Abraham in Arms: War and Gender in Colonial New England* (Philadelphia, 2007), 167–68.
14. Bradstreet to Gould, 21 September 1758, quoted in *PPP*, 133.
15. *Impartial Account*, 26.
16. Courville *Mémoires*, 114–15; C. J. Russ, "Lefebvre Duplessis Faber, François," in *DCB*, vol. 3 (Toronto, 2003–), accessed 23 October 2020, http://www.biographi.ca/en/bio/lefebvre_duplessis_faber_francois_3E.html.
17. Anne-Joseph-Hyppolite de Maurès, Comte de Malartic, *Journal des campagnes au Canada de 1755 à 1760*, ed. Paul Gaffarel (Dijon, 1890), 200.
18. See Marquis de Vaudreuil to Messiac, 1 November 1758, Montreal, *RFF*, 271–73.
19. Courville *Mémoires*, 115–16.
20. Lt. John McKeane to Capt. Horatio Gates, 3 September 1758, Oswego, AB, 586.
21. Wall's Account, 166.
22. Albertson *Memoirs*; *Impartial Account*, 24.
23. *Impartial Account*, 26.
24. Bradstreet merely states that the ships ran aground "on the island opposite to the fort." This "island" may have been the mainland or eastern side of the Cataraqui River due east of the fort, as all eyewitnesses agree that the ships never made it out of the harbor. Becalmed and unable to make headway, both ships became sitting ducks. Peter Jacquet, a boatbuilder and an experienced ship's captain, recorded the fate of the two abandoned ships, stating that the two French crews were obliged "by the hotness of our fire . . . to take to their boats and let the vessels drive; which they did, and went ashore about five miles below the fort." Jacquet wrote "drive," meaning that the southerly headwind "drove" (a nautical term) the ships north back into the basin. He also states "below the fort," which can be interpreted as "downriver." *Impartial Account*, 21.

Lieutenant Sowers's 1758 map prepared after the raid (later published in *Gentleman's Magazine*) clearly shows that the British believed Fort Frontenac to be situated at the "Head of the St. Lawrence" and have mislabeled the mouth of the Cataraqui River just so. A second extant map (most certainly a copy of a seventeenth-century French map because of the place nomenclature used and the fact that the Iroquois are shown as still inhabiting the north shore of the lake when, in fact, they were driven out in the Beaver Wars of the late seventeenth century) shows the Cataraqui Basin as a giant bay with the fort located on the *wrong side* of the Kingston Peninsula. If these maps constitute the collective British awareness and knowledge of the fort's location and its local topography in 1758, then Belle Island, in their minds, was certainly "below the Fort." As no one specifically states which "island" it was, or gives a simple heading such as southwest or northeast from the fort, or some other point of reference, we are left with just a few tantalizing clues and facts that might pinpoint the abandoned ships' final resting place after the siege.

The Yorkers and rangers (who recovered the ships) were stationed on the northwest side of the fort when they first saw them drive aground. Located in the vicinity of the fascine battery, the provincials would have had a front-row seat to watch the ships being "driven" to Belle Island or somewhere on the eastern river shoreline beyond. Bradstreet stated that the boats had to be "refloated" the following morning, which implies a couple of possibilities: (1), the ships had been hulled so badly by shot and shell that they had to be first repaired, caulked, then pumped out, and (2), they may have had to jettison some or all of the two ships' cannons to lighten them to get off the muddy shoreline. The latter is probably the case or perhaps a combination of the two. The ships' guns were no longer required as there were no other ships to oppose them on the lake. Their last voyage would be the transportation of the plunder (and British artillery) seventy-five miles back to Oswego, where Bradstreet intended to unload and then scuttle them.

Interestingly, *if* all the ships' guns were jettisoned, then those thirty-two pieces of ordnance still lie somewhere deep in the mud of the Cataraqui River near Belle Island, waiting for an astute marine archaeologist to discover them someday. My thanks to an old colleague, John Grenville, a former fellow Fort Henry guardsman, a retired Parks Canada mandarin, and an expert on British artillery and fortifications, for pondering on this particular mystery with me as well as helping shed some light on the fate of the other French artillery ordnance found lying outside the fort. My thanks also to Kingston archaeologist Dr. Sue Bazeley for helping me confirm the locations of the two siege batteries based on local archaeological digs and her extensive knowledge of the early cartography and topography of Kingston: the five-gun "breaching" battery established in the French embankment running parallel with Brock Street and along the crest of the hill where Kingston's City Hall and its market now stand; and the two-gun fascine battery, which was located in the vicinity of the intersection of modern-day Rideau Street and the aptly named Ordnance Street.

25. Capt. Thomas Butler to Sir William Johnson, 28 August 1758, Cadaracqui, *SWJP*, 2:889–90.
26. Rea *Journal*, 62.
27. Shute *Journal*, 14.
28. Dorr *Journal*, 459.
29. Dorr *Journal*, 460.
30. Bass *Journal*, 451.
31. "Bradstreet's Orders," 8 September 1758, Fort Bull, Clinton *Journal*, 314.
32. Albertson *Memoirs*; see also Anderson, *People's Army*, 158. It is unlikely that Albertson's share is in pounds sterling. Most colonists recorded values in their local currency. In the mid-1750s, New Jersey currency was the equivalent of about 62.5 percent of the same amount in sterling. So, Albertson's share was more like £4, 12 shillings in sterling.

33. General Stanwix to General Abercromby, 29 September 1758, Camp at Onida Station, *RFF*, 267.
34. See VSOB; Dorr *Journal*, 459–63; [Capt. Richard Atkins], Atkins' Orderly Book, in "The Expedition to Fort Craven, Oneida Great Carrying Place and Frontenac in 1758," *Colonial Wars: A Quarterly Magazine* (Boston, 1913), 178–215; and Sarah Fatherly, "Tending the Army: Women and the British General Hospital in North America, 1754–1763," *Early American Studies* 10, no. 3 (2012): 566–99, accessed 18 April 2020, www.jstor.org/stable/23546694.
35. *Boston Evening-Post*, November 1758. One is reminded of frontline soldiers who survived the rigors of trench warfare in the Great War only to succumb to the ravages of the Spanish flu pandemic.
36. On Daniel Wall's resignation, see entry, 25 October 1758, Fort Stanwix, VSOB.
37. General Stanwix to General Abercromby, 22 October 1758, AB, 471.
38. Albertson *Memoirs*.
39. On Ebenezer Seeley's resignation, see entry, 15 September 1758, Camp Onyda Station, VSOB.
40. Clinton *Journal*, 315.

Chapter 6

1. M. Daine to Marshal de Belle Isle, 17 October 1758, Quebec; and M. André Doreil to Marshal de Belle Isle, 3 September 1758, both in *NYCD*, 10:834, 821.
2. M. de Montcalm to Marshal de Belle Isle, 9 September 1758, Montreal, *NYCD*, 10:831.
3. M. de Montcalm to Marshal de Belle Isle, 9 September 1758, 10:821.
4. Marquis de Vaudreuil to Massiac, 2 September 1758, Montreal, *RFF*, 264.
5. W. J. Eccles, *France in North America* (Toronto, 1972), 195n.
6. Marquis de Vaudreuil to Massiac, 3 October 1758, Montreal, *RFF*, 271. Vaudreuil implies that Bradstreet's men were in "such haste" and fear that they jettisoned their clothing and muskets at Oswego. This is wishful thinking on the French governor's part. If one examines the context of the moment closely, provincials were facing a long upriver slog in which everything would have to be carried on their backs or in their boats. Many provincials, no doubt, donned new shirts, boots, and clothing from their loot, and dropped their older clothing where it fell before getting into the boats. Logically, the same must have occurred with weapons, officers and men upgrading broken or inferior pieces to those found at Cataraqui with newer and better-quality weapons.
7. Marquis de Montcalm, "Reflections on the Measures to Be Adopted for the Defence of the Colony" [n.d.], *NYCD*, 10:874.
8. Col. Peter Schuyler (1710–62) was born in Bergen County, New Jersey, the son of Swantje Van Duyckhuysen (1679–1724) and Arent Schuyler (1662–1730) of Rensselaerswyck (now Albany), New York. By 1710, the patriarchs of his branch of the large Schuyler family were early copper-mining magnates in New Jersey, and on his father's death, Peter inherited nearly eight hundred acres of land along with a large house in Elizabethtown and a third of the copper mines' revenue. A good marriage to the daughter of his father's business partner, a wealthy merchant in New York, increased his holdings, fortune, and status overnight. On 16 July 1746, he was offered the command of the New Jersey Regiment by the New Jersey Provincial

Council and commanded it until it was disbanded in 1747. He was called on again in 1754 to take command of the Blues for the French war and commanded them until he was captured, along with just over half of his regiment, at the surrender of Oswego in 1756. While the majority of his men were released on parole that year, he and the regimental surgeon, Benjamin Stakes, were held at Quebec. In October 1757, Governor Vaudreuil granted Schuyler parole to return to his home "to obtain funds to enable [him] to live in Canada." Schuyler was accorded a hero's welcome, not for his military accomplishments but for his "great Support of many English Prisoners, without whose Assistance several of them would have been reduced to the greatest Extremities." While on parole, Schuyler complained to William Pitt that he was "Impatient of Confinement, . . . [when my] Country needs [my] best Service." But despite Pitt's concern and the repeated efforts of General Abercromby, no exchange could be arranged. In an angry letter to Abercromby in June 1758, Vaudreuil recalled Schuyler, who returned in August authorized to negotiate prisoner exchanges, and he would not be released until after the capture of Frontenac, his freedom explicitly negotiated as a key part of the prisoner exchange agreed upon in the fort's capitulation. Exchanged at the same time as Colonel Schuyler were 143 other prisoners, many of whom had been redeemed from their French and Indian masters by monies out of the good colonel's personal purse. Schuyler would attend to personal business at home over the winter of 1758–59 and then rejoined his beloved Jersey Blues under General Amherst's command for the 1759 and 1760 campaigns. In November 1760, he retired to his "Peterboro" estate on the Passaic River, where he died on 7 March 1762. "Peter Schuyler," *JJA*, 2:34; John David Krugler, "Schuyler, Peter (1710–62)," in *DCB*, vol. 3 (Toronto, 2003–), accessed 12 April 2020, https://www.biographi.ca/en/bio/schuyler_peter_1710_62_3E.html.

9. Robert Eastburn, *A Faithful Narrative of the Many Dangers and Sufferings, as Well as Wonderful Deliverances of Robert Eastburn, during His Captivity among the Indians* (Philadelphia, 1758), 29, accessed 29 March 2020, https://archive.org/details/faithfulnarrativooeast/page/28/mode/2up; Jean Lowry, *A Journal of the Captivity of Jean Lowry and Her Children, Giving an Account of Her Being Taken by the Indians, the 1st of April 1756, from WILLIAM Mccord's, in Rocky-Spring Settlement in Pennsylvania, with an Account of the Hardships She Suffered, &c*, (Philadelphia, 1760), 17.

10. C. H. Winesfield, *History of the County of Hudson, New Jersey* (New York, 1874), 539–41; Annis Boudinot, "To the Honourable Col. Peter Schuyler," *New York Mercury*, 9 January 1758, quoted in Lyman H. Butterfield, "Morven: A Colonial Outpost of Sensibility, with Some Hitherto Unpublished Poems by Annis Boudinot Stockton," *Princeton University Library Chronicles* 6 (1944): 1–15. For a discussion of the poet Stockton, see Carla Mulford, *Only for the Eye of a Friend: The Poems of Annis Boudinot Stockton* (Charlottesville, VA, 1995).

> Dear to each Muse, and to thy Country dear,
> Welcome once more to breathe thy native Air:
> Not half so cheering is the solar Ray,
> To the harsh Rigour of a Winter's Day;
> Not half so grateful fanning Breezes rise,
> When the hot Dog Star burns the Summer Skies;
> CAESARAE's [Jersey] Shore with Acclamation rings,

And, Welcome SCHUYLER, every Shepherd sings.
See for thy Brows, the Laurel is prepar'd,
And justly deem'd, a PATRIOT, thy Reward;
Ev'n future Ages shall enroll thy Name,
In sacred Annals of immortal Fame.

11. *New York Mercury*, 4 December 1758, in *New Jersey Colonial Documents* (Paterson, NJ, 1898), 20:300; William Adee Whitehead, *Contributions to the Early History of Perth Amboy and Adjoining Country* . . . (New York, 1856), 116–18.

12. Sylvanus Johnson (1748–1832) was born 25 January 1748, the son of James Johnson (1725–58) and Susannah Willard (1730–1810). The account of his mother, Susannah, of his family's ordeals as prisoners of the French and Indians entitled *A Narrative of the Captivity of Mrs. Johnson* was first published in 1796. Widely popular, it went through numerous printings, but was substantially different from earlier published captivity narratives in that it avoided any gruesome sensationalism and was actually sympathetic to the Native Americans' plight. True connoisseurs of the captivity narrative claim the ninth edition to be the best version as it was the last she personally edited. Sylvanus did not return with his mother and father, Capt. James Johnson, in a 1757 prisoner exchange. Instead he chose to remain with his adopted Abenaki family at Odanak (St. Francis). Redeemed the following year by Colonel Schuyler and included in the exchange for Frontenac garrison parolees, the eleven-year-old Sylvanus returned home to find his father dead, just one of over 1,000 British killed or wounded at the Battle of Ticonderoga on 8 July 1758. His redemption from St. Francis in 1758, however, was a providential sign, in that he was nowhere near it when it was razed to the ground by Robert Rogers and his rangers the following year. While Sylvanus's freedom was a blessing to a grateful but grieving mother, he was also a trial as he insisted on wearing Indian clothing and spoke only Abenaki and a few words of French. His oldest sister, Susanna, remained in Montreal with a Canadian Catholic family until September 1760 and the British conquest. Upon her return, Susanna Johnson's changeling daughter could speak only French. Henry Saunderson (among other nineteenth-century local historians) claims in his *History of Charlestown, New Hampshire* that Sylvanus Johnson "so much preferred the modes of Indian life to the prevalent customs of civilization, that he often expressed regret at having been ransomed. He always maintained, and no arguments could convince him to the contrary, that the Indians were a far more moral race than the whites." His boyhood captivity apparently had no long-term effects on his life and health, as he died at eighty-four in 1832, "leaving the reputation of an honest and upright man." See also Stephen Brumwell, *White Devil: A True Story of War, Savagery and Vengeance in Colonial America* (London, 2004), 22–26, 29–31, 45–47, 125–26, 237, 260, 281–82; Ian K. Steele, *Betrayals: Fort William Henry and the "Massacre"* (New York, 1990), 10–17, 138, 147, 226n10; Jeanne Holland, "Johnson, Susannah Willard (1729–1810)," in *The Oxford Companion to Women's Writing in the United States*, ed. Cathy N. Davidson and Linda Wagner-Martin (New York, 1995), 448; Colleen Allyn Gray, "Captives in Canada, 1744–1763" (MA thesis, McGill University, 1993); Emma Lewis Coleman, *New England Captives Carried to Canada between 1677 and 1760 during the French and Indian Wars* (Portland, ME, 1925), 2:308; and Henry Hamilton Saunderson, *History of Charlestown, New Hampshire* (Charlestown, NH, 1876), 448.

13. George W. Schuyler, *Colonial New York: Philip Schuyler and His Family* (New York, 1885), 2:210–11; *New York Mercury*, 1 April 1762; John David Krugler, "Peter Schuyler (1710–62)," in *DCB*, vol. 3 (Toronto, 2003–), accessed 24 March 2020, https://www.biographi.ca/en/bio/schuyler_peter_1710_62_3E.html.
14. Americanus, "On Col. Bradstreet's Success," *Boston News-Letter*, 12 October 1758, 31:2925; *New London Summary*, 29 September 1758, 42:8; and *New Hampshire Gazette*, 20 October 1758, 33:107.
15. Bradstreet to Gould, 5 August 1759, quoted in *PPP*, 145.
16. Albertson *Memoirs*.
17. Brigadiers Gage and Prevost to General Abercromby, 20 July 1758, Lake George Camp, [in French] quoted in McCulloch, "Believe Us, Sir" *BFTM*, 101.
18. Bradstreet to Charles Gould, 9 December 1759, quoted in *PPP*, 149 (author's emphasis).
19. Dr. Richard Huck to Lord Loudoun, 13 December 1758, New York, LO, 5971.
20. *Impartial Account*, 31 (author's emphasis).
21. Johnson to Abercromby, 17 September 1758, Fort Johnson, *SWJP*, 10:4–8.
22. See George Washington Papers, *Bradstreet's Journal*, 1 January 1778.
23. George Washington Papers, *Bradstreet's Journal*, 1 January 1778.
24. George Washington to Major General John Sullivan, 31 May 1779, Middlebrook, *The Papers of George Washington*, Revolutionary War Series, vol. 20, 8 April–31 May 1779, ed. Edward G. Lengel (Charlottesville, VA, 2010), 716–19.
25. See Sullivan's Report to Congress, in John Sullivan, *Journals of the Military Expedition of Major General John Sullivan against the Six Nations . . .* , prep. by Frederick Cook (Auburn, NY, 1887), 303.
26. See esp. the important introductory essay in Charles M. Johnson, *The Valley of the Six Nations: A Collection of Documents on the Indian Lands of the Grand River* (Toronto, 2013); Barbara Graymont, *The Iroquois in the American Revolution* (Syracuse, NY, 1975); and Carl Benn, *The Iroquois in the War of 1812* (Toronto, 1998); and "Grand River (Oswekin) . . . ," *Encyclopedia of the Haudenosaunee*, ed. Bruce Elliott Johansen and Barbara Alice Mann (Westport, CT, 2000), 131.

Chapter 7

1. For the best scholarly monograph to date on the St. Francis raid, see Brumwell, *White Devil*.
2. James Austen Holden, "How the State and the Historical Association May Be of Mutual Assistance," *Proceedings of the New York State Historical Association* 13 (1914): 307, accessed 22 October 2020, http://www.jstor.org/stable/42889465. One might also remind Austen and others of his ilk that the history of New York being written by a Bay Colony historian is not as egregious as white people purporting to write the history of indigenous peoples with little or no idea of their language, culture, ethnography, or oral history. See Bruce G. Trigger, *Natives and Newcomers: Canada's "Heroic Age" Reconsidered* (Kingston, ON, 1985), 2–45, 288–301.
3. Frégault, *Canada*, 223.
4. René Chartrand, "Fort Frontenac: Saving Face after Ticonderoga," *Osprey Military Journal* 3, no. 2 (2001): 21–22; see also Susan M. Bazely, "Le fort Frontenac sur la route des Pays-d'en-Haut," *Cap-aux-Diamants*, no. 66 (2001): 15–18.

5. For an excellent assessment of Montcalm's leadership capabilities and limitations, see Michael Boire, "Le Marquis de Montcalm and the Battle for Québec, September 1759: A Re-assessment," *Canadian Military Journal* (Summer 2006), 77–84; for a comprehensive review and discussion of the letter wars conducted from the colony to France by the governor and his senior military commander, see Nester, *Epic Battles for Ticonderoga*, 175–205; and Stanley, *New France*, 211–14.
6. *Impartial Account*, 30.
7. Vaudreuil to the Minister, 30 October 1758, RFF, 271, 456–57; Malcomson, *Warships of the Great Lakes*, 16–20; R. J. Andrews, "Two Ships—Two Flags: The *Outaouaise*/Williamson and the *Iroquoise*/Anson on Lake Ontario, 1759–1761," *Northern Mariner/Le marin du nord* 14, no. 3 (July 2004): 41–55.
8. Malcomson, *Warships of the Great Lakes*, 29–30.
9. For a good overview of the years and months leading up to the 1758 Treaty of Easton, as well as highlighting George Croghan's involvement as Sir William Johnson's righthand man, see William J. Campbell, "An Adverse Patron: Land, Trade and George Croghan," *Pennsylvania History: A Journal of Mid-Atlantic Studies* 76, no. 2 (2009): 117–40, accessed 24 October 2020, http://www.jstor.org/stable/27778883.
10. Dr Richard Huck to Lord Loudoun, 13 December 1758, New York, LO, 5971.
11. Dorr *Journal*, 464.
12. Ian Hamilton, *A Staff Officer's Scrap-Book during the Russo-Japanese War* (London, 1906), 1:v.
13. See Francis Parkman, *Montcalm and Wolfe*, vol. 2 of *France and England in North America* (London, 1884), 134–35; and Richard C. Vitzhum, "The Historian as Editor: Francis Parkman's Reconstruction of Sources in *Montcalm and Wolfe*," *Journal of American History* 53, no. 3 (December 1966): 471–86.
14. Parkman, *Montcalm and Wolfe*, 134–35; J. W. Fortescue, *A History of the British Army* (London, 1910; reprint, 2004), 2:338; Gipson, *Great War for the Empire*, 238–39.
15. Parkman, *Montcalm and Wolfe*, 134–35; Fortescue, *A History of the British Army*, 2:338; Gipson, *Great War for the Empire*, 238–39.
16. Frégault, *Canada*, 223.
17. F. A. Anderson, *Crucible of War: The Seven Years' War and the Fate of Empire in British North America, 1754–1766* (New York, 2000), 264.
18. Steele, *Warpaths*, 213–14. Walter Borneman paraphrases Bradstreet's hindsight observations on Niagara, just as Gipson and Parkman did before him, but cannot resist in indulging in a little creative speculation of his own: "Had the bateau man known that the French garrison there numbered but forty men, [Bradstreet] might have relied on the odds of a speedy victory, raided without Abercromby's permission, and then simply begged forgiveness." He ignores the facts that Abercromby, the operational commander, returned to his senses and priorities after his stunning defeat and denied Bradstreet's request on his return to be allowed to conduct another raid against Niagara. Bradstreet's superior pointed out that no passage of a large armed force through Seneca lands had been negotiated, and more importantly, he had had to refocus his resources and efforts on his assigned operational objectives to the north. This refusal draws Borneman's ire; he then states that Abercromby was "clearly not recognizing the strategic coup that Bradstreet had just

wrought," a perfect example of a myopic historian not recognizing the difference between the tactical and strategic levels of war. Walter R. Borneman, *The French and Indian War: Deciding the Fate of North America* (New York, 2007), 143–50; see also Frank McLynn, *1759: The Year Britain Became Master of the World* (New York, 2004), 47, 153.

19. Benjamin Franklin, letter signed "A New Englander," in *London Chronicle; or, Universal Evening Post*, 10–12 May 1759.
20. *Impartial Account*, 28.

Appendix A

1. "Parade State of Fort Frontenac Garrison, 27 August 1758," *RFF*, 259–61.
2. Three key French officers at the siege who are *not* included on the garrison rolls are the artillery officer, Lt. Louis-Auguste-Joseph-Victor d'Espinassy from Fort Niagara, and the two naval captains, René-Hippolyte Pepin *dit* Laforce and Joseph Boucher, Sieur de la Broquerie. Their crews and men (approximately 20–30) escaped with them.
3. Ens. Pierre-Charles Daneau de Muy (1736–70) was born on 23 September 1736 at Montreal, the only son of Capt. Jacques-Pierre Daneau de Muy, a company commander in the *compagnies franches de la marine*, who had passed away earlier in the year commanding Fort Detroit. Pierre-Charles died on 16 February 1770 (aged thirty-three) at Boucherville, Quebec. "Daneau de Muy," Table 61, in *Tables généalogique de la Noblesse Québécoise du XVIIe au XIXe*, compiled by Yves Drolet (Montreal, 2009).

Appendix B

1. *RFF*, 260–61.

Note: Two civilians mentioned by name in the capitulation (see appendix J), but not reflected on this return because they were visitors, were Madame Barallon and her traveling companion, Mademoiselle Duvivier. *RFF*, 259–61, 451–54. The only "Barallon" or variant that appears in all of New France in Father Tanguay's acknowledged masterwork, *Dictionnaire Généalogique des Familles Canadiennes depuis la Fondation de la Colonie jusqua nos Jours, 1608–1890*, is the foreman of the St. Maurice Forges at Trois Rivières in 1748, Antoine-Claude Raimbault dit Baraillon. *A History of the St Maurice Forges* is more specific: he was an ensign of the colonial troops, a native of Paris born in 1720, who on 2 May 1757 married Marie-Catherine Dandonneau dit Du Sable. Why she and Duvivier were exempted from the POW lists is unknown but may have owed to the fact that Jean-Baptiste Bradstreet was the first cousin of Capt. le Fournier Dupont Viviers of the companies franches de la marine on Île Royale. In addition, a soldier of William Ogilvie's Independents (name unknown), captured the previous year at Fort Herkimer and employed at Cataraqui as the commandant's servant, was liberated. See Clinton's *Journal*, 311.

A more accurate return of civilians taken in the capitulation should thus read: 65 men, women, and children (which includes two wives and three children from appendix A). This figure, combined with 53 military personnel from appendix A, totaled 118 prisoners of war at the capitulation. Every British account inflated the numbers of military personnel in the garrison, ranging from 120 to 200 men, but the truth of the matter lies in the details of the capitulation. The "Bullfrog Effect" was definitely at play here, as no one was willing to admit that the tiny garrison had punched well above its weight. Only one British officer after the raid complimented the French defense, saying "the French behaved very brave before they gave up the fort." John McKeane to Horatio Gates, 3 September 1758, Oswego, AB, 586.

Appendix D

1. Compiled from a "Return of His Majesty's Troops Detached from the Oneida Station—15th August 1758 under the Command of Lieut. Colonel Bradstreet," AB; and "A Return Taken of the Detachment of the New York Regimt on ye Expedition, Camp at Lake Onida [sic] 18 August 1758," in Clinton's *Journal*, 305. These two key returns are the basis of this order of battle, as the numbers initially announced and tasked for provincial regiments to provide on 11 August at Oneida Station in General Stanwix's General Orders had to be adjusted slightly downward the day after, as disease and desertion took their toll, and again on 18 August after the force reached Lake Oneida. Just over 3,000 men made the expedition, with the provincials providing 97.5 percent of the manpower. If one takes into consideration that all of the rank and file for the New York Independent Companies (NYIC) were recruited locally in the colonies, one might say it was wholly a provincial affair. Of the key staff officers and "regulars" above, four of the nine were American-born: Bradstreet (60th Foot), born in Nova Scotia; Capt. William Ogilvie (NYIC), born in Connecticut; Capt. John Butler (Indian Service), born in Connecticut; and Capt. Peter Jacquet (Battoemen), born in Delaware.
2. The NYIC composite company comprised the men of Captain Horatio Gates's Independent Company, in addition to Peter Wraxall's company, two of Gates's lieutenants, Archibald Macaulay and John McKeane, as well as the NYIC staff officers: Richard Shuckburgh, surgeon for all four companies; his surgeon's mate, John Cochran; and the adjutant, Lt. Archibald Montague Brown, NYIC.

Bibliography

Primary Sources
Archival Collections
British Library, London
   Bouquet Collection
   Chatham Manuscripts
   George III Map Collection
   Sir Fredrick Haldimand Papers
Fort Ticonderoga Museum Collection
   Van Schaick, Captain Goose. Orderly Book, 1758.
Huntington Library, San Marino, CA
   James Abercromby Papers
   Earl of Loudoun Papers
Library and Archives Canada, Ottawa
   Bouquet Papers
   MG 11: Colonial Office Papers
   MG 13: War Office Papers
   MG 18-M: Northcliffe Collection
   National Map Collection
Library of Congress, Washington, DC
   Peter Force Collection
   James Grant Papers
   George Washington Papers, Series 4, General Correspondence
Massachusetts Historical Society, Boston
   Israel Williams Papers
National Archives, Kew, Surrey, UK
   Colonial Office Papers
      CO 5: America and West Indies, 1606–1807
   War Office Papers
      1: In-Letters
      4: Out-Letters, Secretary at War
      17: Returns
      25: General Registers

Stewart Museum, Montreal
    William Forbes Papers
William L. Clements Library, Ann Arbor, MI
    Jeffery Amherst Papers
    Thomas Gage Papers

Published Sources

"Account of Men Employed in the Bateau Service, 16–24 March 1756." *Transactions and Collections of the American Antiquarian Society*, 11:145. Worcester, 1909.

Albertson, Garret, Sr. *A Short Account of the Life, Travels and Adventures of Garret Albertson, Sr.* Belvedere, NJ, 1845 (privately printed; reprint, 1918). Accessed 22 February 2010, http://files.usgwarchives.net/nj/hunterdon/military/frenchindian/history/galbertson.txt.

Amherst, Jeffery. *The Journals of Jeffery Amherst, 1757–1763*. Edited by Robert J. Andrews. 2 vols. Ann Arbor, MI, 2005.

The Annual Register; or, a View of the History, Politicks, and Literature for the Year 1763. 7th ed. London, 1796.

[Atkins, Capt. Richard]. Atkins' Orderly Book, in "The Expedition to Fort Craven, Oneida Great Carrying Place and Frontenac in 1758." *Colonial Wars: A Quarterly Magazine* 1 (1913): 178–215.

Aumasson de Courville, Louis-Léonard. *Mémoires sur le Canada, depuis 1749 jusqu'à 1760*. Quebec, 1838.

Barrow, Abner. "Fragment of the Diary of Abner Barrow." *Colonial Wars: A Quarterly Magazine* 1 (1913): 215.

Bass, Lt. Benjamin. "Account of the Capture of Fort Frontenac by the Detachment under the Command of Col. Bradstreet." *New York History* 16, no. 4 (October 1935): 449–52.

Bougainville, Louis Antoine de. *Adventure in the Wilderness: The American Journals of Louis Antoine de Bougainville, 1756–1760*. Translated and edited by Edward P. Hamilton. Norman, OK, 1964.

[Bradstreet, Col. John]. *An Impartial Account of Lieut. Col. Bradstreet's Expedition to Fort Frontenac. . . .* London, 1759; reprint, Toronto, 1940.

Cleaveland, Rev. John. "Journal of the Rev. John Cleaveland, June 14, 1758–October 25, 1758." *Bulletin of the Fort Ticonderoga Museum* 10, no. 59 (1959).

Clinton, Lt. Col. Charles. "Colonel Charles Clinton's Journal of His Campaigns in New York July to October, 1758, during the French War." Edited by Robert E. Mulligan. *Bulletin of the Fort Ticonderoga Museum* 15, no. 4 (1992): 293–315.

Colden, Cadwallader. *The Letters and Papers of Cadwallader Colden, 1755–60*, vol. 5. New York, 1921.

Coventry, Dr. Alexander. *Memoirs of an Emigrant: The Journal of Alexander Coventry, M.D., in Scotland, the United States and Canada during the Period 1783–1831*. Albany, 1973.

Crane, Verner W., ed. *Benjamin Franklin's Letters to the Press, 1758–1775*. Chapel Hill, NC [1950].

Cross, Stephen. "Up to Ontario: Journal of Stephen Cross of Newbury Port . . . : The Activities of Newburyport Shipbuilders in Canada in 1756." *Essex Institute Historical Collections* 74 (1939): 334–57.

Dorr, Ens. Moses. "A Journal of an Expedition against Canaday by Moses Dorr Ensin of Capt. Parkers Company Roxbury May 25 1758." *New York History* 16, no. 4 (October 1935): 449–52.
Eastburn, Robert. *A Faithful Narrative of the Many Dangers and Sufferings, as Well as Wonderful Deliverances of Robert Eastburn, during His Captivity among the Indians.* Philadelphia, 1758 (reprint, 1904).
Forbes, John. *Writings of General John Forbes Relating to His Service in North America.* Edited by Alfred Proctor James. Menasha, WI, 1938.
Franklin, Benjamin. *Autobiography.* Edited by John Bigelow. New York, 1927.
Hastings (Johnson), Susannah. *A Narrative of the Captivity of Mrs. Johnson.* New York, 1841.
Hervey, William. *Journals of the Hon. William Hervey, in North America and Europe from 1755 to 1814; with Order Books at Montreal, 1760–1763.* Bury St. Edmunds, UK, 1906.
Johnson, Sir William. *The Papers of Sir William Johnson.* Edited by James Sullivan et al. 14 vols. Albany, 1921–63.
Kalm, Peter. *Travels in North America.* Translated and edited by Adolph B. Benson. New York, 1937 (reprint, 1964).
Knox, John. *An Historical Journal of the Campaigns in North America for the Years 1757, 1758, 1759, and 1760.* Edited by Arthur G. Doughty. 3 vols. Toronto, 1914.
Lee, Charles. *The Lee Papers.* Vol. 1, *1754–1776.* New York, 1871.
Malartic, Anne-Joseph-Hyppolite de Maurès, Comte de. *Journal des campagnes au Canada de 1755 à 1760.* Edited by Paul Gaffarel. Dijon, FR, 1890.
Mante, Thomas. *The History of the Late War in North America, and the Islands of the West Indies, Including the Campaigns of MDCCLXIII and MDCCLXIV against His Majesty's Indian Enemies.* London, 1772 (reprint, 1970).
McCulloch, Ian, and Earl Chapman, eds. *Orderly Books of the 78th Regiment of Foot, Fort Stanwix, New York, November 1758–April 1759.* Montreal, 2011.
Montcalm, Marquis de. *Journal des campagnes du marquis de Montcalm.* Edited by Abbe H-R. Casgrain. Vol. 11. Quebec, 1895.
O'Callaghan, E. B., and B. Fernow, eds. *Documents Relative to the Colonial History of the State of New York.* 15 vols. Albany, 1853–87.
Pargellis, Stanley M., ed. *Military Affairs in North America 1758–1763: Selected Documents from the Cumberland Papers in Windsor Castle.* London, 1936.
Pitt, William. *Correspondence of William Pitt . . . with Colonial Governors and Military and Naval Commanders in America.* Edited by Gertrude S. Kimball. 2 vols. New York, 1906 (reprint, New York, 1969).
Pouchot, Pierre. *Memoirs on the Late War in North America between France and England.* Edited by Brian L. Dunnigan. Yverdon-les-Bains, CH, 1781 (reprint, Youngstown, OH, 1994).
Preston, Richard, ed. *Kingston before the War of 1812: A Collection of Documents.* Toronto, 1959.
Preston, Richard, and Leopold Lamontagne, eds. *Royal Fort Frontenac.* Toronto, 1959.
Putnam, Rufus. *The Memoirs of Rufus Putnam and Certain Official Papers and Correspondence, 1738–1824.* Edited by Rowena Buell. Boston, 1903.
Rea, Dr. Caleb. *The Journal of Dr. Caleb Rea, Written during the Expedition against Ticonderoga in 1758.* Edited by F. M. Ray. Salem, MA, 1881.

Records of the Colony of Rhode Island and Providence Plantations in New England. Edited by John Russell Bartlett. Vol. 6, *1757–69*. Providence, 1863.

Shirley, William. *Correspondence of William Shirley, Governor of Massachusetts and Military Commander in America, 1731–1760.* 2 vols. Edited by Charles Henry Lincoln. New York, 1912.

Shute, Rev. Daniel. "A Journal of the Reverend Daniel Shute, D.D., Chaplain in the Expedition to Canada in 1758." Edited by James Kimball. *Essex Institute Historical Collections* 12 (1874): 132–51.

Sullivan, John. *Journals of the Military Expedition of Major General John Sullivan against the Six Nations of Indians, 1779, with Records Of Centennial Celebrations.* Prep. by Frederick Cook. Auburn, NY, 1887.

Tinkman, Seth. "Seth Tinkman's Diary, 1758." In *Contributions Biographical, Genealogical and Historical*, ed. Ebenezer Weaver Peirce. Boston, 1874.

Washington, George. *The Papers of George Washington.* Revolutionary War Series, vol. 20, 8 April–31 May 1779. Library of Congress. Edited by Edward G. Lengel. Charlottesville, VA, 2010.

Wolfe, James. *The Life and Letters of James Wolfe.* Edited by Beckles Willson. New York, 1909.

Woodhull, Nathaniel. "A Journal Kept by General Nathaniel Woodhull," 257–60. New York, 1861.

Woolsey, Melancthon Taylor. *Letters of Melancthon Taylor Woolsey: Colonel, New York Provincial Troops in the French and Indian War.* Champlain, QC, 1927 (privately printed).

Periodicals

Boston Evening-Post
Boston News-Letter
Boston Weekly Advertiser
Gentleman's Magazine
London Chronicle; or, Universal Evening Post
New Hampshire Gazette
New London Summary
New York Mercury

Secondary Sources

Books

Anderson, F. A. *Crucible of War: The Seven Years' War and the Fate of Empire in British North America, 1754–1766.* New York, 2000.

———. *A People's Army: Massachusetts Soldiers and Society in the Seven Years' War.* Chapel Hill, NC, 1994.

———. *The War That Made America.* New York, 2005.

Beauchamp, Martin. *Indian Names of Places of New York.* New York, 1893.

Benn, Carl. *The Iroquois in the War of 1812.* Toronto, 1998.

Berleth, Richard. *Bloody Mohawk: The French and Indian War and American Revolution on New York's Frontier.* New York, 2010.

Bonomi, Patricia U. *A Factious People: Politics and Society in Colonial New York.* New York, 1971.

Borneman, Walter R. *The French and Indian War: Deciding the Fate of North America.* New York, 2007.
Boscawen, Hugh. *The Capture of Louisbourg, 1758.* Norman, OK, 2011.
Bronze, Jean-Yves. *Les morts de la guerre de Sept Ans au Cimietiere de l'Hôpital-General de Quebec.* Université Laval, QC, 2001.
Brumwell, Stephen. *Redcoats: The British Soldier and the War in the Americas, 1755–1763.* Cambridge, 2002.
———. *White Devil: A True Story of War, Savagery and Vengeance in Colonial America.* London, 2004.
Charbonneau, André. *Les Fortifications de l'Ile aux Noix: Reflet de la stratégie défensive sur la frontière du Haut-Richelieu aux XVIIIe et XIXe siècles.* Ottawa, 1994.
Chartrand, René. *The French Soldier in Colonial America.* Alexandria Bay, NY, 1984.
———. *Fort Frontenac 1758: Saving Face after Ticonderoga.* Oxford, 2001.
———. *The Forts of New France: The Great Lakes, the Plains and the Gulf Coast 1600–1763.* Oxford, 2010.
———. *The Forts of New France in Northeast America 1600–1763.* Oxford, 2008.
———. *Montcalm's Crushing Blow: French and Indian Raids along New York's Oswego River 1756.* Oxford, 2004.
Chet, Guy. *Conquering the American Wilderness: The Triumph of European Warfare in the Colonial Northeast.* Amherst, MA, 2003.
Coleman, Emma Lewis. *New England Captives Carried to Canada between 1677 and 1760 during the French And Indian Wars.* Portland, ME, 1925.
Dictionary of Canadian Biography. http://www.biographi.ca/en.
Dowd, G. E. *Groundless: Rumors, Legends, and Hoaxes on the Early American Frontier.* Baltimore, 2015.
———. *War under Heaven: Pontiac, the Indian Nations, and the British Empire.* Baltimore, 2002.
Dunnigan, B. L. *Siege, 1759: The Campaign against Niagara.* Youngstown, OH, 1996.
Eccles, W. J. *Canada under Louis XIV 1663–1701.* Toronto, 1964.
———. *France in North America.* Toronto, 1972.
Fauteux, Aegidius. *Les Chevaliers de St Louis en Canada.* Montreal, 1940.
Fisher, David Hackett. *Liberty and Freedom: A Visual History of America's Founding Ideas.* New York, 2005.
Ford, Paul L. *Franklin Bibliography: A List of Books Written by, or Relating to, Benjamin Franklin.* Brooklyn, NY, 1889.
Fortescue, J. W. *A History of the British Army.* Vol. 2. London, 1910 (reprint, 2004).
Fournier, Marcel. *Les officiers des troupes de la Marine au Canada, 1683–1760.* Quebec, 2017.
Fowler, W. M., Jr. *Empires at War: The French and Indian War and the Struggle for North America, 1754–1763.* New York, 2005.
Frégault, Guy. *Canada: The War of Conquest.* Translated by Margaret Cameron. Toronto, 1969.
Gipson, Lawrence Henry. *Great War for the Empire: The Victorious Years, 1758–1760.* Vol. 7 of *British Empire Before the American Revolution.* New York, 1949.
Godfrey, William G. *Pursuit of Profit and Preferment in Colonial North America: John Bradstreet's Quest.* Waterloo, ON, 1982.
Graves, Robert. *French Military Terminology, 1670–1815.* St. John, NB, 1979.

Graymont, Barbara. *The Iroquois in the American Revolution.* Syracuse, NY, 1975.
Guy, Alan J. *Oeconomy and Discipline: Officership and Administration in the British Army, 1714–63.* Manchester, 1985.
Hackett, David G. *The Rude Hand of Innovation: Religion and Social Order in Albany, New York, 1652–1836.* New York, 1991.
Hager, R. E. *Mohawk River Boats and Navigation before 1820.* Syracuse, NY, 1987.
Hagerty, Gilbert. *Massacre at Fort Bull: The de Lery Expedition against Oneida Carry, 1756.* Providence, RI, 1971.
Havard, Gilles. *Empire et métissages: Indiens et Français dans le pays d'en haut, 1660–1715.* Sillery et Paris, 2003.
———. *The Great Peace of Montreal of 1701: French–Native Diplomacy in the Seventeenth Century.* Trans. P. Aronoff and H. Scott. Montreal, 2001.
Houlding, John A. *"Fit for Service": The Training of the Administration in the British Army, 1714–63.* Manchester, 1985.
Jennings, Francis. *The Ambiguous Iroquois Empire: The Covenant Chain Confederation of Indian Tribes with English Colonies from Its Beginnings to the Lancaster Treaty of 1744.* New York, 1984.
———. *Empire of Fortune: Crowns, Colonies and Tribes in the Seven Years' War in America.* New York, 1988.
———. *The History and Culture of Iroquois Diplomacy.* Edited by Francis Jennings. Syracuse, NY, 1985.
Johnson, Charles M. *The Valley of the Six Nations: A Collection of Documents on the Indian Lands of the Grand River.* Toronto, 2013.
Johnston, A. J. B. *Endgame 1758: The Promise, the Glory, and the Despair of Louisbourg's Last Decade.* Lincoln, NE, 2007.
Keegan, John. *The Face of Battle.* London, 1976.
———. *The Mask of Command.* New York, 1987.
Kennett, Lee. *The French Armies in the Seven Years' War: A Study in Military Organization and Administration.* Durham, NC, 1967.
Leach, D. E. *Arms for Empire: A Military History of the British Colonies in North America, 1607–1763.* New York, 1973.
———. *Roots of Conflict: British Armed Forces and Colonial Americans, 1677–1763.* Chapel Hill, NC, 1986.
Little, Ann M. *Abraham in Arms: War and Gender in Colonial New England.* Philadelphia, 2007.
Lossing, Benson J. *The Life and Times of Philip Schuyler.* Vol. 1. New York, 1872.
Lozier, Jean-François. *Flesh Reborn: The Saint Lawrence Valley Mission Settlements through the Seventeenth Century.* Montreal, 2018.
Luzader, John F. *Fort Stanwix: Construction and Military History.* New Hartford, NY, 2001.
MacLeitch, Gail D. *Imperial Entanglements: Iroquois Change and Persistence on the Frontiers of Empire.* Philadelphia, 2011.
MacLeod, D. Peter. *The Canadian Iroquois and the Seven Years' War.* Toronto, 1996.
Mahan, Harold E. *Benson J. Lossing and Historical Writing in the United States.* Westport, CT, 1996.
Malcomson, Robert. *Warships of the Great Lakes, 1754–1834.* Annapolis, MD, 2001.
McCulloch, Ian M. *Highlanders in the French-Indian War, 1756–67.* Oxford, 2006.

———. *Sons of the Mountains: The Highland Regiments in the French and Indian War, 1756–67*. Fleischmanns, NY, 2006.
McCulloch, Ian M., and Tim Todish. *British Light Infantryman in the Seven Years War, North America, 1757–1763*. Oxford, 2004.
McLynn, Frank. *1759: The Year Britain Became Master of the World*. New York, 2004.
Mulford, Carla. *Only for the Eye of a Friend: The Poems of Annis Boudinot Stockton*. Charlottesville, VA, 1995.
Nester, William R. *The Epic Battles for Ticonderoga, 1758*. Albany, 2008.
O'Conor, N. J. *A Servant of the Crown: In England and in North America 1756–61*. New York, 1938.
O'Toole, F. *White Savage: William Johnson and the Invention of America*. London, 2006.
Pargellis, S. M. *Lord Loudoun in North America*. New Haven, CT, 1933 (reprint, 1968).
Parkman, Francis. *Montcalm and Wolfe*. Vol. 2 of *France and England in North America*. London, 1884.
Preston, D. L. *The Texture of Contact: European and Indian Communities on the Frontiers of Iroquoia, 1667–1783*. Lincoln, NE, 2009.
Pritchard, James. *In Search of Empire: The French in the Americas, 1670–1730*. Cambridge, 2004.
———. *Louis XV's Navy, 1748–1762: A Study of Organization and Administration*. Kingston, ON, 1987.
Richter, Daniel K. *The Ordeal of the Longhouse: The Peoples of the Iroquois League in the Era of European Colonization*. Chapel Hill, NC, 1992.
Richter, Daniel K., and James H. Merrell, eds. *Beyond the Covenant Chain: The Iroquois and Their Neighbours in Indian North America, 1600–1800*. Syracuse, NY, 1987.
Ross, Michael. *Bougainville*. London, 1978.
Saunderson, Henry Hamilton. *History of Charlestown, New Hampshire*. Charlestown, NH, 1876.
Schumann, Matt, and Karl Schweizer. *The Seven Years War: A Transatlantic History*. New York, 2008.
Schuyler, George W. *Colonial New York: Philip Schuyler and His Family*. New York, 1885.
Selesky, Harold E. *War and Society in Colonial Connecticut*. New Haven, CT, 1990.
Shannon, Timothy J. *Iroquois Diplomacy on the Early American Frontier*. New York, 2008 (reprint, 2009).
Shy, J. *Towards Lexington: The Role of the British Army in the Coming of the American Revolution*. Princeton, NJ, 1965.
Skaggs, David Curtis, and Larry L. Nelson, eds. *The Sixty Years War for the Great Lakes, 1754–1814*. East Lansing, MI, 2001.
Stanley, G. F. *New France: The Last Phase, 1744–1760*. Toronto, 1968.
Steele, Ian K. *Betrayals: Fort William Henry and the "Massacre."* New York, 1990.
———. *Guerillas and Grenadiers: The Struggle for Canada, 1689—1760*. Toronto, 1974.
———. *Setting All the Captives Free: Capture, Adjustment, and Recollection in Allegheny Country*. Montreal, 2013.
———. *Warpaths: Invasions of North America*. Oxford, 1991.
Trigger, Bruce G. *Natives and Newcomers: Canada's "Heroic Age" Reconsidered*. Kingston, ON, 1985.
Wainwright, N. B. *George Croghan: Wilderness Diplomat*. Chapel Hill, NC, 1959.

Ward, Matthew C. *Breaking the Backcountry: The Seven Years War in Virginia and Pennsylvania, 1754–1765*. Pittsburgh, 2003.
Woodhull, Mary Gould, and Francis Bowes Stevens. *The Woodhull Family in England and America*. Philadelphia, 1904.
White, Richard. *The Middle Ground: Indians, Empires and Republics in the Great Lakes Region, 1650–1815*. Cambridge, 1991.
Winesfield, C. H. *History of the County of Hudson, New Jersey*. New York, 1874.
Zarzynski, J. W. *Ghost Fleet Awakened: Lake George's Sunken Bateaux of 1758*. Albany, 2019.
Zoltvany, Yves F. *Philippe de Rigaud de Vaudreuil, Governor of New France, 1703–1725*. Toronto, 1974.

Articles and Book Chapters

Agostini, Thomas. "'The Provincials Will Work like Giants': British Imperialism, American Colonial Troops, and Trans-Atlantic Labor Economics during the Seven Years' War." *Early American Studies: An Interdisciplinary Journal* 15, no. 1 (2017): 64–98.
Anderson, F. W. "Why Did Colonial New Englanders Make Bad Soldiers? Contractual Principles and Military Conduct during the Seven Year's War." *William and Mary Quarterly* 38, no. 3 (July 1981): 395–417.
Andrews, R. J. "John Bradstreet's Raid: An Account of the Expedition mounted against Fort Frontenac in August–September 1758." *Kingston History* 58 (2004): 10–38.
———. "Two Ships—Two Flags: the *Outaouaise*/Williamson and the *Iroquoise*/Anson on Lake Ontario, 1759–1761." *Northern Mariner/Le marin du nord* 14, no. 3 (July 2004): 41–55.
Bazely, Susan M. "Le fort Frontenac sur la route des Pays-d'en-Haut." *Cap-aux-Diamants*, no. 66 (2001): 15–18.
Boire, Michael. "Le Marquis de Montcalm and the Battle for Québec, September 1759: A Re-assessment." *Canadian Military Journal* (Summer 2006), 77–84.
Brumwell, Stephen. "Band of Brothers," *History Today* 58, no. 6 (June 2008): 25–31.
———. "A Service Truly Critical: The British Army and Warfare with the North American Indians, 1755–1764." *War in History* 2 (April 1998): 146–75.
Butterfield, Lyman H. "Morven: A Colonial Outpost of Sensibility, with Some Hitherto Unpublished Poems by Annis Boudinot Stockton." *Princeton University Library Chronicles* 6 (1944).
Campbell, William J. "An Adverse Patron: Land, Trade and George Croghan." *Pennsylvania History: A Journal of Mid-Atlantic Studies* 76, no. 2 (2009): 117–40.
Cassel, Jay. "The Militia Legend: Canadians at War, 1665–1760." In *Canadian Military History since the 17th Century: Proceedings of the Canadian Military History Conference, Ottawa, 5–9 May 2000*, ed. Yves Tremblay, 59–67. Ottawa, 2000.
Chartrand, René. "Fort Frontenac: Saving Face after Ticonderoga." *Osprey Military Journal* 3, no. 2 (2001): 21–22.
———. "La gouvernance militaire en Nouvelle-France." *Bulletin d'histoire politique* 18, no. 1 (Autumn 2009): 129.
Dagneau, C. "The 'Batteaux Plats' of New France." *International Journal of Nautical Archaeology* 33 (2004): 281–96.
Douglas, W. A. B. "Le Saint Laurent: Une Voie d'Acces Strategique." *Cap-aux-Diamants*, no. 43 (Autumn 1995): 19–23.

Eccles, W. J. "The French Forces in North America during the Seven Years' War." *Dictionary of Canadian Biography*, vol. 3 (Toronto, 1974), xv–xxiii.

———. "The History of New France according to Francis Parkman." *William and Mary Quarterly*, 3rd ser., vol. 18, no. 2 (April 1961): 174–75.

———. "The Social, the Economic and the Political Significance of the Military Establishment in New France." *Canadian Historical Review* 52, no. 1 (1971): 1–22.

Fatherly, Sarah. "Tending the Army: Women and the British General Hospital in North America, 1754–1763." *Early American Studies* 10, no. 3 (2012): 566–99. Accessed 18 April 2020. www.jstor.org/stable/23546694.

Grant, W. L. "The Capture of Oswego by Montcalm in 1756, a Study in Naval Power; with an Appendix of Letters from Captain Houseman Broadley, Commander of the British Forces on Lake Ontario." *Mémoires et comptes rendus de la Société Royale du Canada/Proceedings and Transactions of the Royal Society of Canada*, 3rd ser., vol. 8 (1964): 193–214.

Green, Ernest. "Corvettes of New France." *Ontario History* 35 (1943): 29–38.

Holden, James Austen. "How the State and the Historical Association May Be of Mutual Assistance." *Proceedings of the New York State Historical Association* 13 (1914): 282–308.

Holland, Jeanne. "Johnson, Susannah Willard (1729–1810)." In *The Oxford Companion to Women's Writing in the United States*, ed. Cathy N. Davidson and Linda Wagner-Martin. New York, 1995.

Jennings, Francis. "Francis Parkman: A Brahmin among Untouchables," *The William and Mary Quarterly*, 3rd Series 42, no. 3 (July 1985): 306–28.

Knoublach, E. H. "Mobilizing Provincials for War: The Social Composition of New York Forces in 1760." *New York History* 78, no. 2 (1997): 147–72. Accessed March 20, 2020, www.jstor.org/stable/23181843.

Kopperman, P. E. "Medical Services in the British Army, 1742–1783." *Journal of the History of Medicine and Allied Sciences* 34 (October 1979): 428–55.

MacLeod, D. P. "The Canadians against the French: The Struggle for Control of the Expedition to Oswego in 1756." *Ontario History* 80, no. 2 (June 1988): 143–58.

———. "The French Siege of Oswego in 1756: Inland Naval Warfare in North America." *American Neptune* 49, no. 4 (1989): 262–71.

Marshall, D. W. "The British Engineers in America: 1755–1783." *Journal of the Society for Army Historical Research* 51, no. 207 (Autumn 1973): 155–63.

McCulloch, Ian. "'Believe Us, Sir, This Will Impress Few People': Spin-Doctoring—18th-Century Style." *Bulletin of the Fort Ticonderoga Museum* 16, no. 1 (1998): 92–107.

———. "'Like Roaring Lions Breaking from Their Chains': The Battle of Ticonderoga, 8 July 1758." In *Fighting for Canada: Seven Battles, 1758–1945*, ed. Donald E. Graves, 24–80. Toronto, 2000.

———. "'The Old Squah Who Should Wear Petticoats': General James Abercromby at the Battle of Ticonderoga, 1758." *Battlefield Review*, no. 26 (2003): 39–46.

———. "'Within Ourselves': The Development of British Light Infantry in North America during the Seven Years' War." *Canadian Military History* 7 (1998): 41–55.

Meany, Joseph F., Jr. "Batteaux and 'Battoe Men': An American Colonial Response to the Problem of Logistics in Mountain Warfare," New York State Museum, Albany, [1998], 2–6, accessed 5 May 2017, https://dmna.ny.gov/historic/articles/Batteaux_and_Battoe_Men.pdf.

Moogk, Peter. "Notables, Rank and Patronage: The Social Order of Early Eighteenth Century Canada." *Proceedings of the Meeting of the French Colonial Historical Society*, Vol. 13/14, (1990): 58–85.
Nicolai, Martin. "A Different Kind of Courage: The French Military and the Canadian Irregular Soldier during the Seven Years' War." *Canadian Historical Review* 70, no. 1 (1989): 53–75.
Pargellis, S. M. "Braddock's Defeat." *American Historical Review* 41 (1936): 253–69.
———. "The Four Independent Companies of New York." In *Essays in Colonial History Presented to Charles McLean Andrews by His Students*, 96–123. New Haven, CT, 1931.
Parmenter, Jon. "After the Mourning Wars: The Iroquois as Allies in Colonial North American Campaigns, 1676–1760." *William and Mary Quarterly* 64 (2007): 39–82.
———. "'L'Arbre de Paix': Eighteenth-Century Franco-Iroquois Relations." *French Colonial History* 4 (2003): 63–80.
———. "'Onenwahatirighsi Sa Gentho Skaghnughtudigh': Reassessing Iroquois Relations with the Albany Commissioners of Indian Affairs, 1723–1755." In *English Atlantics Revisited: Essays Honouring Professor Ian K. Steele*, ed. Nancy Rhoden, 235–83. Montreal, 2007.
Parmenter, Jon, and Mark Power Robison. "The Perils and Possibilities of Wartime Neutrality on the Edges of Empire: Iroquois and Acadians between the French and British in North America, 1744–1760." *Diplomatic History* 31, no. 2 (2007): 167–206.
Patel, Kant. "Origins and Development of Government's Role in Health Policy (Colonial Era to Present)." In *US Health and Health Care Policy*, ed. Thomas R. Oliver, 7–36. Los Angeles, 2014.
Rabinovich, Alexander B. "Seiches and Harbor Oscillations." In *Handbook of Coastal and Ocean Engineering*, ed. Young C. Kim. Los Angeles, 2012.
Shannon, Timothy J. "'The Baubles of America': Object Lessons from the Eclectic Empire of Peter Williamson." In *Experiencing Empire: Power, People, and Revolution in Early America*, ed. Patrick Griffin, 27–49. Charlottesville, VA, 2017.
———. "French and Indian Cruelty? The Fate of the Oswego Prisoners of War, 1756–1758." *New York History* 95.3 (Summer 2014): 381–407.
———. "King of the Indians: The Hard Fate and Curious Career of Peter Williamson," *William and Mary Quarterly*, 66 (January 2009): 3–44.
Shy, John. "The American Colonies in War and Revolution, 1748–1783." In *The Oxford History of the British Empire*. Vol. 2, *The Eighteenth Century*, ed. P. J. Marshall and Alaine Low, 300–324. Oxford, 1998.
Starbuck, D. R. "Military Hospitals on the Frontier of Colonial America," *Expedition* 39, no. 1 (1997): 33–45.
Staudt, J. G. "Immigrants, Indians and Idle Men: Long Island's "Rabble in Arms" in the French and Indian War." *Long Island Historical Journal* 11, no. 2 (Spring 1999): 178–89.
Stewart, W. Bruce. "The Structural Evolution of Fort Frontenac," *Northeast Historical Archaeology* Vol. 14. Available at: http://orb.binghamton.edu/neha/vol14/iss1/3.
Stoker, Donald. "There was no Offensive-Defensive Confederate Strategy." *Journal of Military History* 73 (April 2009): 571–90.
Sweeney, Kevin M. "Firearms, Militias, and the Second Amendment." In *The Second Amendment on Trial: Critical Essays on District of* Columbia v. Heller, ed. Saul Cornell and Nathan Kozuskanich. Amherst, MA, 2013.

———. "The Very Model of a Modern Major General." *Amherst Magazine* 61, no. 1 (Fall 2008).
Vitzhum, Richard C. "The Historian as Editor: Francis Parkman's Reconstruction of Sources in *Montcalm and Wolfe*." *Journal of American History* 53, no. 3 (December 1966): 471–86.
Way, Peter. "Soldiers of Misfortune: New England Regulars and the Fall of Oswego, 1755–1756." *Massachusetts Historical Review* 3 (2001): 49–88.
"The Will of Charles Clinton." *Proceedings of the New York State Historical Association* 6 (1906): 166–68.
Yabe, Mitsuyoshi, Chris Jackson, Elizabeth Goins, David Halbstein, Shaun Foster, and Sue Bazely. "Chronological Restoration of Fort Frontenac in 3D for Heritage Visualization." *Journal of Civil Engineering and Architecture* 9 (2015): 1463–73.
Zelnik, Eran. "Yankees, Doodles, Fops, and Cuckolds: Compromised Manhood and Provincialism in the Revolutionary Period, 1740–1781." *Early American Studies: An Interdisciplinary Journal* 16, no. 3 (2018): 514–44.

Unpublished Dissertations and Transcripts

Bratten, Jonathan. "War for the Soul of Empire: Colonial British Protestants in the French and Indian War, 1754–1763." MA thesis, History Department, University of New Hampshire, 2011.
Carroll, Brian D. "From Warrior to Soldier: New England Indians in the Colonial Military, 1676–1763." PhD diss., History Department, University of Connecticut, 2009.
Cassel, Jay. "The Troupes de la Marine in Canada, 1683–1760: Men and Material." PhD diss., History Department, University of Toronto, 1987.
D'Amours, Marc-André. "Entre deux régimes: Louis-Léonard Aumasson de Courville et ses Mémoires." PhD diss., History Department, University of Montreal, 2016.
Gray, Colleen Allyn. "Captives in Canada, 1744–1763." MA thesis, History Department, McGill University, 1993.
Grenier, Benoît. "Devenir seigneur en Nouvelle-France: Mobilité sociale et propriété seigneuriale dans le gouvernement de Québec sous le Régime français." MA thesis, History Department, Université Laval, 2000.
MacDonald, Ian Glenn. "Whaleboats, Row-Galleys and Floating Batteries: British Gunboats in the 1760 Canada Campaign." MA thesis, History Department, Queen's University, 1999.
MacLeod, Malcolm. "French and British Strategy in the Lake Ontario Theatre of Operations, 1754–1760." PhD diss., History Department, University of Ottawa, 1974.
McCulloch, Ian M. "'Dominion of the Lake'?: A Reassessment of John Bradstreet's Raid on Fort Frontenac, 1758." MA thesis, Defence Studies Department, Canadian Forces College, 2009.
Parker, King Lawrence. "Anglo-American Wilderness Campaigning: Logistical and Tactical Developments 1754–1764." PhD diss., History Department, Columbia University, 1970.
Rogers, Greg. "Petite Politique: The British, French, Iroquois, and Everyday Power in the Lake Ontario Borderlands, 1724–1760." PhD diss., History Department, University of Maine, 2016. Electronic Theses and Dissertations, 2506, http://digitalcommons.library.umaine.edu/etd/2506.

Shy, John. "James Abercromby and the Campaign of 1758." MA thesis, University of Vermont, 1957.
Sweeney, Kevin Michael. "River Gods and Related Minor Deities: The Williams Family and the Connecticut River Valley, 1637–1790." 2 vols. PhD diss., History Department, Yale University, 1986.
York, Amoreena L. "The Myth of the Citizen Soldier: Rhode Island Provincial Soldiers in the French and Indian War." MA thesis, Military Art and Science Department, Fort Leavenworth Staff College, 2016.

Index

Abenaki. *See* indigenous peoples
Abercromby, James, 1, 15–18, 21–22, 25, 27, 29, 34–37, 43–44, 46–48, 50–51, 53, 56–58, 65, 91, 106, 108–9, 121, 132–34, 141–44, 147, 179n3, 202n8, 205n18
Abraham (Mohawk chieftain), 54
Acadians, 6, 12, 16, 80
Adirondack Mountains, N.Y., 32
Akwesasne, 24
Albany, N.Y., 4–5, 10, 14, 16, 22, 25–27, 32, 34–35, 37–44, 49–50, 59, 70, 79, 86, 105, 120–22, 184n49, 187n24, 189n37
Albany County, N.Y., 37, 40, 59
Albertson, Garret, 29, 62, 70–71, 73–75, 83, 87–88, 92, 96, 103, 107, 110, 114, 119, 122, 132, 164–65, 198n5, 200n32
Algonquin. *See under* indigenous peoples
American War of Independence. *See* wars and uprisings
Amherst, Jeffery, 15, 17, 34, 66, 74, 86–87, 118, 129, 148, 186n12, 194n3, 195n34
Anderson, Frederick, 91, 119, 143, 147, 180n4, 186n18
Anishinaabe. *See under* indigenous peoples
Annapolis Royal, Nova Scotia, 16
Annual Register. See under newspapers
Appy, John, 43
Arbuthnot, William, 60, 156, 158, 167
artillery, 3, 13–14, 23–24, 36, 43, 49–51, 58, 62, 66, 73, 76, 78, 80, 82, 92–94, 98–101, 104, 115–17, 126, 128, 132, 134, 136, 142, 146, 149, 156–57, 173, 181, 200n24. *See also* weapons
Atlantic Ocean, 4

Babcock, Henry "Harry," 49–50, 60–62, 121, 157
Badgely, Samuel, 44, 159
Bagley, Jonathan, 41, 43, 187n.21
Bancroft, George, 139
Barns, Stephen, 122
Barrow, Abner, 49
Bass, Benjamin, 68, 81, 105, 111, 117, 119, 158, 164–65
Bass, John, 121
bateau (bateaux), 12, 19, 25, 32–33, 40, 51, 59, 62, 67–68, 70, 75–76, 8, 84, 92–94, 105–7, 110, 114–16, 120–22, 125, 160, 173, 179n2, 185n4
battles and sieges: Beausejour (siege), 2, 10, 12, 16, 128; Cartagena (siege), 58; Fontenoy, 59; Lauffeldt, 59; Lake George, 2, 5, 35, 61, 108; Louisbourg (sieges), 1, 12–18, 37, 111, 118, 197n.6; Monongahela, 11, 36, 38, 85; Niagara (siege), 35, 60, 74, 86, 131, 134, 138, 148; Oswego (siege), 5, 11–13, 19, 21, 24, 33, 59, 76–78, 84, 99, 109–10, 115, 127–28, 136, 154–55, 172, 197n6, 201–2n8; Quebec (sieges), 144, 166; Rocoux, 59; Ticonderoga (Carillon), 1–2, 5, 14, 16–18, 20, 26–29, 36–37, 43–44, 46, 49, 52, 54–55, 58, 60–63, 64, 69, 82, 101, 106, 122, 126, 132, 135, 141, 144, 147,

battles and sieges (*continued*)
  180n1, 182n28, 184n49, 195n34, 197n15, 203n12
Battoe Service. *See* regiments, British
Bay Colony. *See* Massachusetts
Bay of Cataraqui, 78
Beaver Wars. *See under* wars and uprisings
Belle-Isle, Marshal de (Charles Louis Auguste Fouquet, duc de Belle-Isle), 125
Bigot, François, 80, 140
Bonnel, Abraham, 122
Bosson, William, 68
Boston, Mass., 16, 110, 186n.18
Boucher, Joseph. *See* Sieur de la Broquerie
Bougainville, Louis-Antoine de, 52, 80, 82, 141, 193n22
Braddock, Edward, 11–12, 16
Bradstreet, John (Jean-Baptiste), 1–2, 4, 12, 15–18, 20–30, 33, 40–41, 43, 46–60, 62–66, 69–77, 81–88, 90–102, 104–12, 114–21, 124, 127–29, 131–36, 139–48, 156–57, 160–70, 179n1, 179n2, 179n3, 183n36, 191n52, 197n15, 200n24, 205n18
Brantford, Ontario, 137
Brehm, Dietrich, 86
Brookfield, Mass., 41
Browne, Archibald Montague, 57–58, 91–92, 156, 207n1 (app. D)
Bryan, Josiah, 122
Butler, John, 63, 137, 157, 207n1 (app. D)
Butler, Thomas, 53–54, 63, 72–73, 76, 82, 95, 108, 115, 130, 156, 160
Butler, Walter, 108
Butler's Rangers. *See* regiments, British
Bull's Fort. *See under* forts and fortresses

Canada, 2, 5, 9, 17, 23–24, 27, 50, 52, 136–37, 141, 145, 148, 194n33, 195n44, 202n8
Canada Creek, N.Y., 67–69
cannon. *See under* weapons
Cape Breton Island (Île-Royale), Nova Scotia, 16, 34

Cape Vincent, N.Y., 84
Cataraqui, 44, 200n24
Cataraqui River. *See under* rivers
Champlain, Samuel de, 85
chaplains, 35, 44, 58, 60, 68, 97
Chartrand, René, 140
Chaumont Bay, N.Y., 84
Chevalier de la Pause (Jean-Guillaume Plantavit de Lapause de Margon), 18, 22, 100–101
Chew, George, 136
Chignecto Isthmus, Nova Scotia, 10
Chouegen. *See* Oswego (Osh-we-geh), N.Y.
Claverack, N.Y., 37
Cleaveland, John, 43
Clinton, Alexander, 45, 123
Clinton, Catherine, 45, 188n28
Clinton, Dr. Charles, 45, 188n28
Clinton, James, Sr., 45
Clinton, James (infant), 45, 123
Clinton, Lt. Col. Charles, 44–45, 56, 70–72, 82, 84, 92, 98, 10, 109, 111, 115–19, 123, 131–32, 148, 156, 158, 161–62, 167, 188n27
Clinton, Lt. (later Brig.) James, 45, 123, 131, 137, 188n28
Clinton, Mary, 45
Cochran, John, 132, 207n2 (app. D)
coffeehouses, 12
Colden, Cadwallader, 45, 52, 92, 188n28, 189n43
compagnies franches de la marine. *See* regiments, French
Congress, 137, 190n45, 194n33
Connecticut (colony), 38, 41, 136, 189n18
Connecticut Valley, 5, 186n18
Continental Army, 11, 132, 190n44
Comte de Frontenac, 18
Corboy, Ireland, 45
Corsa, Isaac, 82, 92, 96, 119, 131, 156, 159, 167, 195n34
courts-martial, 35, 135
Courville, Louis-Léonard Aumasson de. *See* Sieur de Courville
Covenant Chain alliance, 31
Coventry, Alexander, 101

Coventry, George, 101, 156
Croghan, George, 36, 205n9
Cross, Stephen, 74–75
Crown Point, N.Y. *See under* forts and fortresses

d'Argenson, Count, 18
Delancey, Oliver, 40, 44–45, 56, 59, 116, 123, 156, 180n6, 184n49
Delaware (colony), 61, 143
de Lignery, François-Marie Le Marchand, 126
Denniston, Elizabeth, 45
de Normandie, Daniel, 92, 110
de Noyan, Pierre-Jacques Payen. *See* Sieur de Noyan
Deo-Wain-Sta. *See* Great Carrying Place
Deschambault, Jeanne-Charlotte de Fleury, 78
desertion, 48, 50, 57, 59–60, 72
d'Espinassy, Louis-Auguste-Joseph-Victor. *See* Sieur d'Espinassy
de Vassan, Jean, 126
Detroit. *See under* forts and fortresses
Dieskau, Baron Jean-Armand, 2, 5, 11
Dinsdill, John, 68
diseases: dysentery (flux), 51, 56; measles, 45; smallpox, 38, 42, 45, 118, 120–21, 123, 132; trench foot, 70; typhus (camp fever), 51, 123; yellow fever, 131, 190n43
divine service, 39, 57, 111. *See also* religion
Doreil, André, 20, 125–26
Dorr, Moses, 51, 69, 118–19, 145, 166
Doty, Thomas, 48, 50, 57, 60, 82, 157
Douglass, William, 122
Duplessis Faber, François Lefebvre, 112–13
Dutch, 31, 37–40, 79

Earl of Loudoun. *See* Lord Loudoun
Eastburn, Robert, 128
Eccles, W. J., 15
Ellis, Joseph, 60, 157, 167
Erie, Lake. *See under* lakes; Great Lakes
Everglades, 3
Eyre, William, 47

fascines, 94–95, 97, 164
First World War. *See under* wars and uprisings
Five Nations. *See* Haudenosaunee Confederacy
Fontenoy. *See* battles and sieges
Forbes, John, 15
Forks of the Ohio, 5, 10, 14
Forbes, John, 15, 184n44, 187n24
forts and fortresses: Beauséjour, 2, 10–11, 16; Bull (renamed Wood Creek), 33, 54–55, 62, 108, 119, 127–28, 181n14; Crailo, 37; Crown Point, 5, 10–13, 16–18, 144, 180n1; Detroit, 4, 16; Duquesne, 5, 10–12, 14–17, 85, 136, 142, 187n24; Edward, 13–14, 16, 36, 43–44, 57, 129; Frontenac (Cataraqui), 2, 11–13, 15, 17–21, 23–24, 26–27, 31, 36, 47–48, 54, 64–65, 73, 77–78, 84, 92, 95–97, 99–103, 108–9, 111–15, 119, 123, 127–28, 132, 134–36, 139–41, 143, 145–49, 152, 156, 163, 169, 183n36, 189n40, 197n6, 199n24; Herkimer, 33–34, 36, 45, 50, 54, 104, 123; Île-aux-Noix, 127; La Présentation (Oswegatchie, La Galette), 12, 23, 80, 87, 113, 142–43, 183n4, 194n31; Lévis, 16, 184n40; Louisbourg (fortress), 1, 12–18, 22, 24, 34, 37, 80, 110–11, 118, 127, 144, 197n6; Ontario, 131, 195n34; Oswego, 12–13; Montgomery, 131; Newport, 70, 119; Niagara, 4, 10–12, 16, 20, 31, 50, 79, 85–86, 126–27, 134, 138, 142–43, 146–48; Quebec (fortress), 1, 5, 9, 13, 15–18, 20, 22, 79, 144, 197n6; Rouillé (Toronto), 12, 77, 79, 142; Saint-Frédéric, 5, 10, 14, 16, 20; Stanwix, 16, 33, 116–20, 122, 136; Ticonderoga (Carillon), 1–2, 5, 14–18, 2, 27, 36–37, 44, 46, 49, 51, 55, 58, 60–61, 64, 69, 106, 126, 135, 141, 144, 147, 180n1, 182n28, 197n15; William Henry, 13, 16, 20, 25, 38, 59, 68, 79, 82, 101, 111, 195n34; Wood Creek (Eagle), 54, 62, 68, 113
Foster, Jeremiah, 122–23
France, 6, 9–10, 125, 140–41

Franklin, Benjamin, 1–2, 11–12
Fraser Highlanders (78th Foot). *See* regiments, British regular
Frégault, Guy, 140, 147, 189n40
Frey, Hendrik, 44
Frey House, N.Y., 44–45, 123
Frye's regiment. *See* regiments, British

gabions, 94–95
Gage, Thomas, 28, 47, 132
Ganounkouesnot. *See* Wolfe Island, Ontario
Ga-oh (wind spirit), 88
Gates, Horatio, 36, 207n2
Generalissimo. *See* Marquis de Vaudreuil
Genessee, N.Y., 137
Gentleman's Magazine, 46, 199n24
German Flatts, N.Y., 34, 43, 53, 63, 128
Glasserton, Scotland, 101
Gloucester County, N.J., 60
Godfrey, Richard, 60, 157
Godfrey, William, 22, 25–26, 179n1, 184n46
Gould, Charles, 17, 26, 112, 179n1
Grand Council Fire, 137
Grand-Île. *See* Wolfe Island, Ontario
Grand River, Ontario, 137
Grant, Francis, 47
Great Carrying Place (Deo-wain-sta; Oneida Carrying Place), 4, 16, 31–33, 36, 43–44, 47–49, 51, 53–54, 56, 118, 120–21, 184n1
Great Lakes, 3, 6, 1, 18, 22, 32–33, 83, 86, 127, 140, 145–46, 196n48
Great Peace of Montreal (1701), 32
Greenbush, N.Y., 37, 41–42
Gridley, Richard, 68
Gulf of St. Lawrence, 9, 16
guns. *See* weapons

Hacker, Caleb, 62
Haldimand, Colonel Frederick, 47
Halifax, Nova Scotia, 13, 16, 20, 52
Hand, Elias, 44, 159, 188n26
Hare (Hair), William, 157
Hatfield, Mass., 41–2

Haudenosaunee Confederacy (People of the Longhouse), 7, 10, 20–21, 24, 30–33, 35–36, 53–54, 63–65, 76, 78, 80–81, 83, 86–87, 99–100, 107, 110–11, 126–27, 134–35, 137–38, 192n71, 196n48
Haviland, William, 47
Heights of Carillon. *See* Ticonderoga
Hendrik (Mohawk chieftain), 108
Hervey, William, 46
Hill, Thomas, 122
Hingham, Mass., 42
Holden, James Austin, 140, 204n2
hospitals, 39, 118, 120, 132, 194n33
Howe, George Augustus, 26–28, 47, 55, 101, 184n49
Howe, Jemima, 129–30
howitzers. *See under* weapons
Huck, Richard, 133, 144
Hudson River. *See under* rivers
Hudson Valley, 5, 37
Huguenots, 82, 195n34
Hunt, Samuel, 60
Hunter, William, 121
Hunterdon County, N.J., 132

Île au Cochons (Garden Island, Ontario), 87, 89, 115
Île aux Noix (Nut Island, Quebec), 127
Île de Foret (Simcoe Island, Ontario), 79, 87
Île de Tonti (Amherst Island, Ontario), 78
Île-Royale. *See* Cape Breton Island, Nova Scotia
Illinois, 5, 10
Impartial Account (Bradstreet), 25–27, 50–51, 70, 73, 91, 101, 108, 112, 124, 134, 136, 143, 148, 179n3
Indian Service, 34, 54, 58, 156, 207n1
indigenous peoples: Abenaki, 7, 203n12; Algonquin, 7; Cayuga, 54, 185n3, 192n71; Delaware, 45, 126; Erie, 8; Fox, 8; Huron (Wendat), 8, 193n26; Mississauga, 7–8, 64, 79, 81, 84, 89, 93–94, 99–100, 116, 136, 185n3, 186n12, 190n45, 192n71; Mohawk, 24, 31, 37, 44, 53–54, 63, 71, 74,

107–108, 110, 116, 136, 185n3, 186n12, 190n45, 192n71; Mohican (River Indians), 53; Natchez, 8; neutral, 8; Nipissing, 7; Ojibwe, 7; Oneida, 31–34, 36, 54, 62–63, 71–72, 80, 137, 185n3; Onondaga, 20, 24, 31, 34, 54, 62–63, 80, 86, 107, 127, 131, 14, 183n36, 192n71; Ottawa, 7, 36; Potawatomi, 7; Petun, 8; Seminole, 3; Seneca, 10, 31, 52, 54, 58, 63, 126, 134, 138, 140, 191n67, 192n71, 205n18; Shawnee, 126; Tuscarora, 31, 72, 192n71
Ireland, 45, 82, 123, 184n49, 187n24
Iroquoia, 63, 81
Iroquois. *See* Haudenosaunee Confederacy
Iroquois Wars. *See under* wars and uprisings

Jacobite Uprising. *See under* wars and uprisings
Jacquet, Peter, 92, 96, 110, 115, 156–57, 199n24, 207n1
Jamaica, N.Y., 131, 194n33
Jersey Blues. *See* regiments, British
Johnson, Guy, 87
Johnson, Sylvanus, 129, 203n12
Johnson, Susannah, 129, 203n12
Johnston, John, 41, 50, 60
Johnson, William, 11, 34–35, 37, 44, 47, 61, 63, 108, 130, 134–35, 138, 143
Jumonville Glen, Pa., 79

Kah-ne-go-dick (Wood Creek). *See under* rivers
Kak8enthiony. *See* Red Head the Elder
Kalm, Petr, 39
Keen, Marij, 45
Kingston (Cataraqui), Ontario, 44, 200n24

Laforce, René-Hippolyte Pepin de. *See* Sieur de Laforce
La Friponne (The Big Cheat), 80, 194n30
La Gallette. *See under* forts and fortresses
Lake Champlain. *See under* lakes

lakes: Champlain, 4–5, 11–12, 16–17, 21, 36, 127, 142; Erie, 4, 16, 20, 140, 147; George, 2, 4–5, 11, 13, 15–17, 20, 27, 35, 49, 52–53, 59, 61, 82, 91, 97, 108, 120, 132, 146; Huron, 16, 20, 140, 195n38; Michigan, 140, 195n38; Oneida, 33, 57, 68, 72, 119, 159, 160, 207n1; Ontario, 4–5, 10–13, 16, 18–21, 23–24, 31–33, 47–48, 66, 71–72, 74, 76–79, 81–83, 85, 89, 114, 125–26, 133, 135–36, 140, 142–43, 146–47, 161, 187n24, 194n33, 195n44, 196n45; Superior, 140, 195n38; Two Mountains, 36
La Pause, Chevalier de, 18, 22, 100–101
La Présentation (Oswegatchie; La Galette). *See under* forts and fortresses
La Salle, Robert Cavalier Sieur de, 78
Leach, Surg. Mate, 121
Lee, Charles (Ounewaterika), 52, 190n45
Le Moyne, Charles, 20
Lévis, François-Gaston de, 16, 36, 44, 106, 185n10
Little Britain, N.Y., 45
London, England, 1–2, 10, 14, 17, 23, 27, 46, 51, 70, 112, 148
London Chronicle. *See under* newspapers
Longueuil, Paul-Josephe Le Moyne de. *See* Sieur de Longueuil
Long Island, N.Y., 16, 40, 82, 131
Long Sault, 81
looting, 73, 111, 116
Lord Loudoun (John Campbell, 4th Earl Loudoun), 1, 13–17, 20–22, 24–25, 35, 37, 47, 51, 109, 133, 141, 144, 182n20
Louisbourg, Nova Scotia. *See under* forts and fortresses
Lowry, Jean, 128
Longford County, Ireland, 45
Lossing, Benson J., 25
Lotteridge, John, 63, 157
Lyttleton, Richard, 23–24

Malartic, Maures de, 5, 100, 113
Malbone, Godfrey, 61
Malden, Mass., 42

Marquis de Montcalm (Louis-Joseph de Montcalm), 5, 8–9, 12–13, 18, 20–21, 33, 36, 44, 46, 76–77, 82, 84, 90, 98, 100, 104–5, 111, 125, 127, 134, 140–41, 147, 163, 169, 205n5
Marquis de Vaudreuil (Pierre de Rigaud de Vaudreuil de Cavagnial), 8–9, 13, 18, 20–21, 24, 33, 36, 44, 46, 76, 82, 84, 90, 98–100, 104–15, 111, 125, 127, 134, 140–41, 147, 163, 169, 199n13, 205n5
Massachusetts (Bay Colony), 24, 38
Massachusetts Provincials. *See under* regiments, British
Massey, Eyre, 47
Mercier, François, 19, 21
Ministry of Marine (French), 174
Mississauga Point, Ontario, 93–94, 96, 100–101
Mississippi River. *See under* rivers
Mohawk Falls (Little Falls), N.Y., 33
Mohawk River. *See under* rivers
Mohawk Valley, N.Y., 36, 44, 49, 54, 57, 59, 61, 81, 117, 129, 142, 185n12, 187n24
Monongahela River. *See under* rivers
Montcalm, Louis-Joseph de. *See* Marquis de Montcalm
Montreal, Quebec, 4, 7, 16
mortars. *See under* weapons
"Mrs. Nabbycromby." *See* Abercromby, James
muskets. *See under* weapons

Narrative of the Captivity of Mrs. Johnson, 129, 203n12
New Amsterdam. *See* New York City
Newburyport, Mass., 74
Newcastle, duke of, 14
New England, 2–3, 14, 37–38, 42, 69, 81, 139–40, 180n1
New France, 3–10, 15–17, 19–21, 24, 36, 78, 98, 126–28, 140–41, 146, 180n7, 194n30
New Hampshire, 41, 139
New Jersey, 3, 60, 124, 129, 148, 200n32, 201n8
New London, Conn., 136
newspapers: *Annual Register*, 2; *Boston Evening-Post*, 110, 121; *Boston News-Letter*, 110, 130; *Boston Weekly Advertiser*, 110; *English Gazette*, 2; *Gentleman's Magazine*, 46; *London Chronicle* or *Universal Evening Post*, 1–2; *New American Magazine*, 41, 128; *New Hampshire Gazette*, 130; *New London Summary*, 130; *New York Mercury*, 128–29; *New York Post-Boy*, 128
New York (colony), 11, 13, 2, 36–38, 40, 45, 61, 72, 131, 137, 139–40
New York City, 4, 16, 34, 37, 128–29
New York Historical Association, 140
New York Independent Companies. *See* regiments, British regulars
New York Provincials. *See* regiments, British
Northhampton, Mass., 41
Niagara Falls, 10, 31
Niaoure Bay (Henderson Bay), 71, 84
Nipissing. *See under* indigenous peoples
Nistiguana (Niskayuna, N.Y.), 41
Nova Scotia, 10, 12–13, 16, 23
Noyan, Pierre-Jacques Payen de. *See* Sieur de Noyan

Ogden, Jonathan, 55, 159
Ogdensburg, N.Y., 12, 23
Ogilvie, John, 58
Ogilvie, William, 58–59, 62, 85, 95, 131, 156, 167, 207n1 (app. D)
Ohio River. *See under* rivers
Old Dominion. *See* Virginia
Oneida. *See under* indigenous peoples
Oneida Carrying Place. *See* Great Carrying Place
Oneida Lake. *See under* lakes
Oneida River. *See under* rivers
Onondaga (capital), 31
Onondaga River. *See under* rivers
Ononwarogo. *See* Red Head
Oquandageghte (chieftain), 81
Oswegatchie. *See under* forts and fortresses
Oswego (Osh-we-geh), N.Y., 5, 10–11, 13–14, 16, 19–21, 23–24, 31–34, 36, 52, 54, 59, 70, 73–74, 76–79, 83–84, 86,

99, 105, 109–10, 115–16, 118, 127–28, 131, 133–34, 136, 143, 146, 154–55, 161, 165–66, 172, 193n22, 193n27, 195n34, 197n6, 200n6, 202n8
Oswego Falls, N.Y., 72–75, 77, 112, 116–17, 160
Oswego River. *See under* rivers
Ottawa River. *See under* rivers
Ottawas. *See under* indigenous peoples
Ounewaterika. *See* Lee, Charles

Palatine Bridge, N.Y., 45
Palatines, 34, 63, 128–29
Pargellis, Stanley, 14, 182n21
Parker, John, 59
Parker, Timothy, 44, 68–69, 118–19, 121, 158
Parkman, Francis, 91, 139, 144–47, 189n40
Passaic River. *See under* rivers
pattararoes (wall guns). *See under* weapons
pays d'en haut (upper country), 6–7, 21, 81, 147
Peachey, James, 97
Péan, Michel-Jean-Hugues, 80
Pennsylvania, 14, 16–17, 23, 61, 128, 143, 187n24
Pepin, François, 79
Pepin, Michel, 79
Pepin, Pierre, 79
Pepin, René-Hippolyte. *See* Sieur de Laforce
Perth Amboy, N.J., 60
Peterboro, 129
Petrie, Jost Johannes, 128
Philadelphia, 16, 189n43
Picquet, François, 80, 183n40
Pitt, William, 14–17, 23, 25–26, 28, 43, 56, 130, 133–34, 141–43, 147, 190n52, 202n8
Plains of Abraham. *See under* battles and sieges
plunder, 8, 57, 63, 91, 106, 110–11, 114–15, 119, 171, 200n24
Pointe au Baril (Maitland, Ontario), 115, 143

Pointe Montreal (Point Frederick, Ontario), 80, 93, 102
Pontiac's Uprising. *See under* wars and uprisings
Post, Christian Frederick, 143
Potawatomi. *See under* indigenous peoples
Potter, Jonathan, 61–62, 121, 157, 167
Potter, Robert, 61
Pouchot, Pierre, 78, 80, 100
Pratt, Benjamin, 49
Prideaux, John, 86, 138
Princeton, N.J., 45
prisoners of war, 105, 108–11, 114, 128–33, 141, 169, 201n8, 23n12, 206n1 (app. B)
prize money, 112, 119
Providence, R.I., 45
provincial soldiers. *See* regiments, British
Putnam, Israel, 129

Quebec City, 4–6, 9, 13, 15–18, 20, 22, 79–80, 127–28, 140, 144, 202n8
Queen Anne's War. *See under* wars and uprisings
Queen's County, N.Y., 82

Rangers. *See* regiments, British
Rea, Caleb, 41, 43, 72, 116
Red Head (Ononwarogo), 62–64, 86, 94, 107–9, 131, 157, 183n36
Red Head the Elder (Kak8enthiony), 63
regiments, British: 1st Virginia Regiment, 136; "Bradstreet's Battoemen," 2, 15–16, 45, 47, 52, 57–58, 68–70, 75–76, 82, 92, 94, 115, 121, 157, 160, 179n2; Butler's Rangers, 127; Connecticut Provincials, 38, 41; King's Royal Regiment of New York, 137; Massachusetts Provincials, 10, 41–44, 48–50, 55–57, 59–60, 68–69, 82, 111, 118, 121, 156–58, 167, 186n18; New Jersey Provincials ("Jersey Blues"), 3, 15, 29, 41, 48, 5, 59, 62, 71, 83, 92, 96, 107, 119, 122, 128–29, 132, 157, 202n8; New York Provincials ("Yorkers"), 15, 40–41, 45, 48, 50–51,

regiments, British (*continued*)
56, 58–59, 69–70, 72, 82, 94, 101, 116, 167, 184n49, 195n34, 200n24; Rhode Island Provincials, 48–50, 57–58, 60–61, 82, 91, 104, 114, 121, 124, 148, 157, 160, 200n24, 203n12; Roger's Rangers, 34, 44–45, 57–58, 63, 81, 88, 95, 115, 137, 157, 160, 200n24, 203n12
regiments, British regulars: 17th Foot (Forbes's), 34, 186n12; 19th Foot (Howard's), 59; 22nd Foot (Whitmore's), 34; 27th Foot (Inniskillings), 47; 42nd (Royal Highlanders), 47, 180n6; 44th (Abercromby's), 46–47, 52, 190n45; 46th (Murray's), 46–47; 55th Foot (Howe's), 26, 101, 184n49; 60th Foot (Royal Americans), 47, 179n6, 180n6, 184n49, 187n24, 207n4; Engineers (later, Royal), 15, 60, 86, 91, 93–94, 96, 103, 105, 131, 148, 156; Gooch's American Regiment, 58–9; Royal Artillery, 14, 23, 46, 50–51, 58, 62, 76, 82, 93, 101–5, 115–17, 128, 132, 134, 136, 156–57, 197n6, 200n24
regiments, French: *compagnie du canonniers-bombardiers du Canada* (colonial artillery), 78–80, 92, 98–100, 197n17; *compagnies franches de la Marine* (colonial marines), 6–7, 20–21, 34, 79, 113, 174, 181, 206n3; *milice canadien* (Canadian militia), 6, 11, 36, 54, 112–13
regiments, French regulars: Béarn, 18, 78, 80, 113, 185n10; Berry (Berri), 185n10; Guyenne, 185n10; Languedoc, 185n10; La Reine, 185n10; La Sarre, 185n10; Royal-Roussillon, 185n10
religion, 3, 7, 39, 42, 57, 69, 80, 118, 130, 140, 199n13, 203n12. *See also* divine service
Rensselaer, N.Y., 37, 41
Rhode Island (colony), 60–61, 121, 124, 148
Richelieu River. *See under* rivers
Rigaud, Pierre de, Marquis de Vaudreuil. *See* Marquis de Vaudreuil

rivers: Alleghany, 5; Cataraqui, 18–19, 97, 103, 199n24; Detroit, 20; Grand, 137; Hudson, 4, 31–32, 39–40, 49; Mississippi, 3, 5, 10; Mohawk, 4, 20, 32–33, 36, 40–41, 43–44, 47–48, 51–52, 122; Monongahela, 5, 11, 36, 38 Ohio, 4–5, 14–17, 48, 126, 142; Oneida, 70, 74; Onondaga, 160; Oswegatchie, 80, 183n40; Oswego, 2, 4, 11, 33–34, 66, 70, 72, 105; 127; Ottawa, 140; Otterkill, 70; Passaic, 129; Richilieu, 4; St. Lawrence, 3–4, 6, 8–9, 15–16, 18, 22–23, 32, 63, 65–66, 74, 80–81, 83, 85–86, 100, 105, 110, 113–14, 127, 129, 142, 146, 148, 181n15, 183n4, 195n44, 199n24; Wood Creek, 4, 32–33, 51–52, 54, 62, 65, 67–68, 70–71, 119, 136, 160
Robertson, James, 37
Robinson, Beverly, 136
Robinson, Thomas, 23–24
Rogers, Robert, 139, 203n12
Roux, Bartholomew, 82, 195n34
Roxbury, Mass., 43, 51, 186n18
Royal (howitzer). *See under* weapons
Royal Navy, 15
rum, 62, 77, 81

Sabbath Day Point, N.Y., 59
Saratoga, N.Y., 131
Schaick, Goose, 41, 55, 59, 120, 132, 159
Schenectady, N.Y., 16, 32, 32, 34, 36–37, 40–41, 43, 50–51, 53, 56, 62, 121–23
Schuyler, Peter, 59, 108–9, 128, 201n8
Schuyler, Philip John, 25, 132, 135
Seneca River. *See under* rivers
Shaw, John, 60
Shawangunk, N.Y., 45
ships, French navy: *George*, 155; *Hurault*, 154; *Iroquoise*, 143; *Louise*, 154; *Ontario*, 154; *Outaouoise*, 143; *Marquise de Vaudreuil*, 77–81, 89–90, 92–93, 104, 115, 154; *Mohawk*, 154; *Montcalm*, 77, 79, 81, 103–4, 115, 154; *Vigilant*, 155. *See also* ships, Royal Navy

ships, Royal Navy: *Launceston*, 58; *London*, 77, 79, 154. See also ships, French navy
Shirley, William, 12–13, 22–24, 136, 183n36, 184n40
Shuckburgh, Richard, 37–38, 55, 156, 185n12, 207n2 (app. D)
Shute, Daniel, 39, 41–43, 56, 60, 68–69, 118, 165–66
Sieur de Courville (Louis-Léonard Aumasson de Courville), 20–21, 54, 112, 193n13
Sieur de la Broquerie (Joseph Boucher), 77, 79, 85, 206n2 (app. A)
Sieur de Laforce (René-Hippolyte Pepin), 78–81, 85, 89–90, 154, 206n2 (app. A)
Sieur de Longueuil (Paul-Josephe Le Moyne de Longueuil), 20, 54, 73–74, 126–27, 193n27
Sieur de Noyan (Pierre-Jacques Payen de Noyan), 20–21, 51, 54–55, 73–74, 80, 84, 97, 99, 104–5, 112–13, 126, 150, 168–70, 193n13
Sieur d'Espinassy (Louis-Auguste-Joseph-Victor d'Espinassy), 78, 80, 91, 99–101, 104–5, 197n6
Six Nations. See Haudenosaunee Confederacy
Snell, Jacob, 34
Sowers, Thomas, 86, 91, 95–96, 103, 105, 131, 199n24
Speaker of the Council Fire, 63
Springfield, Mass., 41
Stakes, Benjamin, 128–29, 202n8
Stanley, George F., 15, 141
Stanwix, John, 43–44, 47–50, 53–54, 56–57, 60–61, 118–22, 133, 187n24
Steele, Ian K., 147
Stockton, Annis Boudinot, 128–29, 202–3, 203n10
St. Francis (Odanak), Quebec, 16, 81, 139, 203n12
St. Francis Raid (1759), 16, 139
St. Lawrence River. See *under* rivers
Stone Arabia, N.Y., 44

strategy, British, 9–10, 12–18, 23–25
strategy, French, 5–9, 20–21
Suffolk County, N.Y., 82, 194n3
Sullivan, John, 131

Thousand Islands (Mille-Îles), 23, 85, 195–96, 196n44
Ticonderoga (Carillon). See *under* battles and sieges
Tiowestah. See Great Carrying Place
tomahawks. See *under* weapons
Trenton, N.J., 129
Trois-Rivières (Three Rivers), Quebec, 7, 16, 20–21
troupes de la colonie. See regiments, French
troupes de terres. See regiments, French
Tsioqui (Lake Oneida). See *under* lakes

Ulster County, N.Y., 45, 60, 70, 123, 188n28

Valley Forge, Pa., 132
Van Rensselaer, John, 37–38
Vaudreuil, François-Pierre de Rigaud de. See Marquis de Vaudreuil
Vaudreuil, Marquise de. See ships, French
Vernon, Edward, 58
Virginia (colony; Old Dominion), 16, 79, 136, 142

wagoners, 30, 40–41
Wall, Daniel, 61, 91–92, 104, 121
wall pieces. See *under* weapons
wars and uprisings: Civil War (1861–65), 3; Iroquois Wars (1638–98), 18; Pontiac's Uprising (1764), 131, 145; Queen Anne's War (1701–13), 44; Seven Years' War (1755–63) *aka* French & Indian War, 3–6, 8, 12, 22, 28, 50, 131, 140, 146, 187n24, 189n43; War of 1812 (1812–15), 3, 197n6; War of American Independence (1775–83), 4, 14; War of the Austrian Succession (1740–48), 3, 5; World War I (1914–18), 140

Warraghiyagey. *See* Sir William Johnson
Warren, Peter, 58
Washington, George, 11, 79, 131, 135–37
weapons: bayonets, 50; cannon, 18, 62, 8, 84, 90–92, 94–96, 98, 100–101, 104, 111, 113, 118, 129, 143, 157, 162, 164–65, 174, 197n6, 200n24; grapeshot, 89–91, 102, 174; howitzers, 76, 88, 93–94, 96, 100–101, 157, 168; mortars, 94, 99–100, 164, 197n6; muskets, 26, 37, 99, 127, 172, 201n6; tomahawks, 72; wall pieces (patararoes), 115–16. *See also* artillery
Webb, Daniel, 13, 33, 49
Weiser, Conrad, 143
Wells, Thomas, 168
Wendell, Hendrik, 34, 63, 157
West Indies, 8
White, David, 68
Whitehall, 16
Willett, Marinus, 132
Williams, Joseph, 42–43, 49, 56–57, 59–60, 68–69, 82, 111, 118, 121, 156, 158, 167, 186n18
Williamsburg, Va., 79
Wilson, John, 96, 101–2, 104, 156
Winslow, John, 12
Wolfe, James, 147
Wolfe Island, Ontario (Ganounkouesnot; Grand-Île), 87
women, 8, 21, 34, 81, 99, 104, 110, 139, 153, 17, 206n1 (app. B)
Wood Creek. *See under* rivers
Woolsey, Melancthon Taylor, 49, 51, 56
Woolwich Academy (Royal Military Academy), 60
Worcester, Mass., 41
World War I. *See under* wars and uprisings
Wraxall, Peter, 104, 207n2

"Yankee Doodle" (song), 37–38, 55
Yates, Christopher, 132, 159

www.ingramcontent.com/pod-product-compliance
Lightning Source LLC
Chambersburg PA
CBHW020945230426
43666CB00005B/176